Men Who Loved Me

A Memoir in the Form of a Novel

Men Who Loved Me

A Memoir in the Form of a Novel

FELICE PICANO

NAL BOOKS

NEW AMERICAN LIBRARY

A DIVISION OF PENGUIN BOOKS USA INC., NEW YORK
PUBLISHED IN CANADA BY
PENGUIN BOOKS CANADA LIMITED, MARKHAM, ONTARIO

Copyright © 1989 by Felice Picano

Published simultaneously in Canada by Penguin Books Canada Limited.

 NAL BOOKS TRADEMARK REG. U.S. PAT. OFF. AND FOREIGN COUNTRIES
REGISTERED TRADEMARK—MARCA REGISTRADA
HECHO EN DRESDEN, TN, U.S.A.

SIGNET, SIGNET CLASSIC, MENTOR, ONYX, PLUME, MERIDIAN
and NAL BOOKS are published *in the United States* by
New American Library, a division of Penguin Books USA Inc.,
1633 Broadway, New York, New York 10019,
in Canada by Penguin Books Canada Limited,
2801 John Street, Markham, Ontario L3R 1B4

LIBRARY OF CONGRESS CATALOGING-IN-PUBLICATION DATA
Picano, Felice, 1944–
    Men who loved me: a memoir in the form of a novel/Felice
Picano.
      p.   cm.
    ISBN 0-453-00700-7
    I. Title.
    PS3566.I25M4   1989
    813′.54--dc20   89-12762
                                            CIP

Designed by Julian Hamer

First Printing, November, 1989
1 2 3 4 5 6 7 8 9

PRINTED IN THE UNITED STATES OF AMERICA

For George Stambolian,
who remembers Rome in the sixties

ONE

The Most Golden Bulgari

Viola. What Country, friends, is this?
Captain. This is Illyria, lady.
Viola. And what should I do in Illyria?

—*Twelfth Night*

When I'm asked why I ever moved from my "wonderful" Jane Street apartment, I usually cite the basement boiler room fire that gutted two rooms, and the flood from the upstairs apartment that occurred the week after the place had just been replastered and repainted. If anyone ever needed a sign to get out of an apartment, evidently it was me.

More decisive than either catastrophe, however, was the burglary I foiled not a month after the flood had been cleaned up.

I awakened around four A.M., suddenly and totally, aware that something was wrong. I had gone to sleep in the study off the living room, which had become my bedroom several months before when a roommate had moved in to help stave off total financial disaster. From my position on the bed I could see the entire length of the living room and the farthest window, now open, the lightweight curtains fluttering in the night breeze. I could have sworn I'd closed that window before going to sleep: we were still having cool weather and it was too late in the spring for us to expect steam heat. Clue number one.

Not much waiting was needed for more clues. A soft, padding movement upon the carpet would have been recognizable as that of a cat. I needed a moment to recall that my cat, Fred, had disappeared over a year ago. According to the ancient cat ladies on my block who'd held a séance to contact him, Fred was dead, hit by a car on one of his far-from-home-wanderings clear down on treacherous double-laned Houston Street where I would sometimes come upon him, early on Sunday mornings, as I staggered home, unable to find a taxi home from Flamingo. Might this be another cat coming in for the night? Might be.

I turned slowly and noted not the yellow-green glow of cat eyes but the slender, pale white beam of a penlight flash cross the top of a low table upon which my stereo equipment sat. I knew the beam would focus upon me next, and I shut my eyes. I also understood with full clarity what was going on—there was a prowler in the apartment not ten feet away from where I lay totally vulnerable, pretending to sleep.

Dizzy beyond belief as I sometimes can be, I'm somehow or other the perfect person in a crisis. Certain I hadn't yet been spotted by the intruder, I immediately calculated whether I could leap the few yards to the kitchen drawer for the large butcher knife I kept there before the prowler realized what I was doing.

The unevenness of our situation bothered me—so many unknowns. He didn't know I was there, didn't know I was awake, didn't know that I was trying to get rid of him. I didn't know who he was, what he was looking for, if he carried a weapon, if he would use it, or if he could be chased off. I've always suspected that situations exactly like this bring on avoidable tragedies. I wanted to avert that by providing my prowler with more knowledge of his position—I hoped that would make a difference in his behavior.

The first step was to make noise; not a great deal of noise but the kind of sounds one makes while sleeping. I kept my eyes shut and began to murmur. Instantly I felt the penlight beam over my face. The soft padding stopped. He knew I was there.

Now I had to risk doubling his knowledge. From the fact that he'd not noticed me before, I guessed that he'd just arrived in the apartment, not yet gone into the other rooms.

My second step was to make more noise, to pretend to be

awakening. "Bob?" I asked in a sleep-dazed voice, letting him know that he would have to deal with two people—me and my roommate, who usually slept at his lover's Twenty-first Street triplex and only came home to change—rather than one. "Is that you, Bob?" I opened my eyes: no penlight beam.

The soft, padding footsteps had ceased. Seconds later I saw his tall, thin silhouette bent almost double going back out the window.

My adrenaline burning like the first stage of a rocket, I leapt out of bed, ran to the window, slammed down the sash, locked it, and turned to call the police.

They arrived in the two minutes that I needed to pull on a sweater and half-button my jeans against the cold that had seeped into the apartment. One bluecap was fleshy and swarthy, wise-eyed. He let the second one, blond and handsome in a throwaway manner, speak. After I told them my story the blond cop told me they'd been looking for a burglar who'd been operating in our chain of connected backyards for months. As the elder policeman hurried outside to radio for a backup patrol, the younger one looked around the apartment, out the window, and wondered aloud how far the burglar had gotten.

"He take any valuables?" he finally asked.

"Valuables?" I asked. The stereo equipment was still in place, a vintage tube-set Fisher receiver and an almost equally ancient AR turntable. I was certain one look around my apartment would tell him what he needed to know. Books and records were strewn around, sure, but a furniture set from two decades before I got it, and nothing of any apparent worth was otherwise visible.

"Jewelry and the like?" he prompted. "That's what this guy usually goes for. He prefers gold."

I laughed. My telephone had been shut off for nonpayment two months before. My utilities were still on only because when the young, half-attractive Con Ed collector had knocked on my door with a shutoff notice in hand a week before, I'd talked him into letting me blow him—if he would write that I wasn't home when he'd called. Gold, my foot!

Then the blond policeman was back outside with his partner. Shaken now that the incident was clearly over, my adrenaline all raced out, I sat down in my big, cat-torn wing chair and drank apple juice, unable to get back to sleep. I never expected to see those two cops again, so I was surprised to see their flashlights outside the windows, although how they'd gotten there I never ascertained. I was certain this was more a formality than anything else, to placate me and any other neighbors who'd been awakened, to show that they were "doing their job." I went to the bathroom to take a leak.

When I returned, I was surprised to hear shouting, and to see about a half dozen blue uniforms in the glimmering dawn light moving from yard to yard. People across the backyards had been awakened and were at their windows. There was a shout, met by a louder response. I followed one policeman's pointing hand to a roof in the most distant edge of the courtyard where I made out the silhouettes of three men struggling. Then I couldn't see what was going on, except that all the other policemen were running and shouting.

Ten minutes later my blond cop returned. "We got him!"

"You got him?" I was flabbergasted.

"You bet! With a little help from citizens, the Sixth Precinct always gets its man. By the way, this your name?"

I looked at his belt-hooked pad, wondering at the request, wondering even more why only my first name was written there.

"That's me. Why?"

"You'll want to come down to the precinct house to recover your watch."

"My watch?"

"Found it on him. Your name was inscribed on the back. My partner has it in the patrol car. Guess he decided to hit your place first. We didn't find anything else on him."

I was perplexed. I followed the cop out of the building. On the sidewalk I saw a tall, thin, sad, sensitive-looking black man being pushed into the back of a cop car and I immediately regretted my part in his capture. The swarthy cop lifted a transparent "evidence" baggie off the front seat and handed it to me.

"I figured it was yours," the blond cop said, "because of the *F* on your nameplate." He flipped the glittering object over to its gold back, which read:

> *Carissimo Felice*
> *L'Oro per L'Oro*
> *Mai domenticar—Djanko*

"It's mine," I admitted. "It's been lost for . . . years! Where did he find it?"

"He says he never saw it before," the swarthy cop said.

"It's been missing for years!" I repeated stupidly, to hide the extreme embarrassment that suddenly swept over me at seeing the bauble again. I hadn't thought of Djanko in— what was it?—five, six years?

The next morning I went down to the sixth precinct to reclaim the watch. The blond cop was there and he embarrassed me again by saying to the desk sergeant and to several other policemen at the front desk, "This was the guy I told you about. If everyone was as alert and brave as you was last night, we'da caught this guy a long time ago."

"What's it say?"

I translated. "Dearest Felice. Gold for the Golden One. Don't ever forget me. Djanko. That was his name," I added.

He looked me in the eyes and said right out, "Sergeant Herman says that watch musta cost plenty!" On his lips, unsaid, fluttered the questions he wouldn't ask, that I wouldn't answer: Who was this Djanko, and how had I merited such an expensive gift?

"I should thank that burglar. When I sell this, I'll have more money than I've had all year. And I really need it too."

I did sell the watch two days later, wearing my best suit and tie, using my copy of the precinct claim as ownership ID. It brought in several thousand dollars, although less than its value, and in fact got me through the rest of that year. And, as the elderly Hasidic jeweler on Forty-Seventh Street looked it all over for flaws, I sighed and said, "It's twenty-four-karat gold throughout," remembering with a pang the day that Djanko put it around my wrist in that plush first-floor lounge of the shop on the Via Condottiere and whispered in my ear, "As I promised, no? The most golden Bulgari of them all!"

If ever in the gloomiest moment of yet another broken affair I wonder if I was truly loved, I have to stop and recall that watch and Djanko Travernicke. He was not the handsomest, the sexiest, the most emotionally intense, or the most intellectually gifted of my lovers. He wasn't even the richest, despite his munificent gifts. But he was my only European lover and he was the most sophisticated human being I've ever encountered. When I met Djanko in 1966, he was about ten years my senior, in the manly glow of his early thirties, but already as wise and affectionate as a centenarian. A Yugoslav from the mountains of Croatia, he'd moved to Rome in time for the moviemaking boom at Cinecittà, and there had made dozens of films of every type, from low-budget science fiction to costume and muscle epics to Spaghetti Westerns. He even managed to find the time, energy, and money to shoot a few serious low-budget films in the Croatian language, starring some of his Rome-based ethnic colleagues, and I later learned one had received a Golden Bear at the Berlin Film Festival.

Djanko never had the least illusion about art, money, or love. The first time we parted, in a silver Maserati overlooking the Ostia seaplane port at dawn, he said to me in broken English, "One of us shall break the heart. If it must be so, I hope it is my heart. You are too young." His prediction would come true. In fact, I would have had to be as perfect as Djanko thought I was not to have hurt him. Even so, in the instant that policeman held out the watch I knew that while I hadn't thought of Djanko for years—so concerned with the petty madness of my own life—Djanko had probably never ceased adoring me. His adoration was neither pure, nor idealistic, nor unneurotic, yet oddly enough, for about a year I made him happy, and I'm sure that if ever we meet as old men, he will agree I was his finest lover.

In retrospect, it appears to have been utterly accidental— my transformation from a social worker living on the Lower East Side of Manhattan to being a European film director's lover kept in a suite in the most exclusive hotel in Rome. If any two people are to be thanked, they are my coworker, Phil Koslow, who got me to Europe, and an Italian citizen whose name I forget who smashed my motorcycle against a rock cliff outside of the Genoa city limits.

This is how it happened.

"You know Larraine likes you."

"Who likes me?" I asked, with more than a little surprise.

"Larraine Kellogg. She's one of the transcription secretaries," Phil Koslow said.

It was 1966, and we were standing in the hallway of the social service office where I was employed smoking cigarettes, trying not to seem obvious about peering into the glass-framed transcription booths where once a week, come hell or high water, all of us social workers had to spend at least two hours talking into a microphone attached to a machine that contained a palm-sized red plastic disc that would then be dropped into a small square envelope on the transcription supervisor's desk, to be turned into—two days later—perfectly typed and more or less literate versions of what we had said about Oralia Rodriguez's hysterectomy and Jenny Slater's nine-year-old schizophrenic son's third suicide attempt and Mrs. La Rosa's latest eviction notice.

In our large former schoolroom offices on East One Hundred and Ninth Street, all of us younger caseworkers spoke in a combination of slang, argot, and code. "Can't talk to you right now," I would say, rushing past a colleague. Referring to the above three women's problems, I would explain, "I've got an OD requiring a full set of 709s, a Marshall's writ, and a tube tie-off."

But once in the transcribing office, such shortcuts were impossible. These records might be read by high-up city and state social services officials, even federal officials of the Department of Health, Education, and Welfare. They undoubtedly *would* be read by our overworked, harassed supervisors. Thus they had to be full yet precise, set in a rigidly ritualized language, easily read by outsiders, but also with enough arcane terminology ("the worker submitted three sets of 207s as per requirement of Form 905") that another worker inheriting the particular case in some future restructuring of the neighborhoods we "covered" would instantly know that, for example, Oralia Rodriguez needed a year of subtle persuasion by half a dozen of us from various social work agencies to agree to the hysterectomy. (Sigh! Relief, the family stops at ten kids!) Or to convey the absolutely unprovable yet needed suspicion that little Rowan Slater, hardly his parents' favorite, had been fed thirty-one phenobarbitals by his mother—herself in and out of Rockland State Hospital six times over the past decade—in a specially prepared chili, his favorite dish. Or that Mrs. La Rosa didn't dare mention to anyone her eviction notice for months, in fact not until the marshal's men arrived to oust her, because it wasn't (as was most common with our "clients") for nonpayment of rent but due to her neighbors' disgust at the vomiting and rowdiness of the dozen youths from the local night school who Mrs. La Rosa plied with cheap wine and entertained every Friday night to supplement her welfare income—an enterprising if illegal way to do so.

Thanks to my skipping of several grades in junior high and high school, I was barely twenty years old when I went to work for the New York City Department of Social Services, and even though I dressed in a jacket and tie and was equipped with the small black Naugahyde-covered looseleaf that was my badge and my safe passage through the squalid color and exotic odors of East Harlem, the noise and energy and rhythm and violence of One Hundred and Twenty-Fifth Street, I still looked like a kid. Naturally I knew nothing of life. Naturally I was astonished by everything happening around me. I had gone through sixteen years of schooling, ending up in college courses so rarefied that six of us and a seminar professor would spend hours dissecting George Meredith's sonnet structures, or the Christian symbology in Flannery O'Connor's novellas—and actually think we were being educated. Upon graduation at the top of my department and faced with two more years of school in a writing program in a Midwestern university, I thought I would scream. I'd had it with school. I wanted real life.

I got it. Got it paying a call upon a client like David Carew, in the tiny one-windowed cell he called home in a chockablock SRO dive, to make a monthly checkup on the progress of his incapacitation for work due to severe asthma and cardiac arrhythmia. But what I found was small, ink-black, wiry David tied to his metal window gate, buck naked, welts all over his middle-aged, puckered buttocks. As I untied him, he joked about his "young lady just funnin', you know. Didn' mean no real harm." I didn't know. Or I would go to visit Amy Cruz in her apartment in the local low-income housing project, only to have her peephole flick open an inch and to have Amy say, "Give me a minute." No less than ten minutes later Amy would let me into her spotless, well-decorated apartment wearing a negligee and would offer me coffee. We would perch sedately at her Formica dinette set, surrounded by hanging plants, updating her case and pointedly ignoring the hefty, breasty, unintroduced woman in the living room clad in black leather who sat impatiently leafing through magazines, keeping us in view all the while. No more little Cruzes would be conceived, I knew, while this creature hung around, which was great for the New York City taxpayer, but I would have to be careful exactly how I explained that into the microphone in the transcribing room.

I'd vaguely noticed the half dozen or so mostly black women who worked as transcribing typists. I'd also noticed they were obviously different from the black women who worked as caseworkers with us, who were usually younger, college-educated, and socially concerned—not to say preppy, which many of them definitely were (I think of my coworker and friend Greer everytime I see Shari Belafonte-Harper).

Greer and Cathy and even Mrs. Anderson had more in common with ice-blond Debby Henderson or the semitic voluptuary Myra Rosen than with the stiletto-heeled, heavily cosmetized, tightly sheathed, dusky beauties upstairs who wore magenta lipstick, smelled of expiring calla lilies, and who swayed more times per step than I thought possible for the human body as they walked away from you.

"How do you know Larraine?" I asked Phil.

"I go out with Josette."

This was news to me. To innocent me, Phil was the personification of the term "liberal Jewish intellectual," and while I understood that it was considered chic in the sixties for such youths' rebellions from their parents in Larchmont and Far Rockaway to have black girlfriends—hadn't my college roommate?—still, wasn't Josette different? A girl from "the Islands" without more than a high-school degree and "Not of our class, dear?"

"Which one is Larraine?" I asked.

"There she is."

As though on cue, Larraine stepped out from behind her desk in the typing pool and into the corridor, walking away from us toward the ladies' room.

"How does she know me?"

"From your voice, I suppose. Then from seeing you. How would you like to double-date with Josette and me this weekend?" he suddenly asked.

I said sure, why not, and did double-date with them, once. As planned, Larraine got me alone in a bedroom in some rambling apartment in the depths of Brooklyn, and as planned, she seduced me. But while I had no prejudice against sleeping with black women, Larraine was not even close to my type; that became clear to both of us when I said I would find my way home to Manhattan through the confounding alphabet of subway trains at three A.M. rather than stay over.

Larraine managed somehow to get over her disappointment in me, and it didn't bother Phil, either.

During another conversation in the corridor of the transcribing room when Phil brought up the name of yet another secretary in the typing pool, I answered—anguish clear in my voice—"What I'd really like is to get the hell out of this Welfare Center, this job, this city, and go far away. To Europe, maybe."

This was three months later. Phil and I had become buddies, eating lunch together three days per week (we each had to remain indoors one day a week as "emergency worker") and going out after work to an occasional movie or party. Stag, because by then Phil had found Josette's attention to late-night brandies as well as the financial support of her seven-year-old son a pall on their relationship.

I find it impossible to describe Phil Koslow or his actions as a young man without falling into caricature, despite the truth that we were closest friends for almost two years. At the time I was both pleased and amazed by Phil's purely predictable problems, his conflicts and antics. I prized as necessary ingredients of young manhood our all-night drinking sessions with bottles of cheap Scotch and impossibly low-priced brandy and that certain-to-arrive point when, conviviality long passed, all sharing of the most sordid of confidences long shared, Phil would suddenly awkwardly revivify like some marionette suddenly snipped free of its strings and stand up, even get up on a chair or tabletop, and intone with the seriousness of youth poetry of magnificent stropic qualities and depressingly pessimistic content—Thomas Hardy's "Hap," Eliot's "Hollow Men," and, Phil's favorites,

Yeats's later poems. I cannot read "Sailing to Byzantium" without hearing Phil's voice begin muttering "An aged man is but a paltry thing/a tattered coat upon a stick, unless" and he would rant on, eyes glittering with portent within the protection of oval wire-framed spectacles, his large, mobile lips fluttering with a grief too large, too extreme for containment, the veins purpling into perilous erection upon his soft, aristocratically dented temples as his prow of a nose cut through the incandescent night air—before he staggered, uttered a quiet, definitive, "I'm blotto," and passed out.

How couldn't I be thrilled by such shenanigans? If any other friend of mine got drunk and passed out, he was merely a souse, to be avoided. But that was because he didn't possess Phil's finely attenuated weltschmerz, Phil's sense of his distressing lack of power and glory and station. He couldn't begin to approach Phil's assumption—like a burning mantle—of the two thousand years of Hebrew diaspora, the shame, the persecution, the wasted efforts, the sickness beyond despair of life, and his pride in its great failures.

I don't know where Phil Koslow is today, twenty odd years later, whether he's long dead in some rice field outside Saigon, or whether he's still alive, teaching Byron to silly sophomores in some small, well-endowed college in the forests of Oregon. I doubt that I'd actually want to see him again. If he is still living, what he has become must have been tempered by time and sense and compromise—those culprits of youth. I want to and shall recall Phil as the pure spirit I'd admired—the lost intellectual, the sensitive plant exposed to the gritty realities of Spanish Harlem social work, the eternal, overly self-conscious postgrad student.

All that was still part of him, if a bit tamped down by temporary contentment, when after two years as a social worker I called it quits and finally made good on my threat to go to Europe. Phil had already left earlier that year, and I saw him for the last time in a setting far more apt than the huge, noisy admitting room of the East End Welfare Center. Somehow or other, throughout all his suffering, Phil had managed to finagle a fellowship of no small size to Brighton College in England.

When I said good-bye to him for the last time, it was on a late summer afternoon, the sun sparkling off the redbrick esplanades and squeaky-new painted beige classroom walls, as I boarded a train back to London. Although he was living alone—hadn't even considered a girl, he admitted, in the months he'd been in England—Phil was taking supernal delight in being there, in walking me around and showing me the entire, mostly still under construction school, and telling me about the courses by which he hoped to receive a doctorate in English literature.

In fact, we met not at his college but in London, at the Russell Square Hotel, a large structure in Holborn with the external appurtenances of the Houses of Parliament several miles to the west, and the internal accommodations of a vast, only slightly tarnished Windsor Castle.

When he received my letter saying I was on my way, Phil had taken a room with two beds in this improbable structure to greet me in London. I ended up remaining there a few nights more after he'd returned to his bed-sitter in Brighton, then I decided that the place—with its saffron-gowned gurus and ex-India colonels and foreign diplomats galore—was a bit too "high" for me. I moved halfway around the square to the less ostentatious Montague Hotel, an edifice built— and apparently last staffed—around the time of Jane Austen. Despite this hotel's proximity to the British Museum, Bond Street, and many good bookstores, after several weeks I moved again, this time to a boardinghouse on nearby Tottenham Court Road owned by a middle-aged Irish Protestant woman named Mrs. Timmins, who made up for her gross weight and idleness with vivacity, nosiness, and a gargantuan cloud of frizzed cinnamon hair, and whose country Irish young female help made up for their sloth by their easy conversation and their curiosity about how "it's done in America."

I'd not exactly been a great traveler in my life; in fact, I'd hardly seen more of my native country than New York State, New England, and summers in Topanga Beach as a California surfing teenager. Yet the minute I arrived in London I felt totally comfortable, utterly poised. Doubtless this was a result of my two years as a caseworker. When one has been attacked by a psychotic four-hundred-pound woman wielding a kitchen knife and survived, when one has lived several years on Manhattan's Lower East Side with its rival gangs of territorially sensitive Lithuanians, Puerto Ricans, and surprisingly volatile Orthodox Jews, one tends to feel comfortable virtually anywhere in the world—cosmopolitanism, I believe it's called.

Even so, I seemed to know my way around London with only the most cursory glance at the map in the back of my (British) guidebook. Perhaps it was some inner affinity, like that provided by a former incarnation, if one believed—as I half did at the time—in the Buddhist idea of past lives. I've sometimes thought it might also have been the result of a decade of intensive reading in English literature. None of the place or street names were strange to me, and all of them seemed to line up about where I thought they ought to be. Whatever the cause, I could emerge from an absolutely wrong Underground station and always manage to find my bearings. Marleybone for example. There was the arch behind me, and Belgravia to my left. Hyde Park and the serpentine in front: the city my oyster.

It was Phil Koslow's being so close by—ending up summer classes and preparing for the fall ones in Brighton—that provided me with my point of arrival in Europe. My final destination remained hidden from me for more than a month. I had all the time in the world and I had a thousand dollars to spend. A regal sum then, and three fourths of my savings from my stint as a social worker. After my several visits to Brighton's hilly streets (we had to hold on to metal railings to reach some spots, and the telephone booths were an impossible-to-replicate gumdrop-scarlet), I spent the rest of the time wandering about London.

It was there, one day in early September, at the American Express office on Regent Street where I wired home periodically, that I received a surprise. My older brother, Bob, had also contacted my parents and was coming from Hamburg to meet up with me. He'd been in Germany ("Living with some German girl," my mother had intimated) since he'd been discharged from the Paratrooper Division of the Armed Forces. Since all of this particular brother's comings and goings had been—and pretty much have remained to this day—a source of the most impenetrable mystery to me, I took the news of his imminent arrival calmly.

In fact, he turned out even more outré than I would have guessed. He rode a motorcycle—a BMW 500—and after a few days of my riding around the city in pillion behind him, I was persuaded to lay out several hundred dollars to get a bike myself—a Yamaha.

One afternoon, as we sat astride our bikes in the parking lot of London Tower—brother Bob had never been in England and had thrown me into an exhausting roundelay of sight-seeing quite different from my own previous stumblings about the town—he asked how much French I knew. I had no idea, I said. Why? Because we would need to buy international insurance the minute the car ferry let us out in Calais, he explained, and he didn't know any French at all.

Thus we went to the Continent. I won't go into our week-long bi-motorcycle journey through France, nor will I detail the mostly excellent if nearly silent meals Bob and I shared in various restaurants, *auberges,* and hotel bistros in so-and-so-sur-Loire or such-and-such-sur-Mer, except to say that we seemed to be on a schedule that existed only in brother Bob's mind, which declared that we get to—and then out of—Paris, and in fact every city, town, and village we happened to land in for the night, as quickly as possible. We would arrive, bathe, have dinner, and he would retire for the night. I would go out looking for and seldom find something else to interest me, *anything* to interest me.

After we had split up I decided that he was trying to 1) run away from something—either in Hamburg or back home, and that I and our trip was merely an excuse, or 2) that after a stormy relationship as children, he was trying to get closer to me. Only years later did I find the real reason for this trip. He only had a few weeks vacation from his job in Germany and he was dying to be with someone who spoke English—in short, he was homesick.

As a result of his tactics, we grew no closer and he no less mysterious. We arrived in Genoa eventually on a rainy evening and slept at a lovely small pension downtown, with Barococo beds four-fifths the size of the rooms, operated by a Sr. Giuseppi Falcone ("You Americans? Hey! Call me Joe. I lived in Bushwick twenty years!"). Joe guided us to a superb dinner for our single night in the town and gave us names and addresses of other pensions we would be comfortable staying at during our journey through the boot of Italy, following Bob's lightning-flash itinerary.

We sped out of the gray, already fading Italian port city in the rain along the coastal highway, our bikes headed south. About two miles out of town we stopped at a deep turn in the road. Along our left were the brown cliff rocks of the farthest extension of the Italian Alps, ahead of us a tunnel dug deep into the rock. A slender blue-and-white-striped metal rod signaled this to be a railroad crossing, and a train coming occasioned us to stop. Beyond the tunnel mouth, the mountains jagged out to sea magnificently, the road we were to follow circling around.

I stepped off my Yamaha and walked the six feet or so back to where my brother had stopped his BMW and was once more attempting to adjust his suitcases on the rear fender rack of the bike, a problem that had developed somewhere during our tough going of the Grand Corniche the day before. As I stopped to help him I looked up to see the train just now visible in the tunnel chugging toward us, and at the road encircling the mountain, where I could make out a fawn-colored Lancia sedan speeding toward us, its driver either oblivious to or trying to beat the train.

For a second I wondered if the legendary mad driving of the Italians was about to be demonstrated. I even secretly rooted for the lunatic to edge out the train.

"If he doesn't make it," I said to my brother, "everyone in the car will be killed."

The Lancia picked up speed; cruised right by the blue-metal warning signal; bounced over the tracks, which were only partly embedded in concrete; and slid out of control at seventy-five miles per hour.

If the driver hadn't smashed my motorcyle head-on, he and all of his passengers probably would have sailed directly into the rock cliff, with the expected fatalities. As it happened, my sturdy Yamaha took the brunt of the blow, and although it was flattened against the mountainside like a paper cutout, the passengers were only jolted and bruised.

That very instant the train pulled into the station and stopped, and about a hundred people, including at least a dozen men proclaiming themselves *medicos* of various sorts, descended like a Verdian chorus to bewail the cruelty of the fates and to treat the various great aunts and grandmamas in the backseat of the Lancia to lemon-scented handkerchiefs and homilies from Manzoni.

When all the alleged doctors had reboarded, the train pulled out of the suburban station. The dust cleared, and my bike was shown to be a total loss. My suitcases, strapped to the back fender rack, had burst upon impact and my clothing was strewn hundreds of feet across the rocks in all directions.

I approached the middle-aged driver of the Lancia who had just managed to get all the women back into the car, and asked him politely in my so-so Italian what he planned to do about the damage.

"I'll drive you to a *carrozeria*," he had the nerve to say. That being a body shop where Italian mechanics took a week to hammer out a tiny dent.

I pulled out my green card for international insurance and demanded his. He began to wave me off and step into his car.

Infuriated, I grabbed him by the lapel and in my best learned-from-my-father Roman dialect warned him to pay me for damages, calling him a *ladro sfacime,* which is to say a scum-faced thief.

Being a civilized Piedmontese, he naturally took umbrage at this epithet and attempted to sock me. But I had twenty years and far more umbrage on him. I avoided his flaccid punch and plastered him one, at the same time yelling *"Polizia!"* at the top of my lungs, in the direction of six such gendarmes smoking nearby, who hadn't bothered to come investigate the accident.

The upshot was a most unpleasant afternoon at a Genoa police station, and a deal hammered out, whereby the Lancia driver's insurance agent would pay for the destruction of the bike in three steps: a third immediately in cash—for my journey to Rome, a third in three weeks, the final third in six weeks. Before this negotiation could be made, I'd had the driver and the insurance agent dragged in front of the local judge and charged with every crime short of incest. I had pulled in the local American consul and had loudly and in no uncertain terms cursed the race of my forefathers as the most decadent on earth. If performed in the U.S., this eccentrically operatic and childish behavior would lead to at least a psychiatric examination, if not incarceration in an asylum. In Italy, it was, if not expected, at least admired. The judge and even the Lancia driver's lawyer ended up calling me "Sir" when we were finished, and all were satisfied: myself with the settlement, the insurance man with the terms, the Lancia driver that he'd been legally coerced into being a party to the action, and the American Consul that he had managed to swerve off the major international incident I demanded.

The only person not pleased was Brother Bob. In fact, he

was disgusted by the entire rigmarole. The incident so turned him off Italians and Italy that during our late lunch in Genoa he was more silent, more sullen than I thought possible. As we were paying the bill he quietly told me that he had decided not to go on to Rome but would head up toward Turin and then into Switzerland. He even asked me to join him—on the back of his bike.

"I'm not letting these idiots spoil my vacation," I said. "And who knows if I'll get the insurance money if I leave the country. If I'm here, I can drag them into court again."

Bob winced at this statement—he'd all but hidden in the back of all of my day's dealings, pretending not to understand a word of what was going on.

"Just drop me off at the train station," I said. "I'll find my way."

Two years would pass before we saw each other again, and we never once afterward referred to this—for him painful, for me enlightening—episode.

I remember Bob leaving the large, airy train station. The sun had just come out—mockingly, I thought—through all those high windows, and I bought myself a second-class ticket, checked what was left of my luggage, and looked around for a bathroom.

A few minutes later I found myself standing in this tiled booth with a metal-shielded hole in the middle of the floor and no other obvious lavatory facilities. I left the booth and went into a second one, exactly the same, and a third, and a fourth.

"I must be completely out of my mind to stay in this country where I don't know anyone and haven't a thing to do," I said out loud. Before I could fall into total despair, nature took over and I began to piss. Seconds later I hopped on the train just as it was beginning to pull out.

I found a seat as the train jolted forward, sat down, and opened up my copy of *Time* magazine, found with much difficulty the night before in a Genoa branch of Rizzoli, and tried to focus on the words.

"Oh! You speak English," my neighbor said.

He was an extremely handsome Roman about my age, dressed in a dark suit with a pale peach cuffed shirt and smart tie. His name, he told me, among the other hundred or so words of English he knew, was Orazio (Horace never sounded so good before). He worked for the Treasury Department, had been in Genoa as part of a general audit of the utilities company there, and was on his way home.

This conversation perked me up immediately. Orazio promised to show me around Rome once I was settled. He approved my choice of pension—it was second-class but good, located on the Piazza Della Republicana, not far from a train station and close to the Baths of Diocletian. He thought my Italian was fine for a tourist, more than adequate for getting around the city. He would be occupied that night, "*in famiglia*," but he promised to meet me for drinks the following night: "*Certo!*"

Certo means "for sure," and it is seldom meant to be utterly misleading. However, in Rome—a city with three thousand years of the most variegated history—nothing at all is certain; what counts is the intention, not the fulfillment of the promise.

I knew that Orazio had a fiancée. He'd told me about her. Yet that didn't in the least stop me from fantasizing about him. He was the first Italian that I'd met socially rather than legally; he looked like the film star Jeffrey Hunter and he had a voice deep and manly as Raymond Burr's. I'd come to Europe only partly to get away from social work and New York City. My real reason had been deeper, more insidious: to break all my ties with the past—and to become homosexual. I longed for this, knew with naïve certainty it would only happen outside of my home ground.

But perhaps I'm going too fast. I should drop back a bit to explain how I'd arrived at this predicament, how I'd reached this decision, which I knew even then would determine most, if not all, aspects of my future life.

*   *   *

When my college roommate moved out of our Lower
East Side apartment in the late summer of 1964 to begin
graduate courses at the University of Minnesota, I inspected
the three rooms: the small kitchenette, the living room with
its parquet floors sagging in the middle, the single bedroom
through a pair of French doors. I looked over those possessions remaining, which I could honestly now say were mine.
Excluding clothing, which fit easily into a small chest of
drawers, anyway, and, with room to spare, in the one bedroom closet, my possessions consisted of the following:

1) A trundle bed with two pillows, two sets of sheets, and
two blankets.

2) A small, beat-up chest of drawers I'd purchased locally
for eleven dollars, then stripped and stained.

3) A handsome bent wood (not Bentwood) distressed oak
rocking chair, which I'd bought to have a comfy reading
chair.

4) A second, less comfortable trundle bed, left by my
departed roommate, which became a "sofa" of sorts, once I
draped it with midnight-blue corduroy and placed bolsters
and throw pillows on it.

5) Fifteen wooden milk crates, painted various colors,
stacked both vertically and horizontally for effect, to make a
wall of shelves for books, records, and other small objects.

6) A small, circa 1930 tan metal kitchen table, painted to
look like wood, big enough to seat two comfortably, and
four once its single leaf was opened.

7) Two matching dining chairs.

8) A clock radio.

9) A Webcor monophonic phonograph—my graduation
gift from high school some four years before; and about
twenty records, most of them classical, about half from my
collection at home, the rest purchased over the following
four years, carefully, because of my minuscule scholarship
income.

10) Four water glasses, a set of plastic multicolored ser-

vice for six, then merely cheap, now avidly collected as Fiesta Ware.

11) Several small, inexpensive, functional pots and pans.

The mere fact that after all this time I can remember and list all of my material possessions on a single page I find astonishing. Today I look around me and I automatically wonder how can I cut down on all this excess of *things!*

I used to play and know those twenty records I owned in 1964 far more than is possible with my current collection, even were I given all the leisure of retirement: Bruno Walter's *echt*-Viennese performances of Mozart's Jupiter and Haydn's Miracle symphonies; Van Cliburn's glamorous Tchaikovsky concerto; Horowitz's steel-and-silk Rachmaninoff Second Concerto, with Toscanini conducting; the Callas, Gedda, Von Karajan *Madame Butterfly*, left by my roommate's girlfriend when they broke up; two discs of Landowska playing Scarlatti sonatas in ancient sound, one of them recorded in Paris in '41 as the Germans advanced on the city, bombs thudding in the velvet-shrouded studio's background; Rubinstein's later Chopin mazurkas, which I used to play whenever I had to clean house, because they were so danceable, and which Jerome Robbins turned into a ballet; Glenn Gould's eccentric, intelligent piano version of the Goldberg Variations; finely mustached Monteux's truly Napoleonesque Eroica with the Londoners, my first European pressing, which came in a silver double sleeve; Reiner's Fifth and Coriolan Overture with the Chicago Symphony at its apex (pace Solti-maniacs, and *listen!* to it); Guilini's Debussy—*La Mer* and the orchestral nocturnes, fit inside a perfectly apt cover graced with a pointillist Seurat drawing; Stravinsky himself with a fine pickup group doing his "Three Big" ballets: *Firebird, Petrouchka,* and *Sacre*; Ormandy's Hindemith *Mathis Der Maler* and the *Metamorphoses*. My tastes were unformed, catholic. I didn't know that twenty years later I'd still be listening to Richter's *Wanderer Fantasia* and to Michelangeli's *Gaspard de La Nuit*. I was hearing most of it for the first time, second at most, following the after-midnight classical station that exposed me to so much music I'd never heard before, and impelled me to drop actual hard-earned cash on albums.

But when I shut and locked the door, this apartment with its not so readily apparent treasures was now all mine. I paid the rent and utilities and was responsible for its up-keep; others had to ask to be let in, to stay over; this was a big deal to me, as it must be to anyone who's grown up in a large, interfering, social—and not always convivial—family.

All mine, complete with someone to greet me when I returned home—a trip sometimes an hour long, downtown along the eastern spine of Manhattan from One Hundred and Ninth Street, a full five miles away. Mornings, I'd walk up Avenue A to Fourteenth Street, where I'd descend into the subways for a slow shuttle across to the Lexington Avenue line. The train would arrive from downtown empty, crowd up at Union Square, grow denser at Twenty-third and Twenty-eighth Streets, become really packed at Thirty-third Street, empty but immediately fill up again at Forty-second, until past Fifty-ninth Street where the daily workers were gone; the train continued to Sixty-eighth, Seventy-seventh, Eighty-sixth and Ninety-sixth, finally to 116th Street. I could get off at either of the last two stops, since the Welfare Center was equidistant from them. Ninety-sixth was a cross-town thoroughfare, filled with stores, and if you walked west—rather than toward the East River as I did—it became increasingly classy at Park, Madison and Fifth, before being interrupted by Central Park. One Hundred and Sixteenth was more ethnic, more run-down; it all but rubbed your nose in the fact that you were in Spanish Harlem—not always desirable if you had to be there all day. If I was late to work, it was a toss-up whether to get off the train earlier and have to walk uphill, or later and downhill.

Evenings, the subways were far less crowded and a lot faster. I guess by the time we got to midtown, the rush hour there had already peaked. It was always more relaxing. Even when New York had its first total blackout, it was fun:

our train stopped, went black, then started up again, lights on dimly, and stopped to let us off at Twenty-third Street. I walked home in the unprecedented vision of Manhattan, illuminated only by headlamps as autos slowly edged forward in the sudden lack of red/green signals, and a few volunteers on larger avenues boldly directed traffic at major intersections with broad gestures and shrill whistles, just like the cops in midtown and at tunnel entrances. The sun set, and I could make out stars in the melting blue-black skies, candlelight in every apartment house. People were holding spontaneous all-building parties, impulsively inviting in strangers as I wandered through a softer, gloriously changed neighborhood from that I returned to every other night. Inside my own building, votive candles had been placed in the stairway all the way up to the roof, the warm glow of apartments helping to light the corridors, doors astonishingly open, people standing around chatting and laughing in their kitchenettes.

Another slightly later return from work all the way downtown brought on the first real crisis of the period and threatened to bring down the various flyweight elements with which I'd jerry-built my life—as opposed to other's previous ideas of what my life should be like.

Gustave, my cat, was the immediate cause of the crisis. Of all the pets I've owned, this tortoiseshell tabby is by far the least memorable. He didn't possess the sheer eccentricity of my cat, Puppy, or the intelligent personality of my other cat, Fred; nor the beauty of my bluepoint Angora, Owl, so vain that she was renamed and aptly earned the moniker of *Miss* Cat. No, I recall Gustave only for his exit from my life, and for its effect upon me.

Gustave was one of four surviving kittens out of a litter born to a female belonging to Ruth and Barbara, college friends who had also moved into Manhattan, and who'd lived nearby on East Twelfth Street. This female had one day somehow escaped to the roof, where she managed to get knocked up in less than an hour of disappearance. My friends insisted I take "at least one" kitten for company, when my roommate moved out.

Gustave was a pleasant, pliant, unremarkable animal, and I suppose he turned out to be company of a sort, especially as one by one my college friends and neighbors left the city for graduate schools all over the country, and I—never terribly outgoing in the first place—fell into a sort of reclusiveness, in which I spent my leisure hours reading, listening to music, and daydreaming.

I hadn't had a steady girlfriend since my junior year in college, when I stopped seeing Beverly, because she was getting "too serious." This meant that she was making too many plans for us together. But it also took into consideration the fact that so many of our friends were planning engagements and marriages. I was getting antsy about a long-term commitment to someone I didn't feel strongly about—an honorable if misunderstood response.

For the following three years I watched, slightly on the sidelines, as my college friends went into a series of unbelievable contortions over their women. Phillip would fight with Barbara, then arrive at my apartment sodden drunk and threaten for three hours to join the Army instead of going to Stanford Law School. Matthew would break up with Christa and attempt suicide when she announced her engagement to Kenny. Horrified, fascinated, I observed all these goings-on—and wondered. I'd never once felt possessive, jealous, suicidally depressed, furious enough to smash down an apartment door over a girlfriend. Something was clearly wrong with me. I pulled back from the emotional arena, telling myself that although they were my classmates, they were two or three years older than I. When I was twenty-two or twenty-three years old, something a woman did would make *me* want to throw her against a wall or crash my car at high speeds.

Once my friends were scattered and I was settled into my second year of work at the Welfare Center, I tentatively began to date women again, even to sleep with them on occasion. But while I dated Joanna and enjoyed her company, I had to admit it was as much for her knowledge of opera and ballet, for our talk and dining out, as it was for sex. Both of us knew we were merely marking time; we never pretended we were in love. The same with Gail, a coworker on the floor below my unit who was five years older and already divorced; and Larraine, the transcribing secretary. As each of these women wandered away—by mutual consent—from our placid, sexually excellent relationships and got themselves hooked up with married men and garage mechanics and Israeli soldiers, I decided I needed time to mature.

I tried discussing the problem with Billy Lee, a sensible coworker from Springfield, Massachusetts, who shared with me an interest in eventually being a writer. It was Billy who logically, if offhandedly, suggested that I try out men. "Maybe," Billy said between ordering draft beers for us at Stanley's, our crowded Avenue B hangout bar, "maybe you'll discover you can only become emotionally involved with another guy!" I could tell this was as much pure speculation on his part—the writer's "Hey, what if . . . ?" as it was real advice. I was so naïve at the time that once at a party, when slickly dressed, dark-haired, perpetually tanned Gary Schacter mentioned that he'd just come back from Ft. Lauderdale where he'd had a ball, living for two weeks with a girl and three "gay kids," I thought he meant happy. Despite my distant memories of preteen sex with a neighborhood boy, I doubted Billy Lee had the solution. But I felt attracted to some men, so I decided to give it a try.

In the following months I allowed myself to be picked up by men a half dozen times. These brief encounters always began most promisingly, with both of us sexually aroused. That is, until we got undressed and into bed. At which point I suddenly became completely turned off. I wasn't nervous or frightened, I wasn't in the least bit concerned with what someone might think. I was bored, or at least put off in some inexplicable manner. I wouldn't take his cock in my mouth, would barely touch it, and the one time a man tried to fuck me it hurt so much, I almost punched him out. A few times I let myself be sucked off—but this wasn't always possible if I couldn't stay hard. In most cases, less than five minutes after we'd strolled in through the apartment door, I'd be up, dressing rapidly, mumbling asinine apologies, leaving some poor frustrated guy to wonder what he'd done wrong, how he'd turned me off, and why he would have to jerk off alone again.

The sixth time it happened, I promised myself would be the last time. I'd been told both by close friends and by Beverly that I was cold and unfeeling, incapable of love. Fine. I'd accept that judgment. It wasn't the worst thing that could happen to me, was it? Anyway, I was still young. I had time. I could still fall in love. It happened when you least expected it. Happened to the most unexpected people. The right person would still come along. Not the right man, mind you, or the right woman, because by this time, despite my brave front, I was unconsciously so desperate that *anyone* would do, regardless of gender.

These various strands of dissatisfaction and discontent came to a head in a single twenty-four hours. That Friday afternoon proved a particularly difficult one at work. Both Billy Lee and I were emergency workers for our respective case units, and we were still downstairs in the first-floor admissions lounge, known to us as "the pit" (we mentally pictured the entrance sign to read ABANDON ALL HOPE, YE WHO ENTER HERE), at five o'clock when the Welfare Center officially closed. The problem was—what else on a weekend? —emergency opening cases that simply could not wait until Monday. Emergency openings were the most complex, baffling, and frustrating cases one could possibly receive on any day at any hour of the week, requiring batches of forms to be filled out, involving signatures from seemingly every individual in the building—from the Center head down to the assistant janitor. Some bureaucrat in some office downtown had devised the opening procedure in the same spirit that the CIA had devised its jungle terrain training exercises; the general idea was to keep anyone from completing its rigors. Treacherous pitfalls abounded, if not of the physical, then of the procedural sort. Even case supervisors, in charge of hundreds of social workers, were known to miss some unimportant yet necessary form—the 601b, a nonsense health certification, for example—which would require another half dozen phone calls and hours of delays.

Despite this, both Billy Lee and I finally got the damn things completed at around seven. As we ascended the elevator to our fifth-floor offices, I casually mentioned that all my attempts to become homosexual had failed miserably.

"What are you going to do?" he asked, concern evident through his distraction and utter exhaustion.

"Nothing, I guess. I'm out." Then I added, with a sick little laugh for the sick little joke, "At least I've still got my cat."

It was dark when I arrived home. Completely exhausted, I opened my apartment door and quickly closed it behind me, expecting as usual to have to fend off the meows and little lunges with which Gustave greeted me when I'd been at work all day.

No need to that evening; he wasn't there. I dropped my groceries on the counter, put them away, opened a can of cat food into his dish, and expected to hear Gustave scramble across the sagging parquet to knock it out of my hand in his eagerness.

No Gustave. I called him, then did a quick search of the place. I finally spotted him under the bed. When I reached for him, he hissed and scratched me—unprecedented behavior! I managed to pull him out and set him down on the floor near his food. He acted very odd. He couldn't seem to walk straight. He fell down, then stumbled up again. I sat on the floor to pet him and to figure out what was wrong. He hissed unconvincingly and again tried to scratch me. What the hell was going on? I grabbed a bowl of water and brought it to him. As he'd done with the food, Gustave merely sniffed it, looked at me, and meowed humbly. Suddenly he dashed off through the living room into the bedroom and under the bed.

Once again I pulled him out. He seemed to have a pale white froth around his mouth and nose. Fearing that, rather than his feeble attempts at scratching me, I quickly dropped him, and he zigzagged back under the bed.

Now I was alarmed. I called a local vet and got an answering service. They were closed, wouldn't be open until Monday. I dialed the ASPCA, got someone on the line, and explained that my cat was sick, giving all the details.

"You'd better bring him in."

"Can you tell what's wrong with him?"

"Can't say till we've had a look at him. It doesn't sound like distemper. Maybe he ate something—a houseplant or something toxic."

"Could this be serious?" I asked, frightened. Gustave had crawled out from under the bed and was wobbling toward me. He looked pathetic.

"Here's my assistant. She'll take your name. Better bring him in quickly. We close at eight-thirty."

Gustave stumbled over to me, and I reached down to pet him. I couldn't believe this was happening. I'd had the cat for over two years and he'd never given me a moment of trouble.

Getting the suddenly indolent cat into my flight bag to carry him uptown was easy enough, but I had to punch holes in its top, because once in, he got out every time I opened the zipper even a half inch to let in air. As I walked along Tenth Street looking for a cab, Gustave became spastic again, the flight bag leaping about so wildly with his contortions that twice it snapped out of my grip. I managed to hold on and to flag down a cab on First Avenue. Once inside the taxi, he calmed down.

At the ASPCA office, the vet's assistant took one look at Gustave as I let him out of the flight bag and called for a cage. I talked him into the thing and he rolled out of sight.

I waited in the lounge for close to an hour, smoking one cigarette after another. Finally a doctor came out, a tall, good looking, red-haired man wearing a half-open smock.

"How long has your cat been acting like this?"

"Just today. When I got home from work." Thinking that the foam on his mouth might be rabies, and I infected, I added, "He's never been out of the apartment. He can't have been infected by another animal, can he?"

"It's not rabies," he said, and left the lounge. Five minutes later he was back again with a middle-aged woman vet who had a twangy Midwestern accent and the manner of a grandmother.

"Do you want to see your pet?" she asked. "He's calm now. We gave him a mild sedative."

"Is he all right?"

"We had to give him a sedative to do our tests. Now that the X rays have been checked, we're about ninety-nine percent certain."

The man darted out and returned with Gustave, calm now but still in the cage. He meowed in recognition, and I went to him and put my fingers through the wire mesh to pet him. As I stroked Gustave, the grandmotherly vet explained that they had taken X rays as a precaution. She said they had been fairly certain of the diagnosis from his symptoms alone, all of which they'd seen before. My cat had a substantial tumor on the brain. Gustave might live a month longer, but he would have continual fits that would worsen daily. He would stop eating, develop skin rashes, probably lose much of his eyesight, his hearing, and all motor control. He might end up injuring himself fairly badly. He would definitely be difficult to live with.

"We believe," she said, and her fellow vet nodded, "in the *humane* treatment of animals. We do as much for them as is medically possible. When a pet is terminally ill, we advise the only humane treatment possible."

"Meaning?"

"Putting your pet to sleep as soon as possible, so he suffers less."

My hand continued to pet my cat; I couldn't believe what I was hearing. The male vet now began to talk of cats with Gustave's diagnosis who'd been caught at this late, inoperable state; what he said was horrible. I never stopped petting Gustave. At last the woman put a hand on her colleague's arm.

"We can keep your pet overnight, if you would like to think about your decision with less pressure," she said. "You can call us in the morning. And although I cannot recommend it, if you decide to, you may pick up your cat tomorrow at any time. He's so sweet, it's a shame."

The other vet then handed me a sheet of their fees. Included was "humane life termination," only ten dollars.

"We'll give him another, somewhat stronger sedative tonight. But I doubt that it will last until morning. We have a padded cage where he won't hurt himself too much when he goes into convulsions again."

I remained in the lounge stroking and talking to Gustave until they were done with all their chores and it was time to put him into the safer cage and close up the office for the night. I walked home, some forty blocks, trying to think what to do. When I arrived back at my apartment, I didn't turn on the lights, didn't answer the phone when it rang, didn't eat dinner. Exhausted at nine-thirty, which was early for me, I went to sleep.

The phone awakened me at eight A.M. It was the woman vet. Despite the sedative, Gustave had suffered several more fits during the night. Even with the padded cage, he'd sprained a leg and battered his head pretty badly. She implored me.

"Go ahead," I said. "Put him out of his misery."

Later that afternoon I took a bus up to the ASPCA to recover my flight bag and Gustave's neck ID band, to sign the necessary papers, and to give them a check. An autopsy had been done, and the tumor had been as large as an egg, malignant, metastasizing quickly down his throat to one lung. Gustave wouldn't have lasted another week.

I suppose it was the suddenness and the absolute conclusiveness of the event that sent me into such a tailspin the rest of the weekend. I came home Saturday and got stinking drunk. Sunday I lay in bed all day with a hangover, trying to block out the sound of laughter and music from a huge party across the backyard in what I later found out was Coltrane's apartment.

That night Fleetwood played a recording by the Budapest Quartet of a late Beethoven string quartet, the fifteenth, in A minor. I'd always considered these last half dozen works of the long deaf composer to be far beyond my musical or intellectual understanding. This time I didn't care what was on the radio, I was too depressed to get off my bed and walk the three feet or so to turn it off. A half hour later, when the third movement began, I suddenly found myself completely attuned to Beethoven. This adagio is a bleak, despairing night song; and it seemed to plumb the depths of my own befuddled emotions, resonating within me unlike any music I'd ever heard. Then, just when it seemed it couldn't resolve itself into anything but disconnected chords of total despondency, it lifted suddenly, soared in psalmlike splendor to something like acceptance.

On Monday morning at work again, I hardly spoke to anyone except when necessary. At lunchtime, Daisy Spearman, my supervisor, gave me an envelope. Inside was a note from our case supervisor, Mrs. Kurlander, asking to see me at five P.M.

"You know what it's about, don't you?" Daisy asked. She had just finished a pleasant phone call to her husband at his office and was finishing lunch at her desk, a temptingly fragrant take-out fried chicken. Her good cheer was unshakable.

"About the Childress case, I suppose," I said, mentioning the emergency opening of the previous Friday. I was sure someone had discovered a goof-up.

"Naw," she said. "Silly! As of next week, you'll have been here two years. She's going to suggest you become a supervisor."

"Two years!" was all I could answer. People came and went from the Department of Welfare so rapidly, I was considered a veteran. Before I could come up with anything else to say, Daisy's phone rang again, and she wiped her fingers to pick it up.

Later that afternoon I walked into Mrs. Kurlander's office and was surprised that Daisy Spearman had been so on target. I could become a unit supervisor, Mrs. Kurlander said. I could even go back to school, taking graduate courses toward a masters degree in social work. I would be paid for those two years, and my schooling would be taken care of by the department. But once graduated, I would have to work for the department, wherever they assigned me, for the following three years. It was one of the best school/work programs offered in the country, Mrs. Kurlander told me; she herself had become case supervisor via the method only a scant five years before. She added that she, the other case supervisors, even the head of the center had read my case reports and they were all certain I possessed exactly the abilities they were looking for—I had a bright future as a social worker.

At the time I was stunned. I said I would think about the offer and thanked her. The various ironies of the situation weren't lost on me. I couldn't even keep a dumb cat from getting cancer and having to be destroyed so it wouldn't suffer and here I was, being asked to interfere in the future lives of real people, with real—sometimes extraordinary—problems. I was admired for the interference I'd already done, and who knew what real or so far only potential damage, to those people. Admired and told I did it better than most of my colleagues. I was totally incapable of loving or being loved by another person, and here I was praised by my clients for understanding and compassion far beyond my years. Worst of all, I was lauded for my written reports.

One of them, with the names changed, would be printed intact in the following year's instruction manual for new caseworkers, Mrs. Kurlander told me; yet whenever I sat down to dictate a case entry, I did so with trepidation, knowing that I was prevaricating, hiding, modifying shamelessly, at times outright lying—that hardly a word of it was true.

It took me a decade, after my fourth job, to realize that this promotion business had become a pattern in my life as long as I worked for anyone but myself. No matter where I worked, what the field, what my previous experience, I would be promoted higher and higher, led onto a path that was extremely tempting, gracious, filled with hands willingly extended to smooth my rise, financial security, titles, position, influence, all of it promised—if I'd only say yes, if I'd only commit myself fully. It seemed that I possessed the curse of efficiency: I appeared able to handle anything that came my way with poise if not always the best temper. I was seldom awkward. I never backed down no matter how tough the problem. I never failed, and never would fail.

Yet within those tempting, sometimes glamorous offers lay a trap, as elaborate a noose as Fate has ever devised. Had I taken up any of the offers, then I would be committed; I knew I would never become a writer. In my heart I knew that. The fact that so many of those superiors "helping" me had confided at one time or another that they were themselves unfulfilled painters, concert pianists, stage directors, and dramatists convinced me.

Very noble of me, you would think. Yet the truth is, I had nothing to show for this noble attitude but the attitude itself. I hadn't written a page not specifically required by work since I'd gotten out of college, and there I'd only written what had been required for courses. In almost a decade of rejecting some fine career advancement, I was operating under what could benevolently be called blind belief. A harsher description of it would have been utter stubbornness and total self-delusion.

I waited a full week before making an appointment to speak to Mrs. Kurlander again. She received me a bit less graciously this time, a bit more officiously, complacent in my acceptance of her offer. She began by asking if I'd thought about the department's school/work program, a slight smile playing about her oversize lips as though she knew this was all nonsense, but she was willing to play it out for form's sake.

"Yes I have," I said. "But first I wanted to check with you about something else. I was down in Control"—the financial records section of the center—"and I see that I'm due for two weeks' paid vacation and five more days of paid sick leave."

"That's right. Three weeks' paid vacation," she said. "And I notice you're due to take it quite soon."

"I thought that instead of taking up the department's offer that I'd take the time and just resign."

Her smile froze on her lips, and her eyes seemed to glaze over.

"You see, while I really do respect your professional judgment on my work, I disagree. I don't think I'm cut out to be a social worker."

Her lips pursed as she tried to figure out what I was up to, what more I wanted. They almost disappeared into her face, then shot open to say the words I hate most in the English language: "Don't you think you're being a bit hasty?"

Her uttering that odious phrase drowned whatever tiny qualms of indecision I still harbored. "Well, yes. But then I was being hasty when I went along with my friend Ruth to take the exam for this job two and a half years ago. And I was being hasty when I accepted the job and appeared at this center for training two years ago. You see, last week I had to have my cat destroyed. . . . A brain tumor."

"I'm so sorry."

"Thanks . . . and I realized, well, I realized that my cat was the only link aside from this job that I still have with my past. Since I want to get away from the past and go toward the future, it makes sense to get rid of every last thing, right? To become completely free!"

"Completely free, yes," she muttered, uncomprehending. "But what will you do? How will you live?"

"I'll go to Europe!"

"I mean, after your vacation?"

"Don't know. Don't care."

"You can always change your mind, you know. Take a vacation. Once you're away, you'll gain a fresh perspective on things. Take a few weeks extra if you need them. I'm certain we can work something out here. I understand a decision of this magnitude needs mulling over. I assure you the offer will stand. I'll forget this little talk ever happened. I know what, I can grant you a leave, as long as you need to decide . . ."

And so on and so forth, yah-dida, yah-dida, the fear of freedom so desperately apparent in her every clause and, as a result, so perfectly delicious to me.

I was free, two months later, sitting at one of the numerous outdoor cafés on the Via Veneto, sun splattering the side street a shade of orange just a bit dimmer than the nearly tasteless Fanta in the tight little bottle from which I sipped.

Free and impatient. I'd been in Rome a week and I'd still not met with Orazio. I was expecting him any minute. He was already fifteen minutes late. I was certain he was taking the time to stop at his fiancée's to persuade her to join us or, failing that (for wasn't she a good, virginal Roman daughter, not seen out with men in public?), persuading one of Elletra's numerous brood of brothers and cousins to join us.

Free, impatient, and bored. Those first days in the city had told me a great deal about Rome and given me more than enough time to know I didn't care for Rome and probably never would. Something about the scale and layout gave a somewhat sinister edge to my wanderings about the city, as I did on foot most of the time. I would begin each day in a specific direction—toward the Colosseum, toward the Roman Forum, toward the Borghese Gardens—but I'd never know whether or not I'd arrive where I was going, or if I'd end up at the Piazza di Spagna or at Travestevere, or at some tiny row of identical facing residential buildings, neither elegant nor slumlike, with few shopfronts and no people in sight for blocks. A middle-aged woman debouching a doorway I hadn't until that second noticed in the chiaroscuro frontage, who fled from me as though from an armed murderer when I crossed the street to ask directions. Five minutes later, at a curious intersection—Via What and Via What?—the man I'd ask for help would look at me from behind a nose so high and hooked, it could have been knocked off a bust of Trajan, only to bark out confusing instructions in the voice of a very irritated jailer. So I'd wander away befuddled as ever, following not his incomprehensible words, but the mobile trajectory that enormous nose pointed to three times.

That was when I would begin to sense the sound of water and the sudden appearance everywhere of cats. Soon I'd strolled into a tiny piazza, its market unopened—perhaps because it was some local saint's feast day—the cats niched and sprawled and ledged in every conceivable architectural spot of a gigantic stone scallop that appeared to be momentarily, if eternally, closing upon a frenzied scene of legendary sea creatures, man-fish and monsters, all twisted into existence out of charcoal-colored stone but for their verdigris mouths and worn-almost-to-white flanks—and the slumberous tumble and ooze of fountain waters.

After my shock at this unexpected sight had worn off, I would stumble away, block after block, arriving somehow upon the Parthenon, which I'd searched for all afternoon two days before with no success, which now simply sat there, next to a tiny baroque chapel, looking like nothing more than a slightly repainted theater tower and balcony from a New York movie theater. With them naturally, an-

other smaller fountain—and the requisite four hundred cats.
The museum would be closed, of course, with a tiny notifi-
cation carelessly thrust on, even though I was certain my
guidebook said it would be open. No matter, I wasn't interested in going in but determined to find some place I'd
recognize, and so I would move on.

Arriving fifteen minutes later at the Via Vittore Emman-
uele, named after the first king of the Republic of Italy a
hundred years back, a large avenue I'd become quite familiar with, and a block or two away, that enormous—and to
many, tasteless—monument looking like something out of
the background of an official painting from the time of
Napoleon. Behind it, the tourists' *ne plus ultra* of this city,
the Roman Forum, which I'd immediately notice and forever describe to friends as consisting of more water, more
felines, more jumbled-up stone—in short, cats pissing on
ruins.

My pension overlooked the Piazza della Republicana, my
windows in front, so I could sit hours at a time looking
down seven floors to the enormous train station or the
National Museum or the Baths of Diocletian. Although it
was late August, the "bad winds," a sort of Italian sirocco,
hadn't yet arrived, the talkative wife of the pension owner
confided to me, which explained why the temperature outside was only equal to that of a pizza oven, rather than that
of the Sahara. It was a late sunny afternoon when I got off
the train from Genoa—somewhat mollified despite the loss
of my Yamaha by my two-hour companionship with Orazio—
and ascended to my rented room. An hour later, washed
and cool, I noticed that the sunset rush-hour traffic appeared unusually congested in the piazza. It remained that
way—curses, honking, the sudden starting up of engines to
move two feet at a time—for the next twenty-four hours. I
found it difficult to believe that it required an entire day to
untangle a traffic jam. Then I realized how Italian, how
specifically Roman, that was, like the unexpected, instant
closing of museums and shops and restaurants and even

churches anywhere in the city without rhythm or explication, like the sudden drenching rainfalls out of cloudless
skies, like the incomprehensible system of streets and piazzas, like the winding of the Tiber itself, and the decision
where to place bridges across its sluggish waters.

Still, I was free. Free, impatient, bored, and just a bit
queasy. From the second day of my arrival I'd fallen prey
to a particularly Roman form of dysentery: a fever that
came and went, seldom remaining long enough to show on
an oral thermometer; a touch of dyspepsia; a smidgen of
diarrhea; the most minuscule nausea: yet all those symptoms would appear at once, suddenly, without warning.
Anna Maria, the middle-aged pension's housekeeper, recognized the signs immediately. "I thought that you were of
Roman generation?" she asked. Groaning, I told her that
was only partly true. My father had been born here on a
visit by his parents, who wanted him to have Italian citizen-
ship, but he had returned to America when he was still only
a round face, a wisp of hair, and a huge pair of brown eyes
wrapped in swaddling blankets. According to a famous photo
my grandmother kept in her bedroom, he'd still been too
young to smile.

Anna Maria instantly bustled off, returning to my room
with a large blue bottle of Brioschi, instructing me to carry a
score of the twisted little white things in an envelope and to
munch them wherever I went. She explained the problem
was water. Even though I hadn't gone near the fountains
that gurgled, bubbled, spumed, and sloshed everywhere, the
waters still came into the city by thousand-year-old aque-
ducts. In transit, the waters picked up certain deposits—
minerals, sulfur, iron, even carbonates of lead. These didn't
bother native-born Romans, most of whom could take a sip
from a glass and accurately declare exactly which aqueduct—
what spring in what village in the Apennines, even—the water
came from. Unfortunately tourists . . . In addition to the
lemony bicarbonate, Anna Maria recommended a light diet:
rice, bread, eggs, and pasta. Oh, and chocolate to bind me up.

Luckily the breads in Rome were various and delicious, the *risotti* were a meal in themselves, the simplest macaroni dishes splendid enough to live on forever; and I was still too young to worry about cholesterol—I ate omelets and *frittate* at every opportunity. And, not two streets from the Baths of Diocletian, I happened upon a tiny Carmelite convent shop, no more than a Dutch door closet set into the blank wall of the nunnery, where especially elderly and saintly sisters were allowed into the temptation of public scrutiny to sell sacred candles, rosary beads, prayer cards, vials of holy water, and half-kilo-weight bars of homemade chocolate, both bitter and sweet, as heavenly as one might expect from such a hallowed candy kitchen. After I'd found the shoplet, I stopped every day, carrying my foil-wrapped purchases everywhere I went, so in my memory that first week in Rome, although unpleasant, is tinged by the pervasive scent of Ciocolata di Convento Carmelita.

Free, impatient, bored, queasy, and horny.

Orazio arrived and with him the expected brother—no, he was a friend—only a shade less handsome, named Cesco, also a worker in the Italian Treasury Department but with about sixteen more English words. Could Orazio have guessed my interest in him for what it was? Better still, had he found Cesco for me?

No. It turned out that both men were engaged. After many months in Rome I would discover that every unmarried male over fifteen considered himself engaged and that even if he were, in fact even if he were married, this hardly meant that he wasn't open to a little hanky-panky, hetero- or homoerotic, depending upon your charm and his whim. At the time I was still untutored, and the two of them seemed far more interested in their Camparis and in the various women strolling along the Via Veneto, or using narrow makeup mirrors to check their appearance in low-slung pearl-gray sports cars, or sitting in the abutting sidewalk restaurants. Especially the three at a table separated from us by a large, noisy, four-generation family. Even so, during a lull in my conversation with Cesco and Orazio (mostly in my slow, imprecise Italian flavored with college French and Spanish which I knew far better, and in their halting English) I decidedly heard two of the three girls talking excitedly, saying in English, "I'm *certain* he is." To which the other replied, "No. No, he *can't* be."

Until the first one declared, "I'll *prove* it to you."

She wove around the family and came to sit right next to me: a short, pretty girl with light brown eyes so large they shone through all of her eye shadow and lashes, a close-cut "Italian boy" haircut, the palest pink lipstick. She wore a lacy long-sleeved blouse that revealed as much as it hid, and skin-fitting shiny ebony slacks, all of which showed to great advantage her extraordinary physical development.

"You're not Italian, are you?" she asked. "I mean, Italian Italian?"

The others at the table didn't know what she was talking about. I did.

"No, I'm American."

"See," she said slowly, nasally, and I wasn't at all surprised by her next question: "From Noo Yawk, right?"

"Right."

She stood up to face her friends. "I *told* you!" she said in a loud stage whisper. Then to me, "I told them you were one of us. One of us, and American. Not that there aren't tons of Americans in Rome. But they're all tourists and other icky things. Hey!" to the other girls. "What are you waiting for? C'mon. C'mon!"

The girl she'd been arguing with earlier leapt up from her chair to join us. "Hi, guys! Are you really from New York? Where? East Tenth Street? Where's Cicely? Oh, by the way, I'm Tina Ledger. That"—pointing to our first visitor who was now back at their table trying to convince the reluctant third to join us—"that's Donna Slattery. And our friend"—pointing to the svelte, ash blonde who had stood up and was allowing herself to be tugged over—"is Cicely Bowen. We're actresses."

"No!"

Tina slapped my arm. "Smart aleck! Now who are all of you? C'mon, Cis, sit down. He's one of us."

If Donna was short and stacked, and Cicely taller and slender and quite surpassingly Beacon Hill right down to her tweed tailored suit, then Tina was the Corn Belt personified, a flame-haired, curly-headed Wisconsin farmerette, wearing yellow toreador slacks and a frilly, paisley-patterned, off-the-shoulders blouse one wouldn't expect to see outside of a Wyoming saloon.

Without a doubt, separately the three were the best-looking women in the area. Together they were a spectacle. At our table, befriending me, they were an event. My Roman companions were more than pleased by the sudden company; in response, Orazio and Cesco were sweet and attentive, they bought us drinks and coffee and dessert, and they sincerely wished they knew more English for the *"belle attrice Americane."*

I almost wished they did too. Primarily because once comfy, the three women treated me as though we'd known each other for months, rather than for two minutes. On and on they chatted, Cicely remaining the coolest, but Tina and Donna as though they were home in Flatbush or Dubuque, flirting, outrageous, throwing their arms around my shoulder, feeding me dessert on a fork, slipping a hand inside my shirt (three buttons open to my sternum like all the young men in Italy) to play with my nipple, turning to whisper, "I've had dago men up to here, but these two seem sweet."

And I still couldn't for the life of me figure out how I was "one of us," as they kept saying. At one point Donna and Tina got up to greet some pals at curbside in a super-fantastic Maserati. I looked at Cicely and, in the style of our encounter so far, asked her.

"You know"—she said offhandedly— "you're not *bouge*."

I decided this was slang for bourgeois. "How do you know?"

"Pre-cious, we can tell. You're off. Just like we are."

"Off?"

"Off. Daft. Daring. Dangerous. An artist or writer or layabout or . . . God, Donna!" She suddenly tried to get the others' attention. "It's Angel! There in that awful Principessa's Daimler. We've got to rescue him!"

She jumped up and the others joined her in being lifted over the restaurant fence. They dashed into the slow-moving traffic on the Via Veneto and stormed an enormous pre–World War II sedan, pulling out of the backseat a giant young bodybuilder—so pale blond, he might have been an albino Samson—clad only in a pair of pale yellow skivvies, obviously borrowed, far too small for him.

To shouts of *Putane!* from some female inside the car, the three girls hugged him, jumped all over him, then skipped over auto bumpers and had him lift them back into the restaurant.

Close up, Angel looked exactly like his name. He was smashingly good-looking, tanned to a fare-thee-well, and didn't speak a word of Italian other than *Ciao.*

"Well, howdy there," he drawled, sitting down next to me in a chair the girls finagled. "These sweet thangs told me we wuz having a party."

Cesco and Orazio were nonplussed by the arrival of this most competitive apparition. My eyes almost popped out at the sight of his pinwheel periwinkle-blue eyes, his astonishing expanse of flesh, pectorals like dinner plates, waist-sized biceps, tree-trunk thighs upon which Tina and Donna perched, explaining that Angel was a movie actor—he'd been in three films that had opened in the past six months, with *dozens* of lines, and he was another "one of us."

They introduced me, Donna saying, "Isn't he cute, Angel? Couldn't you just eat him up?"

Angel reached around her back to death-grip my neck in greeting. "Ain't these wimmin fine, huh? They're lak sistuhs to me since I came to Rome."

His arrival had not gone unnoticed. Several women from various tables came over, mostly middle-aged and overweight and gigglingly shy, asking for autographs, which Angel provided, slapping one suddenly freed knee (it resounded like a side of beef) at his celebrity.

A uniformed chauffeur pushed the last of Angel's fans out of the way—evidently the abandoned Principessa's driver—and stood arrow-straight, saying something in a low voice and barely restrained fury, to which Angel replied, "You tell her Princesshood I'm all blown out, ya hear! Take me least another hour or two to churn me up some more stuff for her. Ya hear!" To which the chauffeur looked frigid with shock and homicidal mania but merely snorted and stalked away. "Now where wuz we?" Angel asked, all innocence.

He ordered and gobbled down a series of rich desserts ("building up my strength—and my virile liquids"), then promptly dozed off in his chair.

This relaxed Orazio and Cesco, who'd been quietly discussing leaving. But though they remained, it was soon made clear to them in Tina's much-accented and Cicely's superb Italian that the girls were not to be had—at least not that night—and that in fact they were off to some party, late even by Roman standards, at some count or other's palazzo south of the city, near EUR, that fascist monstro-city Mussolini had never completed building. After a courteous period of time the two men begged off and left.

"Not you," Donna insisted. "You're coming to Contino Eddie's with us."

I wouldn't have dreamed of getting up. Partly because I liked them; partly because I didn't have to get up the following morning; partly because in his sudden sleep Angel had flung an enormous tanned arm across me, his giant hand landing precisely in my lap, under which my erection throbbed like a dangerously infarcted heart.

Free, no longer impatient, not only not bored but fascinated; not queasy despite all I'd been spoon-fed; and yes, hornier than ever.

The girls talked on, shouting *ciaos* at friends, suddenly

falling into instant whispered conclaves when someone important from Cinecittá arrived ("we live, breathe and sometimes even *work* in Cinecittá," Cicely confided). "Don't look left," Tina would quietly say to Donna, who of course couldn't resist looking and would reply breathlessly, "It's Piero"—or Mario or Enzo or Luchino or Claude. . . . In less than an hour I knew everything about Tina and Donna's Defoe-like fortunes in the Roman movie business over the past year and a half and, despite her reticence, a bit about Cicely's too. And, as we kept drinking wine, I became even more at ease with them, although I did slur out a slip of the tongue: I called them "Stollywood Harlots." Instead of being insulted, they loved it so much, the name stuck.

Angel reawakened as suddenly as he'd fallen asleep, looked around, and promptly found a waiter and ordered a *suppa Inglese*, which he accompanied with a plateful of cookies and three cappuccinos. When he lifted his hand off my crotch, he shook it a bit, saying, "Dang near burned it!" Before I could perish of mortification, he leaned over to me and whispered, "Boy, you'd best do something about that thang." He asked which of us had a car to get to Contino Eddie's.

None of us did, but Donna remembered a former boyfriend of some weeks before who worked at the night desk of the nearby Excelsior Hotel, and talked the other girls into going to help convince him to loan it to them—an offer with so much acting and mischief potential, they couldn't resist.

As soon as they were gone, Angel paused in his destruction of a massive chunk of chocolate cake to say to me, "Now, I wasn't kiddin' back there, boy. You ought to get into the jakes and whack that thang before it breaks through your trousers," his periwinkle eyes fluttering through naturally long lashes Sylvana Koscina (with four at a table in the next restaurant) would envy, a smile on his lips stained foamy white from the cappuccino.

"I think I could use the bathroom," I said, flushed and

flustered, attempting to gather together the remaining shreds of my dignity.

"Nuthin' to be 'shamed of," he said as I stumbled away from the table. "Only natural."

When I managed my way through the tables into the restaurant proper, I promptly bumped into someone. Still embarrassed from the talk with Angel, I blushed even more and murmured *"Scusi."*

The man I'd knocked into stood back to let me by. The jacket over his shoulders, *à la mode* that season, made his shoulders even larger. A shock of straight, straw-colored hair under an askew bone-white fedora was wetted or oiled so that every thick strand was visible. His forehead was high and wide, a single deep horizontal line creasing it suggested much thought and not a little suffering. Heavy brows and shaggy honey-hued eyebrows shadowed his Slavically angled sea-green eyes. A brush of wheaten mustache hid most of his top lip—the full lower one suggesting both—and cradled his short, asymetrically squashed prizefighter's nose. A cleft in his chin completed the perfect jawline.

"Va!" he said in a mellifluous baritone. *"Prego,"* he added gently, somewhat amused. I'd been so stunned by his handsomeness, I hadn't moved. *"Per piacere"*—please, he now insisted.

I finally got together enough sense to stumble toward the john; but once arrived at the door, I couldn't resist turning around to look at him again. He was stopped, talking to a vampirical-looking black model. What held me was how completely he filled some idealized portrait of The European Man I'd developed, without ever being fully aware of it. It had happened over the years from various foreign films I'd seen, from glossy, glamorous, full-color ads in *The New Yorker* and *Esquire*, where men exactly like him stood aloof, a slight smile on their faces, as someone held their polo pony or a mannequin stepped out of an expensive automobile. Despite the fact that I'd been in Europe a month, in Italy a week, and had seen my share of good-looking men, not a single one had so utterly encapsulated this particular cosmopolitan persona. Without having spoken more than a few pleasantries with him, I knew he was cultured and kind, pensive and provocative, sensual and considerate, deeply intelligent and yet caring. In short, I arrived at a terrifying, exhilarating, Aristotelian recognition that he was devastatingly attractive to me: the first male who had been attractive to me in more than a decade. Then he noticed me staring at him and glanced from my face down to my crotch, which sent me quickly inside.

Slapping cool water on my face helped my flushed color, but when I tried to piss with a steel-hard erection, I couldn't, and finally I had to hold the door shut with one hand (no lock) while I poured cold water over my cock with the other, until I'd finally softened it enough to urinate.

The Slavic god was gone when I got out. No, there he was, at a table not far from ours, sitting with the needle-thin model and a bald, fat man wearing an unseasonal knitted sweater and Ray-Ban dark glasses, despite the fact that it was now past midnight. I looked at my heartthrob and he looked at me as I managed my way back to where Angel was once more snoring away, rejoined by the girls. As I pulled up and sat down, Tina said, "Kit was right there in the bar saying he'll drive us, and he's got an Electra convertible. So we invited him too. He'll be here in a min. Who *are* you glaring at?" she demanded of me.

"He's glaring back," Donna said, angling to get a better look past other diners. "Now he's raising a glass of wine. Cis, isn't that . . . ?"

"Djanko the T," all three girls said at once and in a somewhat hushed tone.

"Who?" I asked. Like a fool, I'd also raised my glass at him. Maybe not like a fool, as he smiled and I saw a row of strong white teeth peeping out of that bushy mustache and those thick lips. I was erect again.

"Djanko Travenicke, *the* hottest director in Cinecittá!" Tina murmured. "Do you know him?" she asked suspiciously.

"I bumped into him before."

"Angel, wake up!" Donna said, "Djanko the T is toasting our new pal."

Angel not only instantly woke up, he also stood up, then did a most amazing thing: Raising up his clenched fists, he began to ripple his muscles at Djanko. Up and down they bumped and thumped and rolled along his arms, chest, stomach, and back, until I thought I would collapse from overstimulation.

Applause and shouts of "Bravo!" greeted this display, and Djanko now raised his glass to all of us in a toast.

"He's shooting what, Cis, three films right now, with two in the can and two more on the boards?" Tina asked breathlessly. "What do we do now?" she despaired.

"I believe we got his attention." Cicely understated it.

Angel sat down again, smiling, and reached forward for more food.

Seconds later an insistent car horn turned out to be Kit picking us up. Before we'd paid, gotten out from the mess of tables and onto the street, the fat man with dark glasses who'd been at Djanko's table managed to take Cicely aside and speak to her. I didn't hear what he said, but she replied in Italian numbers.

Kit turned out to be an Australian sheep heir, a playboy who'd lived in Rome almost twenty years—"long after he was still new or cute," Donna confided—who seemed delighted to have our company in his flashy chrome and acid-green Buick convertible, the newest model, with dove-gray calf leather upholstery and sheepskin throws over everything not expressly needed for driving, doubtless in subtle reference to his endless source of ready cash.

Tina and Donna jumped in front, Angel, Cicely, and I in back, and Kit revved away from the curb despite the slow, tight traffic, with much shouting from the girls and burning rubber from the front tires.

Once we'd gotten off the Via Veneto and finally found our serpentine way to the much faster Via Cristoforo Colombo, which eventually led to Contino Eddie's, Tina turned around, shouting, "What did the Pig want?"

"Our phone number!" Cicely shouted back.

"For which one of us?"

"He didn't say."

"Who do you *think*?" Donna joined the yelling. "The T's got a muscle epic in the works, doesn't he?"

Cicely recalled reading that he was planning a film about Jason and the Argonauts.

"Oh, Angel," Tina cried, "if I didn't love you, I'd hate you." Then she turned around in her seat for the rest of the ride.

Kit took every slight curve in the road as though he were driving in the Mille Miglia. This either tossed the beauteous Cicely into my arms, or more often threw me into Angel's huge outstretched curved arm, where I finally ensconced myself, Cicely's head in my lap so the wind wouldn't mess her hair. With every sharp turn Angel would holler out a bloodcurdling "Whoopee!" and hold me tighter. Contented as I was at that moment, I still couldn't stop thinking about the man in the restaurant: I was certain he was attracted to me if by no means as much as I was bowled over by him.

At the huge Baroccoco gates to the palazzo, we met others driving out again. The party was a drag, they told us in four languages; even Eddie had left to go to Ulrica's place in the Alban Hills.

"Where?" Kit asked.

"Follow us," one carful of revelers shouted.

During the ride I fell asleep. Once we'd arrived (Cicely later told me), Donna and Tina thought I looked so "darling," they convinced Angel to carry me inside and put me into a small bedroom on the second floor of this seventeenth-century country villa, a palace built by some pope or other for his cardinal nephew and their mistresses. I must have napped about two or three hours. When I awakened, I wandered though roomsful of a slowly ending, rather disorganized group of people—the remnants of the party. I found a bottle of cognac but no glasses and sipped from the bottle-neck as I wandered through the large old chambers, looking for the people I'd come with. Outside one room I heard laughter, and the door opened to reveal Tina—quickly pulling up her paisley blouse—with two men. One of them turned out to be Contino Eddie, the other an Austrian Olympic ski champion. They invited me in and offered me a pipeful of burning hashish. I smoked it but left when all three began to undress each other. Finally, in what seemed to be some sort of library, I spotted Cicely, chatting with two tiny dark-skinned women in full Balinese ceremonial regalia (evidently I'd missed their performance). I almost wandered away again, but Cicely motioned to me. The women bowed and left and Cicely took my arm, pointing us outside where an enormous flagstone terrazzo wound around the place. From one side we could look over the Campagna and see the sudden bright aura that she said was the lights of Rome. On the other side we could see the mountains, and behind them the night sky beginning to pale. It was still too early for birdsong.

I was slightly drunk, slightly stoned on the hash, totally at ease. So, apparently, was Cicely. We strolled silently along the terrazzo, turned a corner, passed French doors ajar upon rooms with people sitting talking or sprawled sleeping in chairs and on beds. At one window-door we passed, I saw Angel supine, snoring away, his yellow skivvies pulled down to his ankles; Kit was fully clothed astride those giant calves, his hands separating those large, hairless buttocks, Kit's tongue about to dart into Angel's unsuspecting rectum. Casually Cicely pulled a curtain and murmured, "I swear, that boy could sleep through an earthquake," and we sauntered on. We stopped where a double stairway broke the terrazzo's length of balustrade and we descended to a tiny fountain where a travertine satyr was ravishing an alabaster nymph in graphic detail.

"Would you believe me if I said I was still a virgin?" Cicely asked pensively.

"Why would you say a thing like that?" I asked back.

She stared at me, then giggled. "Donna was right about you. Well, then, would you believe me if I told you that I was a fat and hateful little girl? And that I want more than anything to be a famous actress just to spite all the people I grew up with back in Marblehead, Massachusetts?"

"No. I think you were a beautiful little girl. Your ambition to be an actress is to prove to yourself that you're worthy of all the attention you got."

"You clever thing! That's exactly right! Now, your turn. Go on. What's your ambition?"

"I don't know."

"No holding back allowed."

"Sometimes I think it's writing. But first I have to live, I guess."

"Dramas, novels?"

"I have no idea, really."

"You should write for the movies since you're here," she said.

"I couldn't possibly do that!"

"Well, then," she temporized, "you should at least try your hand at translations. You know they make scads of films here of all sorts, then sell them all over the world. You could help translate them into English. That's mostly what I do in Cinecittá, except of course for fending off lewd offers. I'm the only one of us who works steadily, you know. As a voice-over. I've been dozens of characters already—an English schoolmarm in Mau Mau country, a Slave girl from Gaul, even a Cockney murder victim."

"Well, maybe . . ."

"It's not hard work. And I have the contacts. Really. Promise me you'll at least try it."

"All right. But I didn't come to Rome to work in the movies."

"Don't try to tell me you came to look at the Vatican and all that trash?"

"No." Then it just blurted out of me: "I came to fall in love."

She looked astonished but instantly stopped herself. "Precious! What a lovely idea. I'll help. Do you have a clue who yet?"

Now I hesitated. "Someone I met tonight."

"Please don't say it's me," she begged.

"No," I said, but didn't know how to say more. "I'm not sure, of course. But I think," I went on, checking her aurora-lighted face for reaction, "I think it may be that man in the restaurant. The director," I explained.

Both of her perfect eyebrows went up a bit. "So *that's* why the Pig wanted our telephone number. So Djanko could get hold of you!"

I thought that was rushing to conclusions and said so.

She shushed me. "Djanko is *perfection* for you, Pre-cious. Rich, powerful, restless, temperamental, unfulfilled. I couldn't have chosen better for romance if I'd tried."

"Except," I had to say, "what if he's not . . . interested," I added lamely, not wanting to reveal myself as the *bouge* she thought I wasn't.

She seemed not to hear me. She went on to tell me I mustn't breathe a word about it to the other girls, who would mess it up trying to get jobs through me. "Leave it to me," Cicely concluded.

It seemed impossible, absurd. We walked past the fountain to a little stone platform raised high above a wood, and leaned over the stone parapet, watching the sky redden in the east. Cicely placed one arm over my shoulder, put her face next to mine, rubbing my cheek ever so softly, and said, "This *will* be fun!"

Not too many years later, under a different name, Cicely became quite famous as an actress. She made a dozen films, went on to some plum roles in West End theaters, even had a longish run in one Broadway play and was nominated for a Tony award. Then she disappeared—married, I guess, to a young man from Marblehead, Massachusetts, having proved to herself that she was indeed worthy of all the attention her regal looks had brought her. Of the three of them, only Cicely fulfilled her acting ambitions—if only for a decade. In fact, of all the young Americans at Cinema City I came to know, only she got what she wanted.

So you can assume that such a small and easy thing as matchmaking would be a cinch for her.

I awakened on the floor of the girls' flat about noon, the phone ringing in that particularly insistent way of Italian telephones. I wondered if I could negotiate my way over Angel—slouched next to me in a dead sleep—and through all the pushed-together living-room furniture without serious injury to one of us. I needn't have worried. On the third ring, two pairs of female hands were on the receiver. I sank back into a sofa pillow to hear Tina wrest the phone from Donna and say *"Pronto."* She listened a bit, then shouted, "Cis, it's for you."

Cicely was already up, dressed in a little wraparound smock, her hair freshly shampooed and done up in a pink towel turban. She spoke into the phone, then shooed the others away until they'd retreated into the bedroom they shared and closed the door. She looked to where Angel and I were sprawled—him out of the yellow skivvies—and turned away, continued speaking in a low voice, seemed to be waiting for someone on the other end, then began speaking again in a somewhat haughty tone I'd not heard from her before. After several minutes of exchange, her tone of voice softened considerably. When she turned into profile, I could see her smiling. Still smiling, she said, *"Si, si. Certo!"* and then hung up.

"All right, you two," she said loudly. "Get up. I've got jobs for you."

Tina and Donna tumbled out of the bedroom doorway from where they'd remained, evidently unsuccessfully trying to overhear the conversation.

"Not you two," Cicely said. *"Those* two."

"Oh, Cis! How could you?" the girls whined.

"I didn't do a thing. It was a foregone conclusion. I

merely pretended I was their agent so the Pig wouldn't screw them too much. Wake up, Angel. Flexing time!''

Tina and Donna stormed off into the kitchen, a room separated from the rest of the flat by a long, skylit (eighth-floor walk-up!) corridor. Once there, they could be heard making fresh coffee and loud, rude comments on American boys taking the bread out of American girls' mouths.

Angel was awake enough to hear and shouted, "Hell! I gave you all eight hundred dollars' worth of that there Monopoly money they paid me for my last movie, didn't I?''

Immediate apologies ensued all around, and kisses to make up. Sitting around the living room, we had a breakfast of coffee and day-old Italian bread smeared with apricot preserves. It was a most informal affair. Angel modestly pulled the sheets in which we'd slept up to his midsection, and when I tried to put on my clothing, I was pushed back onto the floor, and so wore only my underwear. Tina and Donna wore bras and panties, their hair in curlers, and sat near us on the floor. Cicely had the only chair, poured coffee, jammed our bread, and played mother.

Once we were all settled and fed, she quietly and effectively explained what she'd set up for us. As we all thought, Angel's impromptu exhibition of the night before had been noticed by the film director. Angel was to be screen-tested for a small role in a medieval historical film Djanko the T was in the middle of shooting. And if he worked out there, he would be tested for a much larger role—that of Hercules in the future Jason and the Argonauts production. This latter role was a costarring one, third name down on the credits, with lots of action and not too many lines to learn.

"When you go there today," Cicely warned, "pick up something heavy in the room and swing it around. And, Angel, wear a jockstrap, will you? Portions of your genitals have been seen in every screen test you've done in Rome.''

Under Cicely's special recommendation, I was to be personally interviewed by Djanko for a position as dubbing translator.

"Whatever you *want* to do," she warned, "resist the impulse and keep to business. I've given him a complete rundown on you. All lies, of course. He thinks you're a Whitney or Rockefeller or something. I told him you're a brilliant writer and just trying your hand at this for what you may learn of the film business for a novel you're planning. He's prepared to treat you like the crown prince."

"But I don't even know if . . . ." I began to protest.

"*I* know. He's willing to pay you —— lire per hour." (Here she named some outlandish amount, which even when translated into dollars was a stiff tariff.)

"The real trick," Tina said, "is to *always* make them pay for it." She was eating the sesame seeds off a small, rotund St. Anthony's roll, biting them off the hardened crust one at a time.

"It's true," Donna agreed sagely. "In fact, it's absolutely expected. In Rome if you get anything for nothing, you consider it worthless."

"Oh, come on," I protested.

"Ask anyone."

"I've never been paid," Angel said with dignity, "except for work."

"Pre-cious!" Tina laughed. "You arrived home this morning with a sheaf of lire notes shoved in your underwear." She reached for the skivvies and, daintily holding them at a distance, shook them. Italian bills fluttered to the carpet.

"Well, I'll be. . . . Where did that all come from?" Angel wondered.

Cicely and I exchanged glances but kept quiet. She took the bills and doled them out to us, tucking a few into her towel turban.

"Carfare," she said succinctly. Then, to me, "In principle, the girls are right. However, there are always exceptions. I don't for a second doubt that you'll continue to be your pre-cious discerning self and know which is which."

Angel stood up to go to the john. He reappeared wearing not the yellow shorts but a tiny pair of sheer black panties he'd obviously found hanging in the bathroom. It looked like a posing strap and fit him spectacularly.

Cicely groaned. "It's ruined!"

"Don't it look good?" Angel asked, turning all around in front of us. "Hell, this is better than a nasty old jock, ain't it? Ain't it?"

What I had told Cicely about coming to Europe to fall in love was true, although I'd certainly never expected it to happen quite so quickly.

Despite that, and given all of Cicely's buildup on the telephone, the first thing I did when I arrived at Djanko's apartment-office suite at the Hassler was to tell him:

1) I didn't really want a job;

2) I wasn't a Whitney or Rockefeller—obvious, I thought, from my name—but merely a middle-class New Yorker;

3) Cicely wasn't my agent, but she was a wonderfully talented actress and surely he had some small part for her.

Djanko wore no hat inside, had no jacket slung over his shoulders. He did have on a sexy, waist-pleated pair of white linen slacks, a royal-blue polo shirt, and two-toned aerated wingtip shoes.

At the time I thought he looked like a fashion plate from *Gentleman's Quarterly*. Years later I would be leafing through our family photograph albums and come upon photos of my father taken in the late thirties, when he was still single, and I would groan, seeing him in a virtually identical outfit. Djanko spoke in a deep voice, in not terrible English:

"Then that's why you came here?"

"Pretty much," I lied.

"You could have told me that on the telephone, no?"

"Yes."

He stood up from behind the desk and came over to where I sat in the office and, to my complete astonishment, kneeled down in front of me and took my hands in his own large, golden-haired hands. His perfectly combed hair glittered golden in the afternoon light, his eyes dancing green. "You came here. Why? To make love?"

"Yes," I said, and immediately wondered that those words had come out of my mouth. *"Certo."*

"You have done this before? In New York?"

"Not really."

"Nor I too much. I was married to a woman. But a little bit, yes."

He kissed my hands lightly, looked up at me again, and I felt like a heroine in a Jane Austen novel receiving a marriage proposal.

"My father, in Yugoslavia, belongs there to the Party. You know what I'm talking about? There he is a very serious Communist. All the time I was growing up, he would say to me, 'Djanko, remember the Americans are your enemy.' At the same time, while I was a small child, he would read to me stories of the old Greeks, their legends and their myths—Hercules, Theseus, Andromeda, Perseus.

"But when I came here to Rome, everywhere I looked, I saw Americans. They were not devils, as my father told me. Yet . . . yet . . . they were not ordinary people like the Italians, like the French people. No. Those girls, that boy Angel, and you—especially you—are all to me like those people in the Greek legends my father told me. Some Italians make fun of you, call you the new conquerors of the world, despite yourselves. But even they wonder how it is that even the most innocent of you come among us as though . . . as though you *know* something."

"Know what?" I asked, confused. He was getting it all wrong: He—the European—possessed all knowledge, all culture, not I the barbarian American.

"I can't say what. None of us know. That you are better, maybe. That we are all small and old and ridiculous, maybe."

"I never thought that." He smelled faintly of cologne, an odor more insidiously disturbing than any after-shave I'd ever inhaled; it enflamed me like an aphrodisiac.

"It's true!" Djanko said. "But what is most puzzling to us

is that you want so very *little* from us, and we wreck our minds to wonder why that is."

"I want you," I said boldly, waiting for him to stand up and laugh, tell me the charade was over, and I could go—fool that I was to dare aspire.

Instead he continued to astonish me. "*Caro.* Since last night in the restaurant I am already yours," he said thrillingly. Then we went into the bedroom and I understood what it was like to be with a member of my own sex whom I adored. Without a thought, without a jot of the awkwardness, distaste, or free-floating boredom of the months before, I did everything with Djanko that all those men had expected from me in New York. Loved it and—excited, panting, sweating—loved him.

That night after dinner (sent up to his rooms from a restaurant below, possibly one in the hotel), we made love again. During an interlude Djanko told me, "I spent all of last night trying to think who of you five were lovers with each other. Then I thought, 'Wait, Djanko. These are Americans. It won't do to think of them in the usual way.' "

"Well, you're right about that. We're all just friends."

"Tonight I fly to Cannes on business. I'll be back tomorrow afternoon. You'll stay here, of course, from tonight on."

Later, we sat in some Via Veneto café watching the Kessler Twins singing *"Danke Schöen"* on the Scopetone—a movie and jukebox duo who never successfully crossed the Atlantic—and Djanko told me more of his childhood as a Young Communist, one of twenty boys and girls in the local party division who'd gone off on a combination summer camp and history/geography jaunt to Dalmatia.

Djanko spoke of the basalt barrenness of those skyscraping rocky shelves, so cleanly broken they might have arisen out of the earth's restless mantle the day before. He told me about the storm-swept sunsets observed from what had once been some Grand Hotel's overdecorated restaurant. Magyar princes and Italian revolutionaries, the principal residents of the previous century, had preferred their bit of nature unpredictable, and few experiences equaled that of a piano recital in the glass-enclosed conservatory, lightning crackling to punctuate someone's attempt at "Reminiscences of Norma."

In his eleventh summer, Djanko's group had stayed a week at a People's Summer Resort in a shell-shocked Romanesque abbey. Somewhere among the warren of tunnels and vaults was inlaid an icon of St. Stephen, a local patron, who Djanko swore looked like me—preordained me: "Greek, Italian, Spanish, Lebanese, *echt* Mediterranean." During one of the many organized activities, young Djanko had run off and hidden in the vault. Discovered, he had been slapped across the face by his leader and dragged back to the others and later on censured for dawdling so long in front of the icon-studded wall with its un-Leninist religious connotations.

Long after midnight, we drove out of the city in his Maserati, past the airport to the Ostia seaplane basin. There Djanko told me one of us would hurt the other and that he hoped I would be the one who left first.

His statement was highly unnerving to me, coming so soon after eight hours of complete bliss. "Why? Why even talk like that?" I asked. "It's so fatalistic. So negative."

"Why? Because I'm a European. What choice do I have?"

"Just get to and from Cannes safely, will you?" I demanded.

Once the seaplane had buzzed off over the Tyrrhenian, I started up Djanko's car and left. Speeding back to Rome through a fog that shredded into mist and turned into a soft, warm rain, I luxuriated in a new emotion compounded of jealousy, anxiety, longing, and desire. I became angry, sad, terrified, hopeful, content again, all within seconds. Jesus, I remember thinking, this is *weird*.

"I count only the sunny hours" reads the inscription on a bronze sundial I'd come across in a château garden in the Loire Valley. Were I to tell of my affair with Djanko for the following months, it would be counting mostly sunny hours, which are virtually alike and frankly more interesting to experience than to read about. I'll pass over the idyll. For in the midst of our newfound romantic and sexual happiness, we also had problems, larger and smaller, and conflicts, which at the time didn't seem at all irreconcilable.

The first problem concerned Djanko's housekeeper and cook, Mafalda, a squat barrel of a woman just past middle age yet still black-haired, who'd been with him since he'd been in Rome. That is to say, all through his early difficult days of living in a dingy flat in the Pincio, where she'd slept in a closet, right up to these palmy days in their seven-room Hassler suite, with hotel help for all the heavy work. That is to say, through Djanko's earliest love affairs with waitresses and actresses and film students through his two-year marriage to Jocelyn, an Anglo-Irish magazine writer, right up through the separation and divorce, to me.

"The Wreck of the *Hesperus*," was how Cicely described Mafalda to the others following dinner with Djanko and me, but while the nautical simile was on target, the condition suggested was way off. From closer experience, especially given her astonishing nosiness, tactlessness, couched rudeness, aggression, and indomitability, I renamed Mafalda the Merrimac, after the steel-plated Confederate ship. All this, despite an exterior that seemed—like an Old Master's mural on a collapsing chapel wall—to be cracked in a million places beyond hope of mere patina repair. All this despite her piteous Suffering Martha Sister of the Madonna face: eyes rheumy and yellowing; eyebrows tilting upward together as though from looking too frequently toward Heaven for succor; a diamond-shaped pair of quivering lips as though about to pursue another verso of endless prayer; berry-sized moles on her cheeks, chin, and on her right temple, upon which green houseflies rested unknown to her and from which wiry hairs bristled despite periodic clipping. Had Mafalda fallen to her knees in the Via Condottore and declared to TV cameras that she'd just witnessed anew the

Assumption of the BVM, not a soul in Italy would dream of contradicting her. By the time I moved into the Hassler suite, she ruled Djanko's establishment and life as though he were an addict and she the only dope peddler in the city.

He would yell at her. He would be moody and irritated for days on end. He would refuse—at first. But Mafalda held her tongue, looked uncomprehending at such ire, sometimes allowed a tear to drip down the cracks of her face, sometimes even flinched as though he were about to beat her—then went off and did exactly what she wanted.

The field upon which these tiny battles took place was appropriately minute—the placement of a bed-table water decanter; the choice of a regional olive oil; the thinness and flatness of the linguine she made by hand; the fact of an unneeded pillow upon his favorite reading chair whenever he wasn't seated in it; the selection of cut flowers on the foyer table (he *hated* whatever she loved); how many rings of the telephone before she finally picked it up (I counted no less than five rings: three, she swore). Even so, their reactions could hardly be more grandiose than if they were Bonaparte and Kutuzov at Borodino. In front of me, Djanko hurled the offending pillow out the window in a fit of rage. Mafalda tossed four pounds of hanging-to-dry pasta into the garbage. Djanko knocked over the decanter at three-thirty A.M., wetting both of us in bed, and screamed her name, oblivious to knocks on the suite door and telephone complaints until Mafalda (and half the Hassler) was aroused. Her hair in a simple, incredibly long pigtail, her body encased in a gray flannel nightdress, she looked into the room with an uncontrite *"Signor?"* He settled down instantly and politely told her that she'd misplaced the water, would she clean up the mess and refill it, "Cara Mafalda?"

I never hoped to compete on this emotional level with the two of them, but Mafalda's indomitability included all of us in Djanko's life, and so it was inescapable that she and I would come horn to horn sometime. At first she assumed I was a toy, an affection of the merest moment. I was treated courteously and always addressed as *"Signor."* This was both a hint that other males had preceded me—despite what Djanko had suggested—and that in Mafalda's rheumy eyes, I was to be treated the same as they'd been. As the days devolved into weeks, the weeks to months and I was more in evidence than ever, Mafalda began to leave off the *"Signor"* at the end of her questions to me, and to sometimes stare at me when she thought I wasn't noticing, as though wondering if she really had miscalculated and must now take me far more seriously—as seriously, say, as Jocelyn; or as his secretary, Valentina, known as La Bernakovka; or his producer, known to all as the Pig; or as his friend and screenwriter, Jiri Bernakovka, one of the most persistently masochistic humans alive.

These three were to be found inside the Hassler suite at any time, day or night, whether Djanko was present or not. At first I would be surprised to step out of the shower in the middle of the afternoon to encounter Jiri asleep on the bedroom chair, or come home from lunch with Djanko at Cinecittá to find the Pig on the phone in the office. After a while I became accustomed to them. Valentina, of course, had a key, and was, after all, working there, but Jiri especially seemed to be underfoot at the oddest times. On a Sunday late morning while Mafalda was off to Mass with her sister's family, Djanko and I would fuck and eat breakfast in bed and fuck again, then hear a timid scratching at the bedroom door, and in would creep Jiri with newspapers, wine, and a smug look on his face. I'd be upset. Later on I would say to Djanko, "But he was out there all the while! All the while!" and Djanko would shush me and say, "Be kind to Jiri. He's a tragedy." But how could I be kind when I saw his pale blue eye through a crack of bedroom door as Djanko sucked me, or when I came home from shopping I would find Jiri on the floor of the master bath, his head in our hamper, sniffing our underwear?

Jiri's "tragedy" seemed to be, in Djanko's words, that he was a superfluous man. I'd read Turgenev's novella in college and considered the idea both frivolously Slavic and too literary to be real. But Djanko insisted on its truth: Jiri was unneeded by anyone. They'd met about a decade before when they were film students in Budapest, studying under the great Russian director Grigori Kozinstev, there on loan from Mosfilm. The two youths' shared interest in American popular movies had brought them together—and almost out of the "communal sharing experience" demanded by the school. Jiri hadn't been superfluous then, Djanko said; he'd just been another slender, large-headed boy who wanted to make movies. In fact, of the two of them, it was Jiri and his deft witty slices of Communist life on sixteen millimeter that had the greater success; Jiri who'd held the more promise. It was because of one such film that the two friends had gone to the Bratislava Film Festival, where Jiri met Valentina, who soon became his wife, and where one of his films won an honorable mention.

That day had been the apex of Jiri's life. While he'd been accepting homages and courting his voluptuous, raven-haired countrywoman, Djanko had been busily getting drunk with an Italian film distributor who'd promised to make him rich and famous; about which they'd laughed and sworn eternal friendship and soaked up bottles of Slivovitz.

But the man's promise turned out good. Less than a year later Djanko was in Rome, assistant director to an aging, deaf Italian has-been from the days of silent movies. And Jiri, who was still in Pest making fifteen-minute wonders in sixteen millimeter, was now saddled with La Bernakovka's considerable cosmetics and clothing bills.

As soon as he was able to, Djanko sent for Jiri. The Bernakovkas arrived in Rome just as the Italian Film Renaissance was getting going. Jiri dreamed of making his own *Cabiria*, his own *Rocco and His Brothers*. Instead he went on Djanko's growing payroll, helping to write and direct films with names like *Theseus and the Cyclops*, *Messalina's Last Gladiator*, *Invasion from the Red Star*, and *Bad Afternoon at the Broken Corral*, where his knowledge of the

idiom of American films added to Djanko's already encyclo-
pedic background, resulted in a chain of spectacularly re-
created, often quite bad, movies.

La Bernakovka instantly assessed the situation and left
Jiri's bed for Djanko's; then, when it was clear he was only
being friendly and not a meal ticket, she leapt into the
flabby arms of the Pig. By this time Jiri's incipient Peeping
Tomism had fully developed—for if he couldn't possess his
wife, it was just as well that his buddy was doing so. Yet
when Valentina moved out, Jiri remained. Unable to watch
his wife, he now peeped on his friend. Somehow or other, his
obsession with Valentina had become transferred to Djanko,
and from him to whomever Djanko slept with, including
Jocelyn and myself. Unlike Valentina, Djanko let Jiri watch,
and so remained a true friend.

In vain did I attempt to convince them that all Djanko's
lovers—myself included—were obviously mere props for their
own unfulfilled affair. Jiri protested; Djanko's nose wrinkled in polite distaste, and he pointed out that Jiri was
flaccid, pale, ugly, and balding badly, whereas I, I was a
golden tan, firmly molded, trim, and "pretty as those boys
in Caravaggio with the dirty feet."

If Jiri was so much fouler and more perverted than his
inoffensive mien suggested, the gross Pig turned out to be a
great deal healthier and nicer all around. His name was
Bruno Tratano and he hailed from some peasant village in
Apulia where his subsistence-farming family still lived in
limestone caves. As a boy, he'd hiked to Rome where he'd
worked in film in every conceivable job—grip, gaffer, gofer—
until his breakthrough making a documentary for Mussolini
about the war against Haile Selassie. To his credit, the film
was both good and useful as political propaganda. But the
sight of pasta-chewing soldiers with machine guns leisurely
mowing down hordes of spear-throwing natives had turned
Tratano's stomach. As soon as the film was successfully
screened, he left for Paris, then London, and finally to
Brooklyn, where he worked in the Navy Yard during the

entire Second World War. Either despite of or because of his superb ethics, he was reinstated in the film business in his native land following the American occupation and was instrumental in getting some of the classic films of the time produced. By dint of persistence and his faultless reputation in the industry, he became a name, only a step below Ponti and De Laurentiis. One method he used was to film as much as possible in every genre and then to give directors a "free" film in which they might be as artistic as they wanted.

The Pig had earned his name through mere appearance. He was grossly overweight and though he wore loose-fitting clothing, it didn't contain his bulk. He wore sunglasses day or night, indoors or out, because of an injury to his left eye when a steel chip had scarred it during his Navy Yard work. Naturally he was accused of wearing the glasses so he might be shifty and deceitful. This theory was supported by Tratano's other facial features: his lips and nose were pushed together as though in a perpetual scowl—and were distinctly porcine. He also had little control over his body—he was always belching and sweating.

Still, he adored Valentina and treated her well. He doted on Djanko, whom he kept in large amounts of much-needed lire, putting up with his Slavic tantrums and never taking offense. He even tried to be good to Jiri, whom, after all, he'd cuckolded.

After I'd gotten over my own initial fear, repugnance, and distrust of Tratano, we talked one long afternoon on the set and afterward he called me the Manhattan Kid. He would sometimes make me sit on his fat knee and would feed me sweets, talking in a garble of Bensonhurst and Calabrese.

That was later. First there was Mafalda to cope with and, after six months of her, our first declaration of open war.

Despite my settling into the Hassler suite and securing a work permit and ID through the Pig, I was still on a tourist visa, allowing only a three-month stay. So, after ninety days, I had to leave Italy for twenty-four hours, then return for a restamping of my visa for another three months.

The first time this happened, Djanko made it the occasion of a jaunt for us alone to Paris where we stayed in the Crillon and ate and fucked our brains out—our honeymoon.

The second time it came around, he was deeply involved in final shooting on a film. Would I mind terribly going alone? I'd never seen Switzerland and had been invited to Locarno for a weekend of skiing by Contino Eddie and Tina, who were something of an item. I traveled with two bags and all was explained to Mafalda. I kissed Djanko good-bye, was driven to da Vinci airport where I met the others. At Milan we changed to Contino Eddie's private plane, and if the rest of the weekend wasn't as spectacular as that TransAlpine plane ride, it was pleasant and scenic enough.

I arrived back at the suite forty-eight hours later to find Djanko at Cinecittá—in the cutting room, drinking brandy, he didn't know *when* he'd be home—and to discover all my possessions gone. Or at least not where I'd left them. I later found them neatly packed in three cardboard boxes, tied up, and addressed to me in "Manhattan, America."

When Mafalda returned home from her food shopping, she affected total astonishment. She'd thought I'd gone back to the United States, she said, again and again, as I made her drag out the boxes, place them on the double bed, open them, and return every single item to the closet, bureau, bed table, or wherever she'd found them. She did all of this slowly, meticulously, as I sat watching, talking to Cicely all the while on the phone, saying in English, "Now she's shaking out my powder-blue cable-knit sweater, the wart-faced old bitch," in an objective tone of voice—as though discussing the weather.

After my initial outburst of fury against Mafalda—which she'd missed, being out—I played it cool. Three days later the film was in the can and Djanko was back in our lives. I told him of the incident in a lighthearted manner, as though for his amusement. But he was deeply offended for me; and while I got him to promise never to bring it up with Mafalda, his eyes did moisten when he promised, and he said he would make it up to me.

My idea was revenge, and I was sufficiently re-Italianized by my months in Rome to be able to take it ice-cold. I waited weeks until Mafalda's two days per month off, when she returned to her family in Gaeta. Then I talked Djanko into taking me to Capri for those two days and further arranged it so that I packed for both of us and picked him up in the car, driving directly from Cinecittá to the seaplane airport. Once on the magic isle, it was no problem to get Djanko to remain another day or two.

Thus we weren't there when Mafalda returned to the Hassler, fit her key in the suite door—and couldn't open it. At the downstairs desk they managed to find a new key for her. Humiliated, she took the lift up and let herself in. Only to be greeted by another housekeeper already in attendance (an elderly actress whose services I'd obtained), sitting in the living room reading a magazine with her feet up on the coffee table. Mafalda rushed to her room to find it stripped bare, no longer hers. She ran down to the desk and was led to the hotel cellars, where after a longish, labyrinthine walk she discovered six neatly packed boxes of her stuff. I later found out she'd almost fainted at the sight and had required salts of ammonia to be revived. But once recovered, she'd charged back into the suite, ousted the false housekeeper, and put all in order again.

When we returned from our weekend in Capri, I held out a bouquet of fresh flowers picked on the island especially for Mafalda.

"Che dolce!" she murmured, thanking me several times, never once looking me in the eye. She never complained to Djanko of what I'd done, and after that never once in my remaining time at the Hassler did Mafalda give me a second of anxiety, never once act even vaguely disrespectful. Weeks after the event, I came upon her and another housekeeper chatting and slid out of sight to overhear them. Mafalda was

saying, "No. No. He's far better than the Englishwoman! He's Italian, you know. From Rome, before America. *Molto gentile. Molto gentile.*"

Only in Rome are you called a gentleman once you've proved that you are willing and able to outsleaze and outtrick others.

Mafalda had just been satisfactorily handled when a larger conflict reared its head—and showed me more clearly than I had any right to expect just who Djanko was. Fool that I was at the time, I pretended I'd seen and heard nothing important.

Given the fact that Djanko's earnings in those mid-sixties years were enormous (according to one Italian magazine I read), it made sense that I was kept. La Bernakovka handled all the weekly folding money and there was always more than enough for my shopping expeditions and lunches out with Tina and Donna and Cicely. Everything else was charged or else somehow or other paid for, and in addition, Djanko periodically dragged me down the Via del Corso to buy me things. In and out of Ginori, Ferragamo, and Ricci we would go, with him insisting that I dressed like a provo when I should be dressing like a marchese. I would try on a silk shirt that I sort of liked yet not be certain of the color. Djanko would buy all six colors the shirt was made in. That way I would have a choice—and no excuse not to get it. Or three pairs of a particular kind of shoe, or a half dozen bathing slips, or three linen suits.

A modest if fine dresser himself, Djanko adored gold jewelry and would stop and stare at ridiculously expensive pieces in Bulgari's windows, while I tried to pull him away. He owned almost no gold himself—which I attributed to residual guilt over being a capitalist, following such a social-ist upbringing. This he hotly denied, so I came to another conclusion: Why should he wear anything to detract from that twenty-four-karat head of hair?

But if Djanko didn't wear gold, he certainly insisted I

wear it. I spent hours in shops with him fending off bracelets the size of manacles, rings thicker than my fingers, neck chains too lavish for a Byzantine empress. In the end, of course, he got his way. My keys to the suite were placed on a golden key ring; he had Ginori take all the brass fittings off the forest-green Gladstone I'd picked out and had it replaced with gold. I had to have *one* gold ring, he insisted (I didn't even wear a school ring), and he found a slender, ancient white gold one I couldn't be too offended by. What, no watch? I'd never be on time: I must have a watch! Soon watches in all sizes and shapes—from vest-pocket pointers to standard wristwear—filled my little leather visa kit. My cigarettes were always getting broken, so I had to have a metal cigarette case—gold again. I was always losing my Zippo lighters, always asking for a match, so naturally I had to have one, then two, then six gold lighters. And a gold-plated fountain pen, of course. Once he'd broken down my resistance, I was inundated in the stuff: I hadn't known how heavy, clanking, clunky, and awkward gold could be. I put my foot down. I complained I had nowhere to put it all; it was ruining my leather kit. Naturally Djanko had a solution to that, too: He bought me a gold jewelry case. Cicely took to calling me "Our own little Danae," in not so subtle reference to the imprisoned mortal woman in Greek mythology (and mother of Perseus) visited by Zeus as a shower of pure gold. I was *not* amused.

Despite all this largesse, I was soon bored and wanted to work. I'd seen enough aging courtesans of all genders in Rome by then to know I didn't want to be one. So, after weeks of nudging Djanko, I was allowed to translate scripts into English with the considerable aid of a vast Mondadori Italian-English dictionary: the work I'd ostensibly been interviewed for months before, the job which the Pig claimed I'd been doing all the while to get me a temporary work permit.

Watching British and American actors lip-synch my words onto audio tape as the film started and stopped every min-

ute was both thrilling and profoundly embarrassing to
me. While half of the films made by Tratano were dubbed
into English and sold overseas, few were ever shown in the
U.S. Instead, Hong Kong, Singapore, Bombay, Capetown,
and Sydney were all larger markets for *Creatures from Rigel
IV* and *Silver Spurs* than were L.A. or New York. I had to
find some sort of recognizable transliteration of the Italian
dialogue (which itself often had been lifted directly—in hom-
age, Jiri claimed—from John Ford and Raoul Walsh's films)
into an English that a Parsi or Aussie or Balinese might
easily comprehend. Once I'd understood this point, I could
clean up slang pretty well, but I still faced incredible hurdles
of idiom.

My job as a translator evolved into devising a language
that was not quite English, yet not anything else, either; a
language that was bigger, broader, more encompassing than
any mere local lingo. Naturally I failed. But my efforts
sometimes paid off. Westerns were unstoppably the most
problematic—"Get 'em up, pardner"—but sci-fi films and
costume epics were often more malleable, especially the
latter. I brought in all of my years of reading to provide
these paper-thin characters with words and phrases to speak,
which their historical counterparts wouldn't have utterly
gagged on. "Unusually literate," reported the film critic of a
large Melbourne daily of my work. "One might almost call
the language dubbed-in Marlovian." One might well call it
Marlovian, Jonsonian, Beaumontian, and Fletcherian, Shake-
spearean, too, as I rifled English literature for rhythms and
meters. And bless them, my voice-over people rose to the
challenge and poured out their own frustrated stage ambitions by keeping to the phrasing I provided them.

It was thankless work, but the Pig read (or more likely
had Valentina read to him) reviews of the films as well as
box-office takes and he told Djanko he believed I was now
ready for onscreen work. This meant spending long, coffee-
drenched afternoons with Djanko and Jiri and the Pig be-

fore shooting began, going over endless revisions of screen-
plays they'd put together.

At first I was shy and put in merely a line of dialogue
here, a clarifying action there, a stroke of characterization
in another place. But as the script meetings devolved into
free-for-alls, with everyone openly criticizing the other's
work, I became more confident. I began to ask questions no
one had considered before: if common water really did kill
the seventy-five-foot rhubarblike Beta Centaurans, then
wouldn't they have all melted in the first substantial sun
shower, rather than having to be spectacularly spray-hosed
by our hero? The others would stare at me in horror and
disgust, then the Pig would laugh, "You've *ruined* us!" And
we'd start all over again.

I called out the word *consistency* so often in these meetings that Jiri mutteringly called me Signor Consistency.

All this naturally swelled my young head a bit and led me
to believe I was more than useful; I was a needed part of
their team. I now know that this was what I've come to call
a Major Avoidable Mistake. I didn't then, and it all fell
down around my head with a film project that Djanko had
been planning for years, and over which Tratano had now
given him free reign, partly because it could be packaged as
a commercial muscle epic.

One of the Greek myths Travernicke Senior had told and
retold his son back in Croatia during those harsh stormy
nights when field work was impossible and party work unob-
tainable and which had especially struck the golden-haired
tyke was that of Jason and the Argonauts. A later reading of
Apollonius of Rhodes' second-century B.C. *Argonautica* in
college had confirmed Djanko's belief that this tale would
make a great adventure film. Why, I'm not certain. It was
loose and episodic, its love interest was spotty (Medea, but
she came and went), and none of the adventures were
terribly unique—perhaps Hercules' labors the most exciting.
Still, the idea of a group of heroes—including Castor and
Pollux and Hercules—out in a boat cruising around seemed

to strike some idealized Communist chord in young Djanko, and he was determined to see it in full color, lavishly produced, with the best special effects the studio's money could buy.

Because I soon knew of its background, and because the project seemed "in development" so long after Djanko and I had met and become lovers, I assumed it would never require my attentions. However, about eight months into our affair, as we lolled around a sunstruck terrazzo at Ravenna, the Pig suddenly pulled out a script I didn't recognize (they were coded by jacket color for easy identification) and asked if we were ready for a script session.

Jiri and Djanko were; they'd been at the script for years. I said, sure, let's go, I would read it later.

"No," Tratano declared. "You'll read it now. We'll have a session tomorrow."

"What's wrong with the script?" Djanko asked.

"Who said there's anything wrong? There are four of us. All of us should know it."

"For consistency," Jiri said.

"That's right," the Pig agreed, "for consistency."

As soon as I could, I got away from them, drove Djanko's little Maserati roadster to a restaurant *sul' mare*, and for two hours drank wine and read the script, overlooking the particolored Adriatic Sea.

It was a beautiful screenplay. It was full of Attic light and Theban nobility, the sweetness of Herodotus and the legendary quality of Homer, filled with the brisk spanking of an Aegean wind and the mysterious monstrousness of Thracian mountain clefts. These Argonauts weren't a pack of idiot teenage boys on a fishing trip; they were demigods, driven to know their world in all its terror and wonder, love and enmity, no matter the consequences—to seek knowledge for its own sake. The script was almost perfectly Hellenic and quite filmic.

That night with Djanko, as the floor-length, lightweight muslin curtains fluttered a sea breeze into our bedroom, I told him how marvelous I thought the script was. I quoted to him Ulysses' lines about his final, fatal, till then unrecorded voyage from Dante's *Inferno*:

> "O frati," dissi, "che per cento milia
> perigli siete, giunto a l'occidente
> a questa tanto picciola viglia
> d'i nostri sensi ch'e del rimanente
> non vogliate negar l'esperienza
> di retro al sol, del mondo sanza gente.
>   "Considerate la vostra semenza:
> fatti non foste a viver come bruti,
> ma per sequir virtue e canosceza."

> "Brothers," I said to them, "who've sailed
> a hundred thousand perilous miles,
> aspire now to the Western edge while
> this brief awareness remains to your senses,
> do not deny an experience beyond
> the sun, beyond all living people.
>   "Consider well the lineage you come from:
> you were not made to live like brutes,
> but to follow virtue and knowledge."

Djanko loved my quote and enthusiasm. He said I understood exactly the tone he'd been aiming for in the film. But I'd also found a few tiny problems in the script, and we carefully corrected each copy we could find.

"Ah! You see!" the Pig said triumphantly the following day in our first work session on the script. "Already we have more consistency." He'd spotted the revisions instantly.

These two or three sessions at Ravenna were easy and relaxed, far different than most of the screaming matches I'd grown used to. The Pig and Djanko discussed actors who might be available for the roles, special-effects people and cinematographers, costumers and set designers, even composers for the score. It seemed smooth as custard.

Too smooth. In the next two months the script was cut apart and put back together again. *Jason* became *Jason II,* then *Jason IV* and *Jason X.* Meanwhile preproduction began in earnest—sets were designed and built, costumes designed and stitched, locations sighted and checked, storyboards laid out and revised to accommodate script changes. All in perfect order.

The actors now arrived to rehearse. Angel as Hercules, Cicely as a statuesque blond Aphrodite. It was an unusually springlike early April day when principal shooting began on *Jason*. The first day's scenes were easy and fast and went down well. That night we all celebrated with champagne.

I'm still not sure what fatal impulse led me to pick up a copy of the script, *Jason XV* by this point, to re-read it. Ennui perhaps, or a desire to be moved as I'd been when I'd first read it. But lift the script I did, and read it through.

It was tighter, of course, less episodic, the love story spread throughout most of the film and less lavish in settings, costumes, and special effects. But it was still grand. I had almost reached the end when I came upon a short new scene I didn't remember seeing in the last version—*Jason II*? *Jason IV*?—I'd read.

In this scene, the goddess Aphrodite, offended by the kidnapping of her favorite priestess, Medea (now completely enthralled by Jason), not to mention the theft of the Golden Fleece from her temple in Colchis, demands a sacrifice from the ship's crew before allowing the Argonauts to arrive home safely. She gets her wish from the Council of the Gods and the next scene reads:

CUT TO: long shot
The *Argo*, sailing over a smooth, moonlit sea.
CUT TO: medium shot
Overhead shot of the Argonauts sleeping on deck.
CLOSE UP: tracking shot
Jason and Medea entwined in sleep, as are Castor and Pollux, Hercules, and Pylades.
CUT BACK TO: close-up
Jason and Medea. In his sleep he moves away from her. She reaches for him, cradles him. He seems to resist, then accepts her gesture.
CUT TO: medium shot

Ship's deck. Turnus at the steering helm.
CUT AWAY TO: medium shot
Cyprus: A grotto. Aphrodite, surrounded by her women, pushes them aside. Begins to spin like a top until she becomes a blur, a wind. The little tornado sweeps through the grotto and out to sea.
LONG SHOT:
The tornado sweeps across the waves toward the *Argo* in the distance.
CUT TO: medium shot
The *Argo*. Turnus at the helm as the small tornado sweeps on board and surrounds only him. He throws up his hands to defend himself but is wrapped inside it instantly, gagged by it, and pulled off the ship overboard.
CUT TO: close-up
Turnus, sinking through the seawater, drowned.
CUT TO: medium shot
The *Argo,* sailing over a smooth, moonlit sea. Ghostly hands keep the steering helm straight.
CUT TO: medium shot
Cyprus. The grotto. The tornado returns, slows down into Aphrodite.
CLOSE-UP
Aphrodite smiles.

It was charming, economical, evocative. It was also absolutely out of place. In fact, the scene had nothing to do with Jason and the Argonauts but with Aeneas and the Trojans on their way to found Rome. It had been lifted straight out of Vergil's *Aeneid*.

I read on to the end, then went and quietly collected all the shooting scripts I could find. They all contained the scene. I was appalled.

The mature me said that I ought to have waited until I could get Djanko alone, then calmly ask about the scene, suggesting it was a bit out of place, no, *caro*? But something about its sudden inclusion had deeply shaken me. Granted it was plagiarism, wasn't the entire story stolen from Appolonius and Hesiod in the first place? What bothered me was that the scene derived from a completely different sensibility, altogether too modern for this rather primitive tale. In

Vergil, Turnus had become an exemplar of destiny, and of its absurdity: a sad grace note that a Roman stoic could appreciate for what it said about his turbulent age. In my mind, the tiny scene grew and grew, threatening to capsize the entire project.

Getting Djanko alone was impossible, and when we went to bed that night, he was so horny—as he always became when freshly into a new film project—that I was tickled into passion and kissed into forgetfulness.

Indeed, I might have forgotten the scene completely. But the next morning at our general business luncheon, held early in the afternoon after morning filming had already taken place, Jiri spoke up.

"So, Signor Consistency," he began with unaccustomed effrontery, "we haven't heard any criticism of illogic from you in a while."

"Jiri," La Bernakovka warned. She looked Amazonly ravishing that day and expected the obedience beauty ought to call forward.

"No, wait, *cara Valentina*," the Pig spoke around a slab of bread soaked in olive oil he'd pushed into his mouth. "This is important. Have you read the final shooting script?"

All eyes were on me.

"I saw him reading it last night," Jiri said.

"I read it," I admitted.

"And it's perfect. *E vero*?" Jiri asked.

"Of course it's good." I turned to Djanko. "I really think it will be your best film."

He accepted that and went on reading *Corriere*.

"Partly," Jiri said, "thanks to you. Your friend makes a splendid Aphrodite. You've noticed how much we're using her? We've even written a new scene especially for her," he went on, clearly baiting me. Two beats passed, then he added, "You read all of it?"

"I said I read it."

"All of it?" he insisted. By now La Bernakovka had stopped fooling around with the spaghettini straps on her

sundress, and the Pig was done swallowing. Both were surprised by the ordinarily obsequious Jiri's insistence. I knew
this was a minuscule point, one that I really shouldn't bother
with, but I was annoyed that Jiri had decided to use it in a
power play. As long as he'd selected the battleground, I'd
stand and fight.

"Are you referring to the scene you stole from Vergil?"

Djanko looked up from the paper.

"Vergil, *caro*?"

"The new little scene with Aphrodite and Turnus." To
Jiri I said, "You might at least have changed his name so
the plagiarism wasn't so obvious." Plagiarism is nothing in
film scripts, so the others weren't yet alerted that something
was happening. But Jiri's face glowed as though I'd actually
and not merely verbally slapped him.

"Still," he said, "it's a beautiful scene."

"It's fine. It's plagiarism. It's Vergil. And it has no place
in the script."

Jiri leaned forward over the table, savoring each sentence, avid for more punishment.

"And since you absolutely must know, Jiri, it's *totally*
inconsistent!"

Jiri could have achieved orgasm under the table for the
sudden relief he showed at those words. He sat back, pleased
and humiliated.

"It's not from Vergil, *caro*," Djanko said, less gently than
before. "We wrote it ourselves, Jiri and I. It was an inspira-
tion, something to give an edge, a flavor of *tristesse* to their
homecoming."

Was I actually supposed to believe that?

"It works exactly as you planned," I admitted. "But I'm
sorry, it's from Vergil's *Aeneid*."

"Where?"

"I don't know. One of the middle cantos. I haven't read it
often enough to know exactly which canto and lines."

"So you could be wrong?"

"I'm not wrong. Look, let's drop it, huh?"

Djanko was up at the library bookshelves searching. Now both La Bernakovka and I said, "Djanko, sit down. Forget it. It's not important."

But no. He continued searching, bellowed out for Mafalda, berated her for moving his books around (she'd arranged them by the color of their spines) then asked where his Vergil was. She shrugged and walked back to the kitchen.

"Help me look," Djanko pleaded. None of us would.

Finally the Pig said, "Djanko, don't doubt our *ouaglio*. We know he's always right on this sort of detail."

Djanko flung a look at Jiri—by now shrunken to the metaphorical size of a mouse in his chair with shamefaced secret glee—then Djanko glared at me.

"So," he said, "Signor Consistency. You don't think my script is any good. My film will be a gross failure!"

"I didn't say that."

"No. But you *think* it. Which is worse."

I stood up to leave the room and made it as far as the doorway from which I could see Mafalda down the corridor in the kitchen, at a great distance from the stove, where she stood stirring a pot with a long-handled wooden spoon, evidently listening. She darted out of sight.

Djanko grabbed my arm, stopping me. "The scene stays in," he shouted into my ear.

"Fine. I'm going to take a bath."

"It stays in," he growled at me.

"Do whatever you want, Djanko. It's your goddamned movie."

"Do you know *why* it stays in? Because it's beautiful. That's why."

"It may be beautiful, but it's not true. 'Truth is beauty, beauty truth,' " I quoted Keats's most mooted dictum at him.

"It's beautiful, therefore it *must be true*!"

"It's untrue and therefore it *cannot* be beautiful."

The color rose up his neck, chin, face rapidly. He let go of my arm and hauled off and slapped me so hard, I fell against the bookcase with the impact. Stunned, I crumpled to my knees.

Valentina and the Pig leapt up from their chairs and grabbed Djanko before he could strike me again. Jiri remained ice-still in his chair, whimpering a little. Mafalda rushed into the room, took one look at me, helped me up, muttering *"Barbaro! Barbaro Slavo!"* at Djanko, and half carried me out of the room with amazing strength and dexterity into her bedroom where she found rose water to mist on my face and spirits of ammonia for my nose.

Two minutes later I stalked out of the Hassler suite. The others were in the library loudly arguing.

I wandered around the city most of that afternoon and finally found myself in a familiar piazza. No wonder, the Stollywood Harlots lived nearby. Their flat was considerably improved in the months since I'd slept over, doubtless from both Cicely and Angel working more or less steady jobs all that while and from Tina's "association" with Contino Eddie, a more long-lasting affair than its dubious origins at Ulrica's villa in the Alban Hills had at first suggested. I didn't more than peek into the two bedrooms, but the kitchen had a new refrigerator, the bathroom held a tiny pair of matching washer and dryer, and the living room now sported a large fawn leather convertible sofa as well as matching leather chairs, scooping bronze arcs ending in globule lamps and various other signs of expensive tastes and well-placed friends in the current Milan arena of Italian modern design.

"I'm worried about Angel," Donna was being serious despite her new hair color—a mandarin orange. She served us espresso out of perfectly matched cups the right size and tiny *cannoli* off matching little plates. She held one pastry between deep red fingernails so sharp and long, she would never stain her fingertips with the sweet ricotta filling.

"*We're* worried about Angel," Tina put in. Her dark hair had grown into a pageboy, turned under à la Streisand on the *People* album, revealing honey-blond roots she was allowing to emerge. She wore a single-piece chemise designed by Rudi Gernreich, made of material similar to that upholstering the new sofa.

"Don't tell me. He's marrying Kit What's-his-name."

"Pre-cious!" Tina jumped. "You've heard it for sure?"

"Heard what?"

"Then you must be psychic."

"What are you talking about?"

"Angel's moved out. Settled in with Kit."

"*Settled* being the key word." Having consumed the dessert in one gulp, Donna was dainty again, wiping her nails with a peach-colored serviette.

"Angel's never been settled anywhere for longer than a week," Tina confided. "And he hardly needs Kit's money with all the work he's been getting."

"Which point worries us the most," added Donna. "At any rate, we think there may be a real blaze behind the smoke screen of them 'rooming' together."

"You mean, this new convertible sofa isn't for Angel?"

"He hasn't slept here in a month. Well, maybe once, but he was nearby and still had the key, so he just came in and crashed."

"It's almost tragic." Tina minced about the room, drawing attention to its new accessories: a crystal table lighter, a matching ashtray, a lamp hidden in a Deco statue. "A wonderful boy like Angel at the beck and call of a tired pervert like Kit."

Recalling the scene I'd witnessed between the Australian playboy and Angel at the villa, I thought her concept a bit much and told her I thought Angel knew exactly what he was doing.

"I suppose so," Tina admitted, then shot her dart: "You American boys all seem to know exactly what you're doing."

"Now, Tee," Donna warned on cue; they'd rehearsed.

"Just following your pre-cious advice," I said, far too smugly. "Remember?"

"I do remember."

"So, and what's your complaint, anyway? It's not as though I don't see Contino Eddie's gross Italian hand at work here."

"Our complaint is that Contino Eddie is not in the movies," Donna said.

"And your boyfriend is," Tina added the obvious.

"Okay," I decided if they were going to be so open, "shoot. What do you want from me?"

The two looked at me, incredulous.

"Well?" I prodded.

"You're not going to bullshit us?" Tina had to ask. "You're not going to tell us that you have no influence whatsoever with Djanko the T?" She seemed somewhat aggrieved, as though an amended script had been handed out which she'd not received.

"Why should I?"

"Because everyone in Rome would deny it," Donna said. "And because we're expecting you to deny it."

"Well, it's not true in my case. Not that I can do anything very big, mind you. . . ."

"Angel, Cicely, not big!" Tina asked.

"However, I do know of a few still uncast smaller female roles in the shooting script." I dangled it. "With lines."

"Cicely's handmaidens," the girls said in one voice. Evidently they'd also read the shooting script or some approximation of it. "Just tell us when Djanko holds an audition for the parts."

"I'll do better than that. I'll bring you to the audition. If"—and here they froze, the room becoming a sudden tableau titled, say, Anticipation—"if I ever speak to the Croat bastard again."

This was my conversational gambit into the problem with the script and our argument, which was so pleasant for me to unburden myself of, and they so eager to hear, it called for another pot of espresso and a dish of anisette cookies, as—heedless of crumbs or spills or indeed of anything but my tale of glamorous woe—they listened wide-eyed, avid for details, putting in small oh-nos or "the rat!" every now and again in more or less appropriate spots.

When I was done, they looked at each other, then at me.

"But you've *got* to leave in the new scene, if it's the only one with *us* in it!" Tina declared, having easily leapt from auditioning for the part to already unquestionably possessing it.

"Pre-cious!" I responded, "I really have no say in the matter. It's *his* movie. Why can't anyone believe me when I say that?"

"He'll take the scene out for you," Donna feared.

"Come on. You don't know the man. He's obsessed. He's . . . I don't know . . ."

"He will," Tina insisted. "He'll especially take it out if you deny him any nooky."

Her hand went up to her mouth in a gesture I could see she'd instinctively adopted back in Iowa. All three of us exploded into laughter, repeating the word *nooky* over and over as though it were brand-new, a neologism we'd that minute coined, saying it in different accents—Russian, French, Chinese, putting it into silly sentences such as, "And would you prefer your nooky glazed or plain, sir?" and other such tomfoolery.

When our attack of the giggles had passed, I assured them that if by some mischance the new scene actually did leave the script, I could try to get some new lines for "their" parts into the film somehow.

"Pre-*cious*!" They flew at me, kissing me. "We knew you were one of us."

Although I remained at their flat until six in the evening, Cicely never returned. Donna and Tina were off to various dinner dates, so I said good-bye and headed for the Via Veneto. By now I'd been in Rome long enough to feel comfortable alone in even glamorous restaurants and to know enough people through Djanko and the studio that I probably wouldn't have to be alone long. It was early April and not cold, indeed not even cool, so several outdoor

trattorias were in full operation and I waved at a few acquaintances. But I didn't feel like sitting down yet and
thought perhaps I might stroll up to the nearby Borghese
Gardens.

In fact, I'd just noticed a large cornflower-blue Bentley
pull up to the post-and-chain barrier at one pathway into the
gardens, a Bentley belonging to a wealthy industrialist from
Turin who lived in Rome. The last time I'd seen the Bentley
had been in the Via del Corso. I had just stepped out of a
men's clothing shop where I'd been trying to make Djanko
happy by spending some of his money, and saw the car's
driver step out his door, glide around to the curb and open
the back passenger door for the industrialist, who'd immediately bustled past me and inside the shop. I'd lingered a
second rearranging my packages and searching through my
pockets to look for a cigarette in one of my half dozen gold
cigarette cases from Djanko. I'd managed to find and ex-
tract a cigarette and was holding the lighter clenched in my
fist when I really saw the chauffeur.

As we all know, Italian men can be appallingly, heart-
stoppingly handsome. But until that moment I'd been, if not
oblivious to their charms (after all I'd been attracted to
Orazio), then at least unimpressed, especially when I had in
front of me the blond All-American gorgeousness of Angel
and the wild Slavic beauty of Djanko. Well, if they were
perfection of their type, so was this chauffeur. His whiplash-
slender body moved so gracefully, he might have been stalk-
ing prey in a jungle; his head was like a still unopened
flower encased in the rigidity of his peaked cap: eyes, mouth,
hair. . . . And with all the insouciance of the amazingly
good-looking, he stood there, leaning against the front fender
of the Bentley long after he should have gotten back into
the car, openly allowing me to look over every well-packed
inch inside that close-fitting steel-gray uniform. I was trans-
fixed, more pinioned than a butterfly in an album.

"Fiammetri?" I heard as though from a distance, and
turned. Two stylishly dressed young women passing by

stopped and offered to light the Sobranie dangling off my agape lower lip.

"*Grazie,*" I said, and they wafted by, complimentarily perfumed, rustling silks, looking back with a smile—and the chauffeur never looked at them, never took his eyes off me and—as in a silent movie—his eyes smoldered.

I sighed deeply, reshuffled my packages and managed to walk away, feeling his eyes burn the tropical wool of my jacket back until I was able to elude his heat-seeking ocular range.

And now he was parked at the Borghese, no magnate in the backseat, and so, I had to assume, out for a walk in the gardens. Sure enough, he stepped out of the Bentley, tossed his cap onto the front seat, shook out the liberated mass of chestnut curls, loosened his tie and strode off.

Lost not in lust but in an almost hypnotic trance of potentiality, I followed him. But he must have soon veered off the path—an old, gravel-strewn side path, anyway—and though I expected him to leap out at me like some wood satyr, he didn't. Annoyed, yet hopeful, too, I walked up the gravel path, slowly revolving my angle to all landmarks as the city began to drop beneath me on one side, until that view, too, was gauzed by tree cover, cypress growth, pines of great girth through which a muted spring sunset flickered.

"You idiot," I said to myself out loud. "Chasing after some chauffeur when the man you love is less than a mile away, wondering where the hell you are."

That resolved, I decided to go back. My resolute stride was broken about halfway down the path by the growing dimness, and by the sudden, startling appearance of the cyclops light of a Vespa—a policeman! Although the Borghese only later developed its totally weird and depraved reputation as an agora of outdoors male sex, it was still fairly gamy in the late sixties. I slid into a coppice until the Vespa had passed, then noted another gravel lane out and headed for that.

A few minutes later I all but stumbled upon two silhouettes in the classic fellatio position—one leaning against a tree trunk, the other in front on his knees—and I moved on with a *"Scusi"* and a glance.

"Hey! Wait a minute, boy!" Angel's unmistakable voice called after me. "Hold on there."

I stopped and felt rather than saw him come up to me in the near total darkness.

"Well, I'll be! Whatcha doing heah?" he asked, grabbing me by the shoulders and thus lifting me off the ground.

"Walking."

"Well, then, I'll walk with you. Where you been, anyway, boy?"

Before I could answer, a shadow came up to us. A man speaking in a Roman dialect too rapid and slangy and excited for me to understand placed something in Angel's hand, then flew off down the hill.

"Now ain't that fine?" Angel said. "And I never even delivered the sweet cream for him." I could hear the lira notes crackling softly in his hand. He asked for my lighter and we counted them. "That there dago's been after my hot dog ever since I arrived. Mnn. Looks like enough here for the night. You eat yet? No? I'm hungry too. How about Ruggiero's?"

One arm over my shoulder, Angel loped me down the hill to the main path.

"What did he say to you?" I asked.

"Damned if I know. Still haven't learned the lingo. Just plug stupid, I guess."

He'd been in Rome for over a year. "You mean you haven't learned any Italian?"

"Boy, I've learned me this much: *aeroporto, Cinecittá, grazie, scusi, cuanto lire? grazie, prego,* oh yes, and *un pompino*, which means a head job."

"I know what it means."

"Shee-it! Well, I guess you do!" He hugged me against him and we strode out of the woods, into the *via*, past the Bentley where the stunning chauffeur leaned against the front fender smoking a cigarette. *"Ciao,"* Angel said cheerfully, and the driver stared at us in such a way that I knew I would be able to get him whenever I wanted.

"So! What's this I hear about you and Kit?" I asked once we were settled in Ruggiero's with drinks and breadsticks and a quickly assembled antipasto for Angel's omnivorous hunger.

"Not a thing, boy. I thought it was time to move on—out of the girls' place, you know. Better all around." He winked one perfect blue eye at me. Angel was wearing a pair of tailored tan slacks, a tight-fitting cotton sweater (probably extra large); his hair had grown out of a crew cut and was long, almost wavy, still yellow-white as the sun on an August beach day.

"Tina and Donna think it's romance. Serious romance."

"Cicely too?"

"I don't know. I didn't see her today."

"Well, boy. It sure ain't romance. Ole Kit likes to put his tongue where toilet paper rightly ought to go. But that don't bother me none. You see Cicely lately? She say anything to you?"

I said I hadn't seen her in a few weeks, a bit surprised by his question. Angel seemed so at ease in the world that he usually appeared to intuitively know where everyone was at any moment—or not care. Before I could probe, Angel changed the conversation around to food, unsurprisingly one of his favorite topics, and—more unusual—home.

"My mama called yesterday. Asked if I was eating enough. She's worried. I'll bet you think I come from some dirt-floor shack. Don't. My daddy's an insurance man. Tycoon, come to think of it. Lived in the biggest hacienda outside of El Paso you ever seen, boy. Right from being a little tyke, I liked the movies. Wanted to be a cowboy like Gene Autry or Roy Rogers. We had a big old ranch up in the hills, but I didn't care for any of that roping and cattle and shit. Nope. I wanted to be a movie cowboy. Wear fancy shirts with lots of fringe on 'em and ride a fine, spirited Palomino named

Dancer or somethin' and sing songs to my guitar strumming. Dumb, huh?"

Between mouthfuls of antipasto he went on.

"When I was seventeen, I was already so big—broad and all—that I could pass for a man of twenty-five, you know. Took some money and hitched off to Hollywood, California. Stood on Vine Street and said, come 'n' git me. Well, I got into the movies, all right. But they were the kind of movies where two of them Sunset Boulevard hookers licked my pecker in close-up, or where I cornholed some other kid from the sticks for about twenty minutes. I was so young and horny then, half the time I'd forget to pull it out so I could decorate his crack with my jizz. They called that the money shot. I kept telling them I wanted to make cowboy movies. So once they put me in a Hopalong Cassidy outfit and I fucked some chick wearing a Dale Rogers getup. Their idea of a joke.

"Paid for some acting classes and my rent. And when that wasn't enough, I'd go sell my pecker. One guy, nice old fella who used to chew on my cigar and pay me a hundred dollars for the privilege, actually listened to what I said and told me, 'Boy! Get your ass out of Hollywood and over to Rome, Italy. That's where all the Western movies are to-day.' He even paid my way. So I got here, and sure enough, they're making a Western on every other set in Cinecittá. But you know what? All the actors they have are what? —five-three? five-five? I'm a giant! So that's how come I'm doin' what I'm doin'."

"At least you're making movies. Even if they aren't Westerns," I said, pleased that Angel had seen fit to confide in me.

"This one with your boyfriend's going to be the biggest part I ever done." He suddenly looked worried. "Listen, boy. You'll come see me on the set, won't you? Help me with my lines?" I said I would. "You know, boy, I done something foolish. Hope you won't think the less of me for it. I know now it was a mistake. It's the reason I moved out of the girls' place. Cicely was sleeping in the living room. Guess Tina and Donna had company in the bedrooms. So I undressed and then lay down next to her. I always been sweet on Cicely, you know. Well, to make a long story short, she woke up while I was putting it to her."

Angel sighed.

"She was real upset. Told me I'd busted her cherry and dishonored her and all. I didn't mean anything by it, you know. Hell, I haven't met a woman yet didn't want to fuck me. Lord, boy, it was a scene, I can tell you. She run into the bathroom and locked herself in. Wouldn't come out till I'd gone. Hasn't talked to me since."

I told Angel I thought Cicely was too smart and good for it to damage their friendship. When he didn't seem convinced, I agreed to play peacemaker. That seemed to cheer him up. A few minutes later we were joined by Kit and the tall slim black model I'd first seen dining with Djanko, who turned out to be not at all vampirish as I'd first thought, but a thigh-slapping Atlanta girl named Wanda Mae Reed.

Kit knew of a party outside of Rome and we all hopped into his convertible to get there. By now I'd been to a score or more of these international jet-set shindigs and knew the people and the scenes. I was far more comfortable than I'd been wandering around Ulrica's villa.

I came upon Angel once during the evening. He was sitting alone in what seemed to be a den—eland and rhino heads on the walls, zebra and tiger-skin rugs complete with heads on the floor—watching television turned down so low, only the flickering light upon his face gave a clue to its presence. He motioned me over to sit on the floor between his legs, so I could see the small black-and-white screen. It was a Western, of course, an American film, and it held his intense interest. Every once in a while Angel would reach down and unconsciously play with my hair as if petting a favorite dog. When the film was over and the screen went into patterns, Angel softly said, "You know, boy. It's a crying shame. Think of the star-bright baby me and Cicely could've made." Then he fell silent. After a few minutes his hand stopped; he was asleep, himself a big baby. Before leaving, I found a Mexican serape and threw it over him.

I left the party with Tina and Donna in the fire-engine-red Triumph TR-3 Contino Eddie (in Alexandria, Egypt, for the weekend) had given Tina. We were all stuffed into the small front seat of the sports car, astonishingly high on vodka and hash, which had been available in quantity during the party.

Tina drove wildly and badly, but we laughed all the silly way to the Autostrada, howled with mirth when she took the wrong turn onto it and we were headed away from Rome, and we went into conniptions when she made the highly illegal turn. The Autostrada was straight and dull, and Tina appeared to sober up a bit and to begin an animated conversation about "their" roles in Djanko's film, detailing how Djanko and I would make up later on. "No nooky," Donna said. "We'll *all* go on strike!" Which was hilarious beyond recounting and caused the Triumph to slither across two lanes at a time.

The precise meanderings of our conversation for the next fifteen minutes is too absurd to recall; Byzantine with allusions and suggestions well known to imbibers of the Islamic panacea but somehow we got into a round of singing "Dancing in the Dark."

"Stop! That's our exit!" Donna yelled.

Tina was so startled, she swerved sharply across two lanes to get onto the curving ramp down.

A minute later we were on the ramp, but it was a ramp *up*. We just missed a car coming at us—horn blaring indignantly, the driver purple-faced with ire—and Tina shouted, "I've got to turn around or we'll be killed."

Going fifty miles an hour downhill on a curved ramp, Tina executed a U-turn. She'd raved about the Triumph's handling before and I guess she actually expected this far-fetched manuever to succeed. We spun around neatly, then promptly stalled. In time for a car coming behind to screech to a stop, tapping our left rear bumper, and adding precisely enough thrust to propel the Triumph into and through the meshwork guardrail.

All three of us screamed going into the air, and again as we tore through the trees. Lucky for us the Triumph had stalled or I don't know where we would have ended up. After fifty yards or so we slammed neatly between the trunks of two stout trees that reverberated like elastic bands with an accompanying rustle of branches—one of which ripped off the TR-3's back plastic window.

We'd braced ourselves for the thump of stopping, so none of us were hurt when we did stop. Wasted perhaps, shocked out of our highs unquestionably, but unhurt.

After all the noise, silence.

Donna pointed through the trees to where the headlights showed a farmhouse on a hill level with us. Lights were turned on. As she pointed, the Triumph shifted beneath us.

"People," she said in a tiny voice. "Help."

"We'd better be real careful about moving," I said, the lesson of Donna's quite minor gesture and its consequence clear. "Let me see how high up we are." I cautiously opened the door I'd been thrown against and tried to gauge the depth of the darkness.

Rummaging through the glove compartment, filled with a hair dryer, movie magazines, and what appeared to be six pairs of Contino Eddie's leather gloves, I located a tiny flashlight and pointed it down. Yikes!

Then we heard the people from the farmhouse running toward us shouting, hand-held flashlights bobbing.

"*Aiuto, aiuto!*" Tina and Donna shouted for help in unison, soprano and mezzo perfectly melded a half octave apart as though Von Karajan were conducting the second act of a Mozart opera.

The responses from below were baritone and tenor, with one aged, cracked basso and a shrill contralto—all crying out variations of "Hold on. We're coming."

Their torches illuminated our Triumph high up in the trees!

"Che cazzo de faaaaaa!" the old man trilled, which could be roughly translated as "What the fuck are you doing?"

"Jesu, Giuseppi, Vergine!" the old lady warbled.

I called down for a ladder, turned my light upon the two younger men—barefoot in nightshirts and underwear.

"Too high," one declared. He shouted for us to climb out of the car and down the trees. They were strong old chestnuts, many branches for footholds and to break our fall.

"Berto, get ropes," the old man commanded. I flashed my light toward the old folks. He was in a yellowed singlet, a pipe in his wise mouth half cracked in a smile. "Good evening, gentle ladies." He bowed in courtesy.

"Don't leave us!" Donna cried. I'd decided to take some weight off whatever branches were holding up the TR and had climbed over the door and onto the hood. The TR shifted beneath me. The girls shouted *"Aiuto"* again and the old man chanted, *"Pazze, che cazze?"* But I made it off the car onto a spur of one chestnut and told Tina and Donna to calm down.

"Eddie will murder me when he finds out," Tina said worriedly. "This car is five days old. *Five days!"*

"Sort of gives new meaning to 'up a tree,' doesn't it?" Donna mused, and they began to giggle. Giggled so much, the car trembled and the trees shivered and I told them to cool it.

When Berto arrived with two ropes, he climbed the other trunk and threw me one rope, which, following his instructions, I looped around an upper branch. He tied his end to a branch and made a noose, which we threw to the girls. They were too frightened to get over the car doors, so we had them bring down the canvas top. With every snap of the roof clamps, the car and trees shook again.

Tina came out first. She kissed Donna good-bye and added, "It's been fun." She looped the other end around her waist and arms, Berto and I pulled and, light as Tina was, she sailed over the windshield. We gingerly lowered her to the ground below, where she yelled up, "It's *fun*, Dee. Like the Parachute Jump at Coney Island."

"I hate heights. I've never been on the Parachute Jump," Donna declared. She caught the rope but refused to put it on. After some talking to, she also was lifted out. Before we could lower her to the ground and while she was fluttering about in midair, the car—suddenly relieved of all weight—suddenly shifted and began to slide backward. It was so tightly wedged at the front bumpers, it slid vertically, cracking branches beneath its ton and a half weight, until it stopped, its headlights pointing at the sky through the tattered tree cover.

All this was more than ample cause for colorful swearing, moans of disaster, cries of warning—a sort of Rossini mixed-chorus finale, punctuated by Donna's terrified rope-slung screams, which at times actually surpassed C in Alt.

She kissed the ground when she finally reached it, and I half climbed, half shimmied down the chestnut—remembering that other chestnut tree I'd climbed so often a decade before, an ocean away, to visit Ricky Hersch. The old man hugged me against his pipe-stained white-mustached face, muttering *"Che bravo, che bravo!"* His wife was offering us a homemade white cherry brandy just as the police pulled up, whistling sirens and blue roof lights aglitter.

One stepped out of his car, turned a flashlight upon the hamstrung Triumph, looked at us, and said with total Catholic authority, "It's a miracle."

Ten minutes later the reporters and paparazzi appeared and bribed the police to allow them to photograph Contino Eddie's sports car, wedged between two chestnut trees, its gleaming fenders illuminated by arc lights.

I doubt if a lover ever had a better excuse for the old question, "Where have you been?"

Feted by the farmer family, snapped by the paparazzi, questioned by reporters, written up in all the morning papers (and later in a weekly magazine), questioned more officially with ultra courtesy by the local police—after all, we were living miracles, and Italians have a true respect for the Hand of Destiny—I arrived back at the Hassler near eleven, newspapers in hand as alibis.

Mafalda seemed out, probably at the Friday morning fish market. At first I didn't see Djanko. I made a cup of coffee and walked through the suite deciding he'd gone to the studio. Only when I sat down to look at the photos of me and the girls and the TR-3 did I notice him.

Djanko was sitting on the little balcony off the living room, wearing a jacket against the still cool morning air, his head in his hands. I'd never seen a more forlorn human being.

He greeted me as though I were a ghost: utter disbelief, then with wan smiles and finally a big hug and mumbling into my shoulder. I dragged him inside and showed him the newspapers. They didn't seem to register on him, and I realized he'd reverted to Croatian in his speech and so probably made no sense of the print.

"Don't you even want to know where I've been?"

"When you walked out," he finally managed to say in English, "Tratano said to me, 'Idiot! Italians you slap, they swear a vendetta. Slavs you slap, they start a revolution. Americans you slap, either they kill you on the spot or they go away forever. It's a big country, America. Every day the newspapers tell about men who wake up one morning and instead of going to work, go away forever. They go west to Wyoming, to Nevada and are never heard from again.' I thought that you'd gone away to Nevada forever," Djanko added.

"Without my passport? My visa?"

"You could always get new ones."

"It almost seems like you wanted me to leave."

"No, no, never." He placed his head under my hand, as if I were to give him benediction, and promised never to strike me again.

I extracted a few other promises from him—among them

a trip to the Dalmatian coast of Yugoslavia he'd always talked about once the new film was in the can. So we made up, and despite Mafalda's scandalization, we went to bed for the next three hours. Where the Pig or Jiri or La Bernakovka had disappeared to I never discovered, though they returned after the weekend in full force. When Djanko and I finally did decide to get up that Friday afternoon, I turned from pulling up my trousers to see him still on the bed looking at me not as a fond lover three feet away but as though I'd just returned from a lengthy trek over plains and Rockies.

When he read the papers, Djanko was angry and thrilled and fearful too late for my safety. "How close it came to being true," he mused.

Naturally he promised to take the disputed scene out of the script. He also agreed to test Tina and Donna for the parts supposedly now shortened. I tried to get him to agree to write a new scene in place of the one cribbed from Vergil that would contain lines for the girls but he shushed me. The radio was on, playing a tenor aria of great mellifluousness and poignancy. We listened to it rapt, almost afraid to release our breath until it was over. The announcer identified the singer as Fritz Wunderlich, whom I'd never heard of. The aria had been from Ambroise Thomas's *Mignon* and was titled simply "Adieu Mignon" (or in his German rendition, "Leb Wohl Mignon").

"I wish he'd play it again," I said. As though he'd heard me, the announcer did: Djanko and I moved into a silent, immobile embrace to listen.

Later on I joked about the incident, saying, "I've never even been to Ne-va-da."

The following day Djanko dragged me to the Via del Condottiere and bought me the ridiculously expensive gold watch. The clerk at Bulgari opened up the back to show us how every gear and cog and wheel inside was either a gold alloy or pure gold.

The incident never came up among the others. But on

Monday morning, when we were all gathered for lunch at the studio, Djanko pointed to my watch. "Look Jiri, Valentina, Bruno. Lovely, no?"

In his *Secret History*, Procopius notes that Dalmatia was the sore spot of several Byzantine emperors' reigns and the direct or indirect cause of two imperial downfalls. The conquering Seljuk called it "the barbed coast," and although the Turks marched as far as the gates of Vienna, they never succeeded in bringing the benefits of the Sublime Porte to those rocky shores—partly because of the Venetians who had wrested all sides of the Adriatic as early as the twelfth century, so that it became known as the Primo Lagoon, the vestibule of St. Marks. Even the wily and violent Venetians had difficulties in La Ragusa—as the area was called. Uprisings, sudden unrest in the wealthy satellite city-states, boycotts, trade wars, betrayals all feature in the history of that seemingly insignificant strip of earthquake-tossed granite and schist from Trieste down to Dubrovnik.

I'd read all this in various places, mostly in Rebecca West's *Black Lamb, Grey Falcon,* but had I learned? Apparently not.

As *Jason and the Argonauts* moved into principal shooting and daily rushes, and ultimately into the editors' and translators' and dubbers' booths, it became clear that Djanko had no time for me. Understanding this still didn't keep me from being bored.

Not completely bored. Four of my friends were now on board and that was a great excuse to call the studio and have a car sent for me at lunchtime, to have Mafalda fix a luncheon basket and to drive onto the set just as everyone's nerves were shredding. Bottles of wine and pignoli cookies in hand, I'd pull Djanko into his office—or into a van if we were outdoors—and make him tell me what had gone wrong that day. Two of those not on his shit list for the day would be rounded up for a bright lunch, kicked out again for "siesta"—read sex, which always cheered Djanko up—and bammo! he was ready for a later afternoon shooting, as fresh as a film-school grad.

Nor was Djanko my only responsibility. I had to keep an eye on Tina and Donna, who were like bad chemistry: apart quiet, together doubly catalytic. Cicely was no problem being a pro, and she looked so great in her silver off-the-shoulder gown and star veil as Aphrodite that we all started to say "Di-vine" instead of "Pre-cious," sometimes even "Di-vine, like Cis." Angel and she shook hands and made up. When I told her Angel's comment about their potential offspring, she seemed surprised. Touched too.

"Can you picture it? My first time and I'd get pregnant. Angel marries me and suddenly I'm Mrs. Dwayne Lodge of El Paso, Texas, with babies shooting down the hatch one a year. Babies so beautiful, it hurts your eyes to look at them. What?" she asked at my unrestrained surprise. "That's Angel's name, you know—Dwayne Lodge."

"At least," I tried, "they'd be sleepy babies. They wouldn't keep you up all night."

"And I'd have no problem getting them to eat," she added, and we laughed and laughed.

Angel knew his lines, sailed into and through scenes like the professional he was by that time and altogether made everyone fall in love with him. Jiri stole Angel's yellow posing strap—no surprise—and once an elaborately set-up shoot was halted an hour while they searched fruitlessly for Angel's Nemean Lion spotted loincloth. Mr. Lodge acted, slept, and ate. He became a regular at our pre-siesta luncheons, and with his blond hair tinted bronze and his new bronze-dyed mustache, his muscles, his excellent movement and not terribly wooden readings of lines, everyone on the set spoke of him as the new Lex Barker.

Following each day's shoot we ate together, sometimes a dozen of us, at one of the outdoor restaurants: Djanko, I, Cicely, Angel, Tina, Jiri, Donna, La Bernakovka, the Pig and others from the film, and we were like one big family.

But when they were away on a shoot—"It's only two days,

caro," Djanko would say, "it's crazy for you to come. The budget is already over"—then, *then* I'd become bored. I'd wander around Rome, seeing the city not as a tourist but as a resident: places now had reference points, allusions, personal history. On one such jaunt I found the little hole-in-the-wall-convent shop and bought chocolate. On another I found the Pantheon, for once open, and finally got to see its interior.

I began to notice men and women looking at me; sizing me up sexually. One character followed me all around the Colisseum trying to convince me that he was a sculptor and wanted me as a model. It was a startlingly hot afternoon about five P.M., all good Romans at their siesta, and the place was deserted. I said "Fuck off" in Italian and walked away.

A few days later I was walking out of a cinema that showed English-language films with Italian subtitles when I bumped into Kit. He expatiated upon the flick—Kim Novak as Moll Flanders—then took me for a drink at the not-famous-Venetian, but less-famous-Roman Harry's Bar. There he described what he would do to me using only two pinkie fingers and the tip of his tongue, and I let him take me back to the Excelsior. While I read issues of *L'Uomo Vogue* and ate an apple and talked to Djanko by phone in Sardinia, Kit rimmed.

More serious encounters happened. A group of Swedish hippies congregated in various piazzas, recreating in colored chalk the murals on the ceiling of the Sistine Chapel, the Last Supper of da Vinci, and Fra Angelico's frescoes all over Rome. There were a dozen of them, boys and girls, sixteen to about twenty-five years old. Their leader was a pensively handsome dark blond who looked like a novena-card Jesus and who played up the resemblance by dressing like the Nazarene: ironic Norse Provo provocation, of course, but local women would fall to their knees at sight of him and whip out their ever-present rosary beads.

I'd seen this group around and noticed his slender, tight

body and firm little buttocks more than once, and heard him being called Gun—short, I surmised, for Gunnar. One afternoon at the Spanish Steps, I was sitting reading Rimbaud in the Pleiade edition when Gun came up to me.

"Read aloud one of the *Illuminations*," he said in French, in a tone of voice that expected to be obeyed.

"Read it yourself," I answered in English. Then, to soften it, "Here. My French stinks."

He found what he wanted. The others, working on an Ucello battle scene, froze so Gun could read aloud the little poemlet "Royalty," one of my favorites, in idiomatic French.

They murmured approval and went back to their art. Gun returned to me, still sitting on the steps, and handed back the book. "And you? Who are you?"

Thinking fast, I responded with the famous last line from "Parade"—I alone have the key to this savage sideshow—in my unidiomatic French.

He placed his hand to stop the last word—*sauvage*—from coming out. "What do you want?" he asked in English but in such a pretentious manner that I now understood his attraction, could see a younger, or more spiritual me, think about that question so deeply intoned, wait a minute as the light struck, then answer, "To follow you, of course, Lord."

Instead I said, "I want to fuck your ass."

A smile rose to his lips, his eyes lost their sacred light and became mischievous. "Yes. Yes," he said, as though I'd said something profound. "That would be pleasant."

We did, shortly afterward, on a thin narrow bed pad in a small, nearly unfurnished room in some dreary suburb south of Rome, surrounded by a vast, astonishingly unattractive concrete housing project. We were alone, no disciples, no Nilses or Christas to disturb us, and we went crazy over each others' bodies like starving scavengers over freshly killed carcasses, coming again and again until it was dark and we couldn't get hard again if our lives depended upon it.

The next time I saw the Chalk-Provos a week later, Gun

again asked for the Rimbaud and I gave him the book to keep; and I knew I would be able to fuck this mock Jesus whose pale blue eyes had widened in almost terrified surprise as he'd climaxed without volition through my pumping, anytime I wanted.

Shooting on the film was finally over and I became an editing-room widow for weeks. That's when I once more encountered Maurizio, chauffeur of the cornflower-blue Bentley. It was Mafalda's day off and I went out hunting for Gunnar. Sick of screwing him in puddled basements, in abandoned houses, for once I wanted it clean, ironed, comfortable. After checking various piazzas and asking the group's whereabouts, I ascertained that they had moved along to Lucca, possibly by the Roman police—it was unclear. In a semi-snit, I went shopping.

Once more as I stepped out of an expensive shop on Via Condottiere, the Bentley pulled up to the curb. No magnate inside. The driver got out and opened the back door—for me. I got in.

"Where to, Signore?"

"Wherever you like."

"I would like a large bed."

"Fine," I said, and told him to drive to the Hassler. He picked up my packages and once inside the door to the suite he put them down and grabbed my face hard in one hand, kissing me as though he wanted to eat the features off me. He was well—and gamily—hung, and it was half passion, half technique; no bells, no romance. My suspicion that Angel was somehow behind this encounter was confirmed when Maurizio casually asked bout the big blond. I told him that we worked together in films. Maurizio frowned, then declared, "For him only would I make myself into a woman." I was about to say that wouldn't be necessary, that Angel slept with men, too, when I realized he meant it figuratively: he'd let Angel do to him what he'd just done to me.

Thinking of Maurizio's remark worried me. In fact, it

brought into focus all my relationships with European men. Could all that cultural baggage they carried really have taken over their minds? Did Gunnar actually feel a Triune melding of Father, Son and Holy Ghost whenever I porked him? Had Maurizio's machismo stripped to invisibility my genitals, mustache and beard so he might screw me? Did Djanko buy me gold because the Pig bought Valentina gold and that was how one treated courtesans, no matter their gender or upbringing? What exactly was Jiri sniffing for in my underwear—the Elixir of Youth? the Holy Grail? some specifically American alchemical secret? When I was next with Djanko, I said, "You Europeans are all really sick about sex, do you know that? Do you?"

"What can you expect, *caro*? Too many people all living too close together for too many centuries . . ." As though that explained anything.

Of late, Djanko had moved into this mode of non sequitur with me, and with everyone else. Who knew what Djanko meant when he introduced me to strangers as his *fidanzato* (fiancé) *Americano* and answered me in desperation, "But *carissimo* . . ." as though every statement was grounds for argument. "Let him wait," he'd told an assistant director when I appeared on time at the studio to drag him off to a business dinner he wanted to—said he *had to*—attend. These inanities and little betrayals could not be kissed and caressed away. I knew it meant completion of the film was imminent and that the philosophical despair that usually followed was even nearer.

All would change in Yugoslavia, I was certain; so I looked forward to the trip, counted the days till we could go.

Partly, I admit, from Djanko's own fascination with the place. He'd told me the first night we'd met about that icon of St. Stephen in an underground vault of some half-destroyed monastery which he'd fallen in love with as a child, and which allegedly prefigured me. Another, less completely refurbished official spa Djanko's young Communist group visited had been an embassy of the Venetian Serenissima,

right to the day that Napoleon forced an end to that anach-
ronistic republic. The boys had slept four abreast in giant
beds, testers draped in soft-with-decades blue and gold satin.
"We'd never felt any material like it," Djanko said. "We
pulled it down and rubbed it all over our bodies." In the
morning, the satin was wrapped around their legs under the
blanket. Like a lubricious sponge, it had drawn semen from
them and lay there, bi-colored, inert again. He had been
thirteen.

In all these stories, sun glare magnificence and modest
youth, omens and insinuations and the omnipresent obser-
vance of party hacks were apparent. I could smell the sea
wrack, see the granitic goat paths, feel the arc of starlight
upon mica in his memories. A storm scene in *Jason* had
been filmed near Split, and though the crew was there only
three days and Djanko himself barely an afternoon, it had
been long enough for him to come upon a vacant villa he'd
told me about which commanded perfect views and location.

Yugoslavia came to seem to me a sort of utopia, where
Djanko and I could recapture those first golden days of our
love. Several factors—conscious and not completely conscious—were behind this belief. Like all Americans of my
generation, I'd been taught to see the U.S.S.R. as a thun-
dering, warmongering bear. Conversely, its satellites in Eastern Europe were overcultured states that had fallen into
Communism through the vagaries of history and the fifth-
column betrayals of their intellectuals. The uprisings in
Hungary so terribly quashed, the raising of the Berlin Wall
to keep East Germans from flocking out every day: all
seemed to show how put-upon these poor countries were.
With its forceful, independent leader, Tito, Yugoslavia alone
of this bloc seemed happily, pleasantly, willingly Communist. Yes, happily, because after all, while I was as patriotic
as the next person, I also had enough college-bred liberal-
ism to believe that intellectually, Communism might be a
good thing, possibly the only true future political state. Not
the Leninist-Marxist debacle, not even the Maoist mess, but

a pure Communism, where the people would be proud and individual and sharing, scorning what my parents wanted for themselves and their children so badly—bank accounts and investments, a degree in law or medicine, a larger suburban split level—scorning what these crazed filmmakers in Cinecittá hungered for—renown, worldwide fame, universally recognized success. I reasoned that, returned to his homeland, free of all artificial pressures, Djanko would become the true Djanko whom I alone knew in those ever fewer moments when, after lovemaking or just waking up mornings, we'd camp out in his queen-size bed in the Hassler like Adam and Eve arising that first morning to name the birds and flowers and animals of Paradise.

I began to prod La Bernakovka about our trip, to insist, and finally to demand she do something about it. Within days she'd arranged to rent the villa outside of Split on the Yugo Riviera Djanko had come upon, obtained visas, the car and driver's papers, everything.

No celebration ended the completion of the Jason movie, but bitter, venal disputes among Djanko, Jiri, the Pig, and the film editor. Naturally Djanko had gotten his way about ninety percent of the time. He'd been born on the cusp of Taurus and Gemini and so possessed the doubly dangerous ability to issue the most insane of arguments and then stick to them with bull-like persistence in the face of all realities.

Still, he was exhausted by the entire process by the time he finally got into the studio car—a gigantic Rolls extended limo with bar, stereo system, sunroof, and a trunk as large as my bathroom—to drive into the Apennines toward Venice. Djanko slept all the way to Verona, where we stopped for dinner, and he slept again the minute his head hit the pillow in our hotel suite in Trieste.

He was far more alert the following morning. We frolicked for the first time in a month, had a late breakfast in the sea-view dining room, and drove across the border into his native land an hour later. Cutting across the Fiume Peninsula, we were already rather high up in the Dalmatian range—we would climb all morning—and the sun had come out to wink mischievously in a postcard-blue sky free of the idea of humidity.

I noticed but didn't think much at the time of the awed, even apologetic fawning manner with which the Yugoslav border guards asked for our visas. So close to the bustling port of Trieste, I assumed they were already completely corrupted by its capitalistic values.

Three hours later we had passed through Zadar, left what seemed more or less to be the main highway over a ridge of mountains and began a twisting descent, looping back and forth until we eventually reached a coastal hamlet high on the slate-gray cliffs above a churning baylet with a long, flat island: like a sunken fortress blocking the Adriatic. The driver didn't know the road, and after a while, even optimistic Djanko decided to stop to ask directions.

I'd noticed long narrow plots of vegetables and what appeared to be small barley fields along the road, hedged in by the sharp gray rock hills, obviously farming of merely subsistence level, with square, squat men hoeing, raking by hand, and even pulling plows as though they were oxen. Our driver pulled up to a tiny village at a crossroads and these same square earthen potato-eaters looked at the yacht-sized Rolls as though a flying saucer had landed, bowing their heads and literally pulling at their forelocks in feudal respect to the imperial chauffeur.

"Ask if we can get something to drink here," Djanko said to the driver.

Our chauffeur Ermes's Italian was understood by the farmers. One old man cuffed a younger one into motion toward a farmhouse, then bowed again and mumbled something.

I was already feeling uncomfortable. First, because I'd never laid eyes on true peasants before, and these ragged, stolid, calflike creatures simultaneously disgusted and provoked a bizarre compassion in me. Second, I felt awkward in the presence of Djanko's astonishing acceptance of his own superiority over them by virtue of his wealth, his driver, his ostentatious automobile.

Blind to all that, he pulled me out of the backseat when the younger man returned, leading two women in babushkas. One carried a pail of sweet milk, its cream still yellow clots upon the surface, the other with two obviously old, dented, and somewhat ceremonial pewter goblets and a towel-wrapped loaf of braided bread into which whole hard-boiled eggs had been baked.

"Marvelous!" Djanko enthused, and we were treated to blushes and smiles and curtsies and the distant stares of shy, dirty children hiding behind their elders as Djanko drank the milk, ripped off chunks of the eggy bread and pronounced it all wonderful, urging the driver and me to join in.

I wouldn't, sulked, smoked a cigarette. When Djanko finally goaded me with a singular lack of unawareness, I said, "Djanko! Can't you see we're taking the bread and milk out of these children's mouths? Can't we at least pay them?"

"Don't be such a sentimental tourist, *carissimo*. This is the biggest event in this village in a year. If we tried to pay, they'd stone us. It's an honor. Go on, eat, drink," he added between mouthfuls. He then went on to explain me to the villagers as ailing, to which the flat-faced women frowned in commiseration and insisted upon giving me the remainder of the loaf to take with us in the car along with a cup of freshly made soup. Djanko was gleeful at this turn.

All were smiles, forelock pulling, and curtsies as the Rolls finally glided away from the village, the driver now in command of the directions, a chunk of bread at his side. Disillusioned as I was by this little occurrence in which the joys of the brave new Communist world seemed nonexistent, I nevertheless let Djanko chat me into a better mood. Still, following so quickly upon the scene with the border guards, it was a second sign that matters would not be as I'd envisaged them in Yugoslavia. And I blamed Djanko and his need for showing off the Rolls.

The afternoon before we'd left Rome, I'd gone to a record store to find the Ambroise Thomas aria that had played as background music to our reconciliation. In those days Ricordi, the music publisher, had a shop that not only sold scores and records but also provided listening booths in which one might audition discs. I'd said the name Fritz Wunderlich and the clerk had given me an LP containing eleven arias: Mozart, Handel, Donizetti, Lortzing, Verdi, Wagner's "Steersman's Song" from *The Flying Dutchman* and of course the "Adieu Mignon" Djanko and I had so much loved. But as I played through the album in the listening booth, it was another aria, from Tchaikovsky's opera *Eugene Onegin,* which most impressed me—even though I didn't have the words in front of me and despite the German in which Wunderlich sang all the cuts.

I'd never heard this aria before; indeed I didn't even know Tchaikovsky had composed a half dozen operas. I bought the record, and when Djanko and I arrived at the ultramodern white brick-and-glass-wall villa high above the Adriatic, I took it from our luggage and handed it to him. Ever sensitive to exactly the right gesture, Djanko was delighted. He played the *Mignon* aria as we sat on the huge outdoor terrace. Miles of sheer cliff lay at our feet, birds of prey wheeled in vast circles almost level with us, far out to sea.

In the weeks to come at the villa, the Wunderlich recital would be constantly on our turntable. But when I put it on I would play it right through, enjoying almost all of the pieces equally; when I wasn't there Djanko played the Tchaikovsky cut, Lensky's aria, over and over, using a clever repeat mechanism on the German-made stereo.

Wunderlich and Nicolai Gedda (in Russian) are my favorite singers for the aria still. Every modern lyric tenor has done it and for good reason: it's a marvelous little character study. I was already familiar with the Pushkin novel-in-verse the opera was based on, from a college lit class, and so I knew at least the context. Count Lensky, Onegin's best friend, has found his bored, cynical pal flirting with Olga, Lensky's own intended. When he demands an apology, Onegin refuses. A product of his time and class, Lensky has no choice but to demand satisfaction. Onegin accepts the challenge. It is now the next morning, minutes before the combatants will meet, and Lensky is preparing for the duel. Combined in him (and in the music) is his intuition of death as a result of his rash challenge and his unwillingness to give up life and love at this moment when he is so young, so full of both, so much heir to all in life that is desirable.

Djanko didn't play Lensky's aria much during our first few days on the Dalmatian coast. Those were for unwinding, relaxing, he said. This mostly consisted of sleeping, sunning upon the enormous mesa of terrace surrounding the villa on three sides and eating Mafalda's snacks and larger meals. Making love, too, at all hours of the day.

Yes, Mafalda had come along. Rather, she'd preceded us to Yugoslavia by two days to hire help, to "air out" the villa, to get it ready for us. Dancing attendance upon her was a young girl named Milo and a half-witted handyman, Stromo. I came to enjoy Milo's high spirits and pale gray eyes, her surprise at what could be purchased—object or service—with money. Stromo was a bit more difficult to approach. His sheer ugliness stopped me, especially as there was so little in the way of that sparkle of humanity in his eyes which often turns the physically plain into delicious companions. Even Ermes didn't associate with Stromo. In fact, all Ermes seemed to do was read dozens of paperback mysteries left by the previous tenant and drive to the nearest town to make phone calls to his middle-aged girlfriend, Aurelia, back in Rome.

All was so quiet, so relaxed, so private those few first days, I almost persuaded myself that I finally had Djanko to myself and could work undisturbed on repairing our troubled relationship. The third morning there, however, when I returned from a dip up the steep rocky part-path part-steps carved out of the cliffs, I came upon Djanko talking on the telephone, expostulating in that precise, irritated manner that instantly told me it wasn't a personal call but film business. Almost the second that Djanko noticed me, he signed off.

At lunch, he announced that Tratano would be joining us soon. Djanko was in profile to me (he wouldn't dare look me in the face) as he said, "Bruno needs a vacation too." I didn't say a word but quietly steamed. Before dinner, I ran down the cliffs to the sea and didn't climb back until Djanko and the other servants had called my name for half an hour.

Clambering up the slippery wet rocks, the incoming tide just behind me in the dark, I came upon someone climbing down: Ermes.

"I'm on my way up," I told him.

"Didn't you hear us?"

I tried pushing past him, but he blocked the narrow path. He repeated his question.

"I heard you."

He grabbed my arm nearest him. "If I were the Signor, I would spank your bare behind," he shouted hoarsely over the rush of the tide. But it didn't come out so much a threat as it did an erotic promise.

I pulled away, pushed past him and climbed up, Ermes behind me.

"Ca-ro!" Djanko boomed in basso when I appeared.

"When are they coming?"

"They?"

"Jiri, La Bernakovka and Tratano." I dared him to deny it.

"Tomorrow afternoon," he admitted.

The next morning the phone rang at least a dozen times and Djanko always took it. I suspected that a new film was in the works but didn't know why it was coming so fast on the heels of the last one. He certainly didn't need the money or the credits. Annoyed by how often Djanko would look around to see if I was watching him on the phone, I called out that I was taking the car to town, did he want anything? Only cigarettes, perfumed Turkish ones, he called back. Then: "Make Ermes drive. Your license is no good here."

I rapped on Ermes's bedroom door. Stromo was nearby, kneeling on the parapet staring at a frog. The chauffeur was stretched out on his unmade bed, reading Agatha Christie. He leapt up, happy to drive me, to do something, anything.

The nearest town of any size was fifty miles away, hours there and back given the quality of the roads, but I'd grabbed a fat handful of lire (highly valued here) and had decided to buy magazines, gum, almost anything. Although the downtown of Split suggested a real city, it took us a long time to locate a place to spend money, despite Ermes's intuitive ability to find shops in any three-horse hamlet in Italy.

He finally pulled up to a good-sized store in the main plaza, officially flanked by a party headquarters and several other government buildings. I bought like a madman: magazines, candy, postcards, wrapping paper, three more Agatha Christies for Ermes, hair ribbon for Milo, a woven basket for Mafalda, an American-made snap lighter for Stromo to obsess over, four brands of Turkish cigarettes for Djanko ("Ca-*ro*, who will smoke them all?"), lipstick for Valentina, eye patches (plastic, white, Dada) for the Pig, who detested sunlight. I was stumped by Jiri. Jiri. Jiri. What could . . . ? Then I spotted just the thing, a pair of women's underwear, extra large, as roughly textured as burlap and—grossly—a shade of bubble-gum pink. By now the salesclerk was so startled, embarrassed and finally stupefied by me, he didn't even blink as I tossed the panties into his arms and started toward their ghastly selection of sweets.

Ermes thanked me for the paperbacks, which were offered as casually as possible, but otherwise didn't say another provocative word to me. Not on that drive, nor on the one or two we made every day for the next few weeks. He no longer even asked where I wanted to go when—the telephone ringing, the four of them arguing—I would knock on his bedroom door and he would leap up in such a rush that he'd still be putting on his driver's jacket and cap as he opened the passenger door for me. He'd simply set off on some road and at a fork slow down and ask, "Here?" and unless I said no, would go wherever it led.

We ended up in tiny little villages at lunchtime, the elders with their fezzes and pipes, drinking bracing tea and coffee the consistency of sand. Or at an abandoned abbey or half-ruined castle not yet brought into an official party reconstruction program. Anywhere we drove, even in Ragusa, our car was the largest, the most extraordinary—always the center of attention. I dressed in jeans and T-shirt, cowboy boots or sneakers; on hot days I'd put on my olive Boy Scout shorts with red pocket piping, a faded Izod shirt and Djanko's crocodile espadrilles. Still, on streets and in shops, people parted for me as though I were Grace Kelly. I could see amazement in their eyes, surprise that a boy in beachwear and sunglasses could be recognized as important. "Movie star," I heard said in English more than once. "Popsinger" almost as often. It made no difference that they didn't know my name, couldn't place me. I became increasingly annoyed at such a people for whom a nobody with a large car was respectable.

One morning I said to Ermes, "Find the Grand Hotel. The one with the glass-enclosed dining room." He did, following a half dozen sets of often contradictory instructions. We arrived at the place and I walked past middle-aged adults obviously in charge, toward the sound of children's voices. Ermes asked about the dining room and was told that it was now an enclosed pool. Alas, merely a pool! I was turning to leave, but two of the Yugoslavs came up to me, shook my hands and, delightedly chatting away, in crude Italian and worse French than mine, led me through the entire place—now a Resort Spa Deluxe. The last group of children were drying off at the pool when we arrived, and I stared at them, wondering what legends their memories would make for future lovers.

We found the Venetian embassy too, now a waterworks control for the region. I could have walked in and been shown around there, too, I'm certain, even sporting my "Future Farmers of America" T-shirt, but I passed it by. It would have no beds, no testers, no satin in the colors of the Venetian Republic.

Although Ermes worked at it, we never did find the monastery with the purportedly precise (hah!) likeness of me. Twice I took Valentina out driving with me, but she kept up a running monologue of such astonishing vapidity that even the driver (who tilted the mirror to look at her tits) was relieved when I appeared alone the following day and never invited her again.

The last of these jaunts to the surrounding countryside ended with a surprise. I'd barely acknowledged Ermes forking off onto a small road. It was late on a hot afternoon, no cooler despite the sun setting, and I was dying to get back to Djanko and a shower. For the guiltier Djanko had become about our vacation turning into business, the better his lovemaking had gotten; sharper, more daring. As if to repay me for his treachery, Djanko had taken on new hungers, a new submissiveness . . . it was eerie if exciting, and I wished I had a psychiatrist to ask how common this behavior was for neurotics—it was now clear that Djanko was a complete neurotic.

Musing on this in a half-awake state, I was jolted by ruts in the road. The Rolls suddenly stopped.

After fooling around with the gears, trying to rock back and forth, Ermes turned around to me and made that Roman gesture which signified "I've done everything I can."

I looked outside: fields in one direction as far as the light still showed; fields and ridges in the other; fields ahead; fields behind. I opened the passenger door: a dirt—no, a mud—road. We were stuck.

Ermes had shut off the engine and come to open the door for me.

"I will try again in a few minutes," he said in a strangely

husky voice. "But if we cannot get out, we will have to spend the night here."

He stepped into the passenger compartment and sat facing me on a fold-out seat.

"Don't be anxious. I will protect you. I knew . . . I knew this moment would arrive."

"Now Ermes," I began calmly, but he had already leaned toward me, and I squirted past him and out the door.

He climbed out after me. The sun was setting. It would be dark in no time.

"Look, Ermes, why don't you start up the car. Put on the lights and I'll push."

He was all over me, squeezing me against the car.

"Every day . . . every day . . ." he whimpered with what I had to assume was passion in mind.

I shoved him off me. "Get in the car and do as I say."

"But why not . . . why not?"

"Because you are middle-aged, unattractive to me, heterosexual, and already affianced. That's why not."

"But this growing affection I've noticed, this subtle passion . . ."

"Is all in your mind! Tonight you'll go off to Split and find yourself a woman. I'll pay for it."

That stopped him, although he was still breathing all over me.

"It's because I'm only a chauffeur."

"It's because you do not interest me, Ermes. I have a man, thank you very much, and I'm not even sure I want *him*. Now get in the car . . . and do what I told you. We'll be out of here in no time."

"You cannot *push!*"

"Why not? I'm not made of glass. I'm twenty-two years old and healthy. I've done this before. Get in."

He did, and after a few pushes, the Rolls was out of the mud. His little scheme for seduction foiled, Ermes was rewarded with an Ithacan harlot later that night by my express command.

No sooner had I gotten Ermes off my case and curtailed our drives than I realized that Jiri was following my little walks. I was down at the water's edge, sunning on a flat shelf of basalt far enough away from the villa that I couldn't hear even half phrases of talk when I suddenly looked up and there he was, ineffectively hidden within a fallen tent of mica, staring at me. I picked up my novel and read on, but I could no longer concentrate. When I looked up again ten minutes later, he was gone—or better hidden.

The following day my walk along the shoreline was punctuated by looking around to see Jiri sneaking behind me. The afternoon had turned gray and damp and I'd pulled on my shirt and sneakers, feeling extra annoyed with my lot in life: unable to understand why Djanko wouldn't step foot out of the house, or at any rate not beyond the terrazzo to help me find the monastery of his youth with the preordaining icon, to go anywhere, to do anything but rant on in story conference and then, mournfully alone, to listen to that damn Tchaikovsky aria. Was he having a nervous breakdown? Or rather—and a worse thought—was this how he usually was, and would always be?

Two boys came along, laughing lads fourteen and sixteen or so, with a box net containing two fat eels. The boys were tanned, their hair the same wheat color as Djanko's, but they were brown-eyed, good-looking. We talked about the eels. I said I lived up at the house on the hill—the "glass house," they called it. When I told them I was from America, they didn't believe me until I turned around to show them the genuine Levi patch on my denims. Then the older boy hugged me and said dozens of American names, Coca-Cola, *Goldfinger,* Jerry Lewis, Dave Brubeck. They were about to leave when the younger one stepped up to a rock overlooking the tide and suddenly unbuttoned to urinate. I turned to check if Jiri was looking. He was. I, too, unbuttoned and stepped up to the rock and told the older brother that he should, too—three pissing was lucky, but not two. He was agreeable, and we lined up so that Jiri got a great vista of the three of us. The next morning when I came out onto the terrazzo with my coffee, Jiri was alone. He said "Thank you" so softly and without looking at me, I wondered if it was an illusion.

A few days later I was back on the flat rock, sunning in my bathing briefs when someone came by, awakening me by stumbling over the rocks on purpose so that I would hear. A young man my age, so resembling the boys of the day before he might be their brother.

"American?" he asked.

"Blucky?" I asked, recalling the boys' surname. No, another name, Cepo. He, too, held a box net with eels inside, many more than two, and he took them out to show me. I wouldn't touch them, but I noticed a movement in the rocks behind Cepo—Jiri. I looked past Cepo's large, fishy hands to his open shirt and his flat hairless chest, up to the hollow of his throat, the jutting dimpled chin and wide mouth and sea-green eyes, and I thought perhaps I should really give Jiri something special to look at today. Cepo was already blushing, his glance not on my face but slowly sweeping along my body, and when I looked level again it was clear that he was aroused, probably had been when he'd stopped. I panicked at the thought that such open infidelity as I was now moving into was probably exactly what Jiri was looking for to make a scene with Djanko. I simply gave Cepo a cigarette, lighted it and said good-bye. Still blushing, he went off cheerfully—half relieved, I think.

At the villa, the others were napping, Djanko at his desk strewn with scripts, listening for the eleven hundredth time to the Wunderlich aria.

"Why do you play it so often?" I asked.

"It's so sad. So fated. The poignancy comes from him— and from us, too—knowing it's the last beautiful thing he will do before his life is ended."

I sighed.

"And you?" Djanko asked. "What do you hear in it?"

"I hear a young man rebelling. Rebelling against everything his foolish society stands for. Its values. Its stupid customs that would allow a man to die for nothing."

"But he *does* die."

"Not in the song he doesn't. He lives on forever. Onegin doesn't have nearly as great an aria. Only Lensky."

"And Tatiana. In the letter scene. But they both fail. Only Onegin goes on."

"What is this all about, Djanko? You haven't failed. You've made a wonderful movie of the Jason story."

"*Caro*, they're all failures. The compromises, the alterations, the fraudulent scenes from other sources. Never as I conceive them. Never once pure."

"Is that the reason for all this gloom? Why not make the movie you told me about, the one about your great uncle the tuba player? His adventures in the mountains during the war. That's the film you really want to make: *Great Uncle's Tuba*."

"Ah." He smiled wistfully. "That would be a wonderful film. But no, for that to be filmed and then to fail, too . . . I couldn't bear it. It's best unfilmed, kept pure."

"I'm going for a walk on the rocks," I said. "Want to come?"

"You go, *caro*. I'll stay here."

I headed not for the rocks, but toward the garage, where I took the Pig's Maserati and drove at high speeds for hours over bad roads.

Have you ever noticed how days that will turn out to be momentous and awful begin so appallingly ordinary? You're driving to work as usual in unsnarled traffic, lightly tapping the steering wheel in time to a Kenny Rogers song, when the mammoth semi across the divider jackknifes through the metal fence directly into the oil tanker in front of you, which bursts into flame, and suddenly it's mayhem and headlines. You're in your office at ten o'clock wondering whether to send out your assistant for a glazed cruller or just have coffee when she rushes in to tell you the company president was just found hung, a suicide, in his rec room, a nearby note detailing his embezzlement and the company's bankruptcy.

That Thursday, three weeks into our month-long stay at the villa, began just as ordinarily. Bored to distraction, afraid to go down to the water and be dragged into more of Jiri's voyeuristic games, reduced to watching Stromo's attempts to keep alive a tiny herb garden for Mafalda in the only spot near the house not saturated by salt spray or sun glare, I decided to drive to Split. Everyone needed something—Mafalda and Valentina handed me detailed lists—and it would keep me out of the house for hours. Since his *affaire Greque* was going so well, I was no longer worried that Ermes would attempt another flat-footed passion upon me: he was now again merely an indifferent, obedient driver.

The long drive was almost delightfully dull. The shopping in three stores nearly as fulfilling—I even found a month-old English-language copy of *Newsweek,* although no one in the store would admit to knowing how it had gotten onto the shelf with *Agricultural Heritage, Tractor Features,* and *Anecdotes of the Great War,* the typical Yugoslav-Soviet magazine-rack fare. I was in serene spirits as Ermes loaded all the groceries and other goods into the Rolls' vast trunk and settled in for the drive back up the coast.

Perhaps it was that serenity which caused me, some twisting miles outside of Split, to notice a young man limping along with a broken bicycle, staring at the horizon, over which, after some twenty more miles, I knew a small town would at last appear. As we slowed down to pass him, I saw he was an ordinary youth, dark-haired, plain, wearing a student's uniform.

I told Ermes to stop, and when the boy and his bike limped up, the chauffeur asked if he'd had an accident. The youth looked at me to answer, but though he seemed to understand Italian, like two thirds of the people in Dalmatia, he seemed to speak only Serbian.

"Tell him to get in," I said. "We'll take him where the

bike can be fixed. You can attach it to the rear rack, can't you?"

Ermes conveyed my offer. The youth looked at the ground, frowning, then asked something.

"He asks if you're with the government."

"Of course not! Tell him I'm a tourist, vacationing here."

The boy heard me and quickly, almost angrily asked another question. One Ermes didn't understand.

"Tell him I'm a capitalist devil," I said in Italian, staring at the youth.

He spat on the ground, grabbed the handlebars of his bike and went on, dragging the bike.

Ermes snarled a curse, but I was delighted. I'd finally met someone in this rotten country who wouldn't fall all over himself for me.

We waited until the youth had ascended a rise in the road, then I tapped for Ermes to go on slowly. I knew the road, knew that just over this point the road looped wildly for miles, with no habitation in sight. If there was a place where the youth would change his mind, it was there. Right over the crest, I made Ermes stop, get out and wait for the youth.

Reluctantly, crossly, he let the driver take the bike and tie it down. Even more reluctantly, he got into the front—no, Ermes wouldn't allow that, the driving laws—into the backseat with me. He sat at the farthest extreme from me, frowning, unwilling to speak, and I tapped for Ermes to drive on.

I didn't speak to the boy, either. Didn't offer him a cigarette, though I smoked one myself. All this seemed to relax him a little. After a while I could see the youth was not unhappy to have allowed himself to be picked up for the ride. He suddenly asked in poor Italian if I was Italian. No, I told him, American—a true capitalist devil, I added. His dark blue eyes fairly glittered as he looked around himself at the pale gray leather upholstery, the charcoal plush carpets, the gleaming burled wood paneling on the doors and backs of the seats, the tiny bulbs recessed in chrome. He looked me over shyly: my tanned health, my Porsche sunglasses polarized low for indoors, the gold on my fingers and at my wrist, the Hermés silk sport shirt fluttering in the breeze, my linen shorts and Djanko's crocodile slip-ons.

He sort of grunted; a sound, I assumed, of total satisfaction. It was as if he'd been taught that good peasants would always wear itching wool and worn gabardine and the wicked rich silks and gold. That was life in the Leninist-Marxist struggle—and I proved it!

We arrived at the little town and he stepped out without a thank-you or a good-bye, grabbing the bike out of Ermes's hands. Before the driver could start up again, I espied what seemed to be a food store and thought I'd pick up some local pastries for tea time. Indeed I found some charming-looking and tasting—I was allowed to sample—almond-flavored cookies.

I was only in the shop five minutes, but when I looked outside a dozen villagers had gathered around the Rolls. Thinking to elude them, I went out the back door into a little yard. I walked along a wall, behind which I could hear the voices of young men speaking in the guttural Italian of the region.

"Was he very beautiful?" one asked.

"Like the moon," a voice I thought familiar replied. "His clothing was silk, and oh, I don't know, clothing even Tito can't afford."

"A gold watch?"

"Gold links, each one thicker than my thumb. More than twenty links. And a gold cigarette box, and a gold cigarette lighter with green flames. Inside, the car was all silver and gold and satin and the hide from a rhinoceros."

"American, you say?"

"An American prince," the voice gushed. "Or a movie star. He lives here in a villa with thirty-nine rooms and sixty servants. He owns *five* cars like that one."

"How fortunate you are, Hedi, to meet such a one."

"And to talk to him and to smoke his American cigarettes. If he would have let me, I would have—"

"What? What would you have done?" The others laughed and began to horseplay. I walked past the wall at that moment and saw them, saw Hedi was the frowning young Communist of the broken bicycle whom I'd given a lift.

I hurried past, unseen, out to the Rolls where I barreled into the backseat, hearing the boys chanting "An American prince. A movie star!" in dialect. I tapped for Ermes to drive, hurry!

It was another twenty minutes before what had occurred completely struck home. It's happened since to me. Several years ago in Key West, I was speeding on a bicycle over rain-slick streets, way out by the Boca Chica Mall, when I took a sharp turn to avoid a car and slid nearly to a crash, landing on my left hand, drawing a tremendous arc of water out of the surrounding puddle to spray me. I was more annoyed than hurt as I biked two miles to my apartment. Once there, I felt pain in my hand, but not enough to stop me from having lunch and reading the paper. I took an aspirin and napped. When I awakened two hours later, my arm was swollen to my shoulder and I was in excruciating pain. X rays at Key West Memorial revealed a hairline fracture of my left wrist, necessitating a week of codeine and a Velcro splint. It had been hours before I knew something terrible had happened to me.

Same with the bicycle rider we'd picked up. He hadn't at all been an ardent Communist, contemptuous of my car, my clothing, my life. He'd been afraid, shy, then thrilled, delighted. He'd become a hero to his friends as he told them of the ride and of me, embroidering freely to fit their—and his—absolutely materialistic fantasies and desires.

I'd borne months of Djanko's betrayals, culminating in this giant one of the vacation on the Dalmatian coast that wasn't really a vacation, but somehow I couldn't bear this simple little deception of a Yugoslav student. It seemed to sum up, to encapsulate, all that I'd been experiencing—Jiri's spying and voyeurism, Djanko's neuroses, Ermes's weird passion—and something inside me broke. It hit so hard, I felt pain in my chest, as though—Lord, how cliché it was, I thought even as it happened—as though my heart were breaking!

When the car stopped at the flagstone steps to the villa and Ermes opened the passenger door, he found me convulsed with sobbing, deaf to his questions, his entreaties.

A few minutes later Djanko was there, angrily asking the driver what had happened, holding me as I continued to cry, prodding poor Ermes, who told him nothing had happened, as indeed was true, then detailing the day's activities until Djanko sent him away.

I let him hold me, let him talk me into some kind of quiet, let him wipe my face, find and put on my shoes. I was still shivering, all emotion drained out of me.

"*Caro,* what is it?" he gently questioned. "Tell me, *carissimo.*"

I looked at his kindness and thought: I can't stand this anymore.

"I want to go home," I said in English. "Home," and I broke down again.

"*Certo, caro, certo! Subito,* right away, tomorrow morning."

He half led, half carried me into the house and into the bedroom, where I slept through tea and dinner. The following morning we drove to Rome.

A week and a half after we'd returned to Rome, I told Djanko that I had to leave the country because my tourist visa was up again. He blustered on about how he would have Tratano fix it so it would be a permanent visa, but he'd already said that the last two times and still hadn't done anything about it. Anyway, he was too involved in final preparations for the *Jason and the Argonauts* premiere—to occur soon.

I'm not sure what was in my mind at the time. I suppose I merely needed some time and distance from Djanko and

Rome. Two college friends had written that they were to be in Paris. I told Djanko I'd visit them and get my tourist visa at the same time. He seemed amenable to the idea. In fact, he and Jiri and the Pig had hammered out a scenario for an international spy movie based more or less on the James Bond films, with lots of sex, death and special effects (not to mention Jiri's own brand of kinkiness), and between that and the premiere he was in a far happier and busier state than he'd been in months, still in the realm of contemplating the idea before it would become besmirched by reality.

When I packed for the trip, I decided to take little. I reasoned that I couldn't very well show off all my jewelry to Barbara and Phillip and explain how I'd gotten it. So I took but one good ring, one gold cigarette case and one lighter of the dozen or more that I now owned; and it was, after all, only for the weekend.

The day before I was to go, the final check for my destroyed motorcycle arrived in the mail—only six months late, not bad for Italy—and I decided on the spot to buy another motorcycle. I appeared that afternoon on my slick new Ducati 500-cc in front of the Stollywood Harlots' apartment, and Tina and Donna ran all the way downstairs to take rides on the backseat, holding me around the waist, screeching into my ears as their hair slapped my cheeks and forehead. Cicely had gone to London the week before, they told me. "A big part in a Rank Organization Film," Donna added, almost beside herself with envy.

I found Angel at Ruggiero's on the Via Veneto eating a *millefiore*, surrounded by a group of Germans. He got up immediately and came to tell me of their plans to have him star in his own real Western, to be made in Spain. He, too, came for a motorcycle ride, insisting we go to the Vatican, which we circled round and round until he was done yelling "Yippie" and the Vatican police began to come after us, at which point I took off through Trastevere. When I told Angel that I was going to Paris for a few days, he said, "Boy, you've got wanderdust in your face. Not me. I'm not ever going back to El Paso. I like it here just fine." I repeated that I was only going away for the weekend, less than the three weeks I'd been in Yugoslavia, but Angel hugged me close and said, "Sure, sure. I won't say nothing to no one," leaving me utterly bewildered.

When I got back to the Hassler, the phone was ringing. It was Valentina. She told me that although she hadn't yet seen it, nearly fully edited rushes of *Jason and the Argonauts* were being shown to distributors, publicity and advertising people connected with the studio. I thought it would be a good idea if I went to a viewing where Djanko wouldn't be present, so that night I could tell him I'd seen the film and tell him how good it was.

The film was good: grand and wild. Angel was a god as Hercules—his blond crew cut grown out, the tips of his hair, mustache and beard frosted bronze like a living helmet. The Italian Jason wasn't half bad. All the Argonauts were scrumptious, especially the two Greek twins who played Castor and Pollux. Medea was a bit too Martha Graham for my taste, but Tina and Donna were fine in their small parts, and Cicely was magnificent, beautiful as the goddess Aphrodite.

Indeed, I got a chance to see more of Aphrodite than I'd expected: I saw her in the scene where Aphrodite turned into a whirlwind and drowned the *Argo*'s helmsman. Djanko's one concession had been to change the doomed steersman's name from the Vergilian Turnus to the more Hesiodic Actaeon.

I remember sitting in the deep velvet upholstered chair of the studio screening room, watching the scene stolen from *The Aeneid* and thinking how curious it was that it no longer seemed as inappropriate as I'd been certain it would.

It wasn't until I was driving back to the Hassler that I realized that the screening manager had called the film we were viewing "as close to complete as we'll get short of the premiere." Djanko had never for a second dreamed of taking the scene out of the film. Despite our argument.

Despite his fears that I would run away. Despite our reconciliation. Despite his promise.

I was shaking so badly, I had to pull the motorcycle onto the curb, finally get off and walk around. I even stopped at a café to have a cup of espresso to calm down. That night I didn't mention the screening to Djanko. He was exhausted, anyway, which made it easier—I didn't know how I would have gotten out of lovemaking had he proposed it.

Early the next morning I drove out of Rome. By six thirty P.M., I knew exactly what Angel had seen in my face that neither I nor anyone else had noticed. I'd just driven a long stretch of coastal highway curving from Leghorn through Rapallo along the Italian Riviera when the scenery seemed achingly familiar. Oddly so. I'd certainly never driven this way before. Then I saw it—the road curving around the mountain and once around it the little railroad station, the tunnel, the cliffs opposite. I crossed the tracks and turned the Ducati around to look.

I was at the very spot where the accident with the big Lancia had happened, almost a year before. Although it was much later in the day than that morning and clear rather than raining, the place was so etched in my memory, it seemed exactly the same. And there, across the tracks, around the mountain, was the road I'd just driven upon to arrive here. Yet it still remained the Road Not Taken because I hadn't driven it that day, no, but had gone back to Genoa to court, then to lunch with my brother, then to the main railroad station, onto the train where I'd met Orazio in whose company a week later in Rome I had met all of them, Cicely, Tina, Donna, Angel, the Pig, Djanko, and had spent almost one entire precious year of my young life, to set into motion my true sexuality and to fall in love and to fall out of love too. I turned the bike around and drove on to Genoa.

Luckily I found the same restaurant my brother and I had dined in. There, on the table, just to the right of my coffee cup, I wrote a letter on borrowed stationary to Djanko, telling him I wasn't coming back, even though I hated the idea that I was proving his prophecy of our first night together. Then, quickly, so I couldn't change my mind, I had the letter stamped and mailed at a nearby tobacconist.

That accomplished, I left Genoa, drove past Ventimiglia, across the border into France, high up on the Grand Corniche, which enfolds the entire principality of Monaco, through Nice, Cannes and St. Tropez. I drove like a madman, crazy, yelling out loud at times so I wouldn't have to think, speeding on through the hot, damp night.

I might have driven all night and the next day, too, if I hadn't taken a wrong turn somewhere outside of Cannes and three quarters of an hour later found myself suddenly in a dark, misty section of old downtown Marseilles. It was late, perhaps one, one-thirty, and everything seemed dead. I drove slowly around empty streets, shuttered shops, past rotting wharves, then newer piers with ships moored to them, yet all was still dark. Dark and wet. A mist lay over everything, not cold but sickly, clammy against my skin. At length I drove into a small trapezoid of a plaza with one light on—from a café—and more amazing still, sounds from a jukebox that I recognized as Wilson Pickett singing "Please, Please, Please" that throat/gut/heart-torn plea for a lover to return.

I parked the bike and walked into the café. I don't know what I expected to find inside. But while the jukebox had six songs each by Jackie Wilson and Otis Redding and even Little Richard's "Maybelline," it was a totally French and almost private neighborhood place frequented by harbor rats, most of them merchant marines on leave, some retired, all of them ugly, scarred and dangerous-looking. In my black T-shirt, jeans and boots, stepping right off a motorcycle, I wasn't that much out of place. Though I was heavily glared at, I feigned indifference. I ordered two Marc brandies, went over to the jukebox and began to play all the gut-wrenching soul music on it.

With each brandy, with each play of the jukebox, it sunk

deeper into me that I'd just that day left the man I'd lived with for months, slept with every night, shared my laughter and fantasies with, been comforted and gifted by. That realization was so terrifying that it required more brandies, more music.

At one point a bruiser with a scar slicing asymmetrically through his left nostril and both lips pushed me away from the jukebox and threatened me. He wanted to hear "The Little Sparrow" not any more "Nigger Man laments," he said. We were pulled apart by the others only an inch from a real fight, and I was shoved out the door onto the street.

A wan dawn was beginning somewhere through the infected-looking fog. I walked out to my bike but I was too drunk, too depressed to drive it without intending suicide, so I sauntered over to a large pier, filled with house-sized crates, yet with no ship alongside it. I sat down at the far end and began to think about what I'd just done to poor Djanko, who would go through all of tomorrow no wiser, then wake up for the shock of the mail the following day. How would he react? What would he do, say . . . ? Would he try to track me down in Paris? Would my leaving be the final blow to his tenuous grasp of sanity? Or would he just sigh and say to Jiri that he'd predicted it?

" *'Nuit,*" someone barked a greeting. I looked around: one of the men from the café. Not the one who'd jumped me, but someone else. He was about my size, older-mid-thirties—very slender, wearing an open vest with no shirt, worn denims, heavy engineer's boots. I wanted to tell him to go away. Instead I said, "It's almost morning."

"Your lover leave you?" he asked.

I looked at him again. Very pale skin but dark, dark eyes in a very French face, bent long nose, large, almost blubbery lips. "No. I left. Today."

"*C'est dommage.*" It's too bad. He kept looking at me. Not a murderer, not a thief—at least not with me, not now. What did he want? Why didn't he go away?

"Sometimes," he said slowly, "you can fuck it away. All of it. You can fuck away the whole rotten world."

I shrugged.

"Do you believe me?"

Again I shrugged.

He came closer, put an arm solidly over my shoulder. I didn't shrug it off.

"Let's go," he finally said. "I'll show you."

We got up and walked off the pier, past the café into a boardinghouse with a badly tilted stairway up to a sixth-floor room where this nameless French sailor taught me that neither love nor even attraction was needed for sex, and that indeed, somehow it became sharper, more encompassing, when it was free of all that.

Years later I encountered Donna Slattery again. She was working as bartender, sporting a rakishly aslant Derby, candy-striped shirt, suspenders and bow tie, in a hokey sort of nineteenth-century saloon uptown. She'd come back a year before, finally given up on the movie-star dream after a decade of trying, after two marriages, three kids, "with their Grandma in Flatbush," and a life of some outrageousness and freedom.

Donna told me over a giant schooner of beer (with a perfect head on it, gotta hand it to her) about the others. Of course I'd read about Cicely's success, seen her in a film uptown at the Thalia, then in the British play she'd done on Broadway—but somehow I'd funked it at the last minute and hadn't gone backstage. ("You jerk!" Donna said. "Cis would have creamed in her undies to see you!") I'd also kept up with Djanko's career. For a mere two years after I'd left him, he'd taken a sabbatical, gone back to Prague without Jiri or Mafalda or the Pig and had made the small, lovely black-and-white film which, while not about his great uncle's tuba, was close—and wonderful. I'd seen it at the Film Festival at Lincoln Center, and though it was a "wistful comedy, almost a farce," I recognized Djanko so completely in the characters and lines that I was tearstained when I exited into the glare of the lobby of Avery Fisher Hall afterward.

Donna was most vehement about Tina's betrayal. It seems that she'd met a tall, gangly, pockmarked Oklahoman boy with "no money, no brains, no talent, no ambition, nothing but a pecker on feet"(—Donna). Sensible girl that Tina turned out to be, she'd fallen for Wade and had allowed herself to be dragged away to a ramshackle hotel in Tobago where Tina had grown fat, Caribbean brown, and her hair had resumed its real color ("puke yellow" according to Donna).

Angel's story was a bit more complicated and far less happy. Kit had invested money for him. Good thing too, as the German film deal had been a fiasco—never completed—and although Djanko used him in other roles, Angel never again achieved the eminence he had in *Jason and the Argonauts*. When Kit's father died, the two of them had flown to Canberra, Angel to become a real cowboy—or at least a sheep rancher—despite himself. Within a year of their return, however, his narcolepsy had returned with new force, defying all medical treatment. Angel was now sleeping away what remained of his life in some Antipodean sanitorium ward, intravenously fed, his giant, beautiful body shriveled like a carcass left out in the desert, destined never again to awaken.

The afternoon I unpacked my bags in my West Village apartment, I discovered the gold Bulgari watch folded inside my navy turtleneck sweater.

For three or four days I thought of wrapping up the watch and mailing it back to Djanko in Rome. Then I thought of all those jewelry boxes, probably still sitting atop the dresser in the Hassler suite, and of the unintentional slap he'd get receiving the watch. So I put it away, among socks and underwear, with my passport and birth certificate and college diploma where I'd never see it. Without a qualm, I'd already sold the single gold cigarette lighter and case—the only other of Djanko's golden gifts I'd kept. But now, with the Bulgari's reappearance, I was in a quandary; although I was desperate for cash and knew it would pay expenses long enough for me to complete the first novel I'd begun to write, I was sure that selling the watch would also be a symbolic act, finally cutting all ties with Djanko. Did I really want that?

I was wrong. Even now, having sold the watch, having written about him, hoping I'd exorcised him, I still see Djanko Travenicke on a set, hunched down in his director's chair, barely containing his fury and frustration as something impossibly wrong occurs; still see a pencil tapping his teeth at our script sessions, listening impatiently just before he bursts out, "No. No. No!"; still see his golden shock of hair reflecting like an ancient Athenian's plumed helmet in the illumination of some luxurious Via del Corso shop and his sea-green eyes light up as a salesman places upon my neck or wrist or finger something expensive and glittering and gold.

Interlude

I'd lived nearly a quarter of a century, and to my continuing astonishment, I'd found the truth to be more a hindrance in my life than it was either useful or profitable. Like Cervantes's hero, I'd come to battle with reality several times already, and like the noble La Manchan, I'd already been trounced quite thoroughly. Because of the truth, I'd lost Ricky Hersch in the seventh grade and Djanko Travenicke just a few months after my twenty-second birthday. Because of the truth, I'd ended one potential career as a fiction writer before it could even be thought of as an apprenticeship a decade before, and another potential career, as a film writer, only a few months past. I'd seen it coming this time around, of course, but I'd been in no way able to help myself. Reality intruded, made itself all too clear that it was something quite different than illusion. I'd jumped for the bait and bam!

This being so, when I left Europe, part of my plan was a quite conscious decision to jettison the truth wherever it seemed problematic, to let reality fall by the wayside whenever it appeared to clash with what I perceived as my best interests.

I'd already made this decision by the time I'd boarded the jet that took me back to New York City. If the passenger next to me in coach happened to ask my name, I'd tell him or her I was Herbert Stoller from Rego Park, Queens, a certified public accountant for a large insurance company, traveling on business. Or Alan Stern, from Mamaroneck, a

Peace Corps volunteer, on the last leg of a journey home from Sri Lanka, or . . . anyone! As it turned out, no one did ask. And a good thing. Because if I was planning to return to the States free of the hindrances of reality, I couldn't have chosen a better circumstance to do it in than that which Fate selected for me.

Without knowing it, I was returning to an America about to burst into a decade of Learyesque hallucination. Without knowing that I would become part of this counterculture, I was already within it. You see, I boarded that plane stoned on hashish, continued for much of the six-hour-long flight to become even more stoned, and arrived at the newly re-named Kennedy Airport so thoroughly smashed, I might have been landing at a moon base a hundred years in the future. Naturally, this was unintentional. It was also a most appropriate omen: I had left the States with a taste for grass and an occasional drink. Aside from one bizarre and to this day inexplicable incident—in which I drank absinthe at a party in Copenhagen, passed out and awakened twenty-seven hours later in the backseat of a Volkswagen driven by strangers on the outskirts of Rotterdam—my stay through-out Europe was relatively drugless.

This is how I happened to fly back ripped to the tits.

In the autumn of 1967, I was in my digs south of Sloan Square, all dressed and packed and ready hours early to fly back to New York. Eager too. I was shaking the dust of Europe off my heels, a dust accumulating with a singular oppressiveness in the last months I'd lived through an impermissibly dreary London autumn and a despicable win-ter. They've cleaned up the pollution since then, but in those days when I was feeling a bit bored on a December evening, I used to go through the center of local squares picking up, helping home and sometimes taking to hospitals the barely breathing bodies of elderly pensioners who'd thought to find a shortcut home and instead found their lungs stopped by London's concentration of yellow-black fog and putrid air. I generally rewarded myself for these good deeds at a local Winpy's with gluey kidney pie and a tankard of warm beer the tint of a slightly hepatitic urine.

Picture me then about to make my great escape: I'm barbered, shaved, dressed in a pale blue button-down Oxford, a school tie left behind by someone I'd slept with, charcoal flannel trousers, Scottish walking buffs, my gray Harris tweed jacket—all recently purchased on Regent or Bond Streets: the very portrait of a Rhodes Scholar, you'd say. I was that clean-cut.

Then I remembered the hashish.

The loveliest green-brown Turkish hashish you've ever seen, it was the consistency of handmade chocolate kept in the refrigerator and taken out ten minutes ago. Using a razor blade, you could carve it into strips that bent almost double but didn't break, thin as a perfect *carpaccio*. The hashish was still wrapped in the baroquely embossed and highly decorative gold-and-pink foil I'd bought it in for several hundred dollars a few weeks before. Hell! It was even stamped through the foil with a Turkish government tax mark. It was an inch thick and about the size of the palm of my hand. Yet my luggage was already belted up and in the downstairs hallway under the ever scrupulous eye of my red-haired Dundee-bred landlady when I remembered the hash and took it out of the ginger jar where I'd been hiding it.

Smuggling drugs was hardly on my mind, though it would be a bit difficult to explain that to the authorities. "Gee, Constable, I was going to keep it and smoke it a little bit at a time for the next ten months." But that was *exactly* what I'd been planning to do when I bought it.

More to the point, how I'd gotten the hashish had given it such a personal stamp, I knew I simply had to have it. I could see myself comfily ensconced in my apartment in Manhattan with puffing friends on either side of me, as I began to narrate the adventure.

I'd been in Istanbul, staying at the Hilton during my last jaunt out of England. I can't remember what possessed me to go there, except that I'd never been, and someone I'd met in a King's Road pub had told me he could get me tickets for a quarter of the price on the Orient Express, which ends up in the Turkish city.

About five minutes after I'd arrived in Istanbul I wanted to leave. If the antiquity of London, Paris and Rome had begun to get on my nerves, Istanbul expressed the worst aspects of all rolled into one. It was old, it was noisy, it was crowded, it was filthy, it smelled as though its two million inhabitants had forgotten to put out the garbage. The walls of even the most modern shops and hotels were already crumbling in the miasma of taxi fumes, horse dung and mists off the Sea of Marmora. The place was undeniably picturesque, but I'd had my fill of picturesque. I avoided the Hagia Sophia, narrowly averted being dragged to Suleiman's Castle with its seven towers and to the Mosque of Muhammad II, I fought my way out of the streets that led to the Bucolean Palace, where Theodora once held court, and to the Hippodrome and to John Crysosthomos's tomb and I almost paid money to avoid the Topkapi Museum. My one stroll through the huge souk that had once been Constantine's Forum in the center of the old city the afternoon I detrained had been enough to last me a lifetime. I determined to spend the next two days, until my train left, in the hotel, which being American was clean, had a good bar and television, and where I might be bored by meals but not anticipate food poisoning. I envisioned a perfect, sterile ennui. I took showers repeatedly, I ordered hamburgers and french fries and root beers. I was awful.

This might have lasted if it weren't for lust.

Going up to my room from the lobby where I'd just purchased weeks-old *Time* and *Look* magazines, which I was dying to peruse, I was suddenly struck by the pale green eyes and superb physique of the young elevator operator. I stared, he stared back. I stared harder, he said hello in broken English. I said I think your eyes are lovely. He said would I like to see more of him. I said yes, all of him. His name was 'Thrakis, short for a much longer name I never quite caught, and he was Frankish, i.e., mostly of European lineage, and lived with a huge family across the smaller bridge in Pera. He agreed to meet me when he got off a few hours later and didn't name a fee, but he did insist we meet on the roof, which had a pool with a cabana, closed by then.

We did meet up there, and with the mist swirling over most of the baleful city, we smoked some delightful hashish he'd thoughtfully provided and made love for an hour upon a dampish chaise longue in a humid cabana.

Almost to make conversation afterward, I told 'Thrakis how much I'd liked the hash and I asked how I could get more. He told me a friend of a friend of his would sell me some. Two ounces of the stuff for only two hundred dollars. American dollars. He gave me the address and suggested I go the following night, as the friend of a friend was a construction worker and wouldn't be home until after dinnertime—i.e. about ten P.M. Although neither his family nor the friend of a friend had a telephone, 'Thrakis promised he'd get word to the man that I was coming. I was to ask for Ulema.

The next night I had dinner and caught a cab in the Hilton's porte cochere. The minute I told the driver where I wanted to go, he stopped the car (causing a backup and blowing horns) and said he wouldn't take me there.

"Why not?"

"It's a danger place. Very danger. I wouldn't send my mother with a pistol to that place."

That made so little sense, I insisted: "I'm visiting a friend."

"What kind of friend do you have?" he asked.

"A construction worker!"

"A murderer!" he insisted. "I won't drive to that place."

I left the cab and returned to my room. There I sat and thought. 'Thrakis was a sweet boy, and it was possible the friend of a friend was not a murderer. However, drug deals were notoriously perilous and I might easily be killed and thrown into the Hellespont. I had to plan this a bit better.

The silverware from my meal tray was still outside the door where I'd left it. I picked up the steak knife, cleaned it off, and tested its edge. It would do. Then I changed from my preppy clothing into an outfit I thought might be both less conspicuous and a bit more menacing: motorcyclist's leather jacket and square-toed boots (for a good kick to the nuts), worn denims and a torn shirt. I messed up my hair and beard. I slipped the knife into my pocket where it bulged, then slid it into my left boot, where it fit perfectly, and where if I was sitting down I'd be able to grab it instantly to defend myself.

Garbed for the back alleys of Istanbul, I walked away from the hotel until I'd arrived near the souk. There I found a particularly battered old Vauxhall taxi with four different-colored fenders and a one-eyed driver. I addressed him in French, which he didn't know, then in Italian, which he did (Venetian merchants all but owned the city for centuries, even after the Ottomans had made it the capital of their Empire). I told him where I was going and told him I wanted him to drive there and wait for me—he'd be well paid. If he left me while I was out of the cab, I'd go out of my way to find him the next day. I showed him the haft of the knife in my boot. I spoke fast and hard, and he thought I was a criminal. He drove me to within a hundred feet of where I wanted to be. The instant I got out of the taxi, he began to read a comic book.

It had been raining in Istanbul, but once across the Golden Horn, the rain plunged in sheets. Galata's main roads were reduced to a series of puddles, and Tophane, the northern dockside area we'd finally stopped in, was even worse: the wind howled across the Bosporus and fog from Scutari whirled off the water. For about a minute I asked myself what the hell I was doing. Then I found the house I was looking for, entered a deep foyer in the windowless facade and knocked on the wooden door.

A very stooped old woman with Ghirlandiao eyes opened

up, arranging her kerchief to hide the rest of her face from the stranger.

"Ulema!" I said.

She nodded and let me in, looking around outside before shutting the door. She guided me through a short corridor past a room where people seemed to be silently sitting amidst a haze of cigarette smoke, up a short stairway, around a bend and into another room with its door ajar. She gestured me in.

An elderly man with a scar cutting one nostril and across the cheek to his ear was sitting on one side of the built-in bench. He looked up and I thought, Could this be Ulema?

The woman said something in Turkish. The man grunted. I noticed that he didn't look at me. She gestured at me again, which I interpreted to mean that I should take a seat and wait. I did so, as far away from Scarface as I could in the small undecorated room. She disappeared.

By the clock it was only about five minutes, but it seemed an hour before anything happened. The old man was cutting his fingernails with an astonishing Swiss army knife bristling with contraptions for a dozen unknown purposes. In general he ignored me, but once he said "Ulema?" And I replied in Italian, "I'm a friend of 'Thrakis." He grunted and mumbled something, then went back to hacking at his fingernails.

There was no doubt in my mind that this old brigand was psyching me out and sizing me up, "softening" me up until Ulema arrived, at which point they'd show me hashish, ask to see my money, and kill me. Even so, I avoided any outward nervousness, looked at a point straight ahead where I could distract the penultimate moments of my suddenly too-short life by following the intricate traceries of a wooden screen. I still kept an eye on the old man.

Finally he said something, or rather grunted out an entire sentence, not one word of which I understood. I asked him to repeat himself, and this time he asked in very poor Italian if I was *fratel'd'amo,* i.e., "love-brother" of 'Thrakis. I didn't know what to answer. Then I decided I was doomed no matter what I said and might as well admit it. *"Certo!"* I answered.

"Bell'figl'," he said, meaning a handsome lad.

Once again I answered, *"Certo!"*

Then he said something to the effect that Ulema wouldn't be coming.

Uh-oh! I thought. Here it comes!

He asked to see my money.

I pulled out a wad of twenties and laid all ten out for him on the space of bench between us.

He looked at them, without moving.

My left hand went to the lip of my boot, found the haft of my knife, gripped it. I'd never done anything even vaguely homicidal, didn't know if I could, even to defend my life. And even if I should, I didn't know my way out of the house, was certain to have to pass the roomful of men who would doubtless stop me by any means, chase me outside to where the deceitful taxi driver had long taken off, and I would stumble through a neighborhood I didn't know and pound on the doors of people who wouldn't answer as I was attacked again and again, like Caesar in the Senate anteroom, clawing at the stone walls as I slipped bloody into the mud and piss and dung!

Suddenly I saw a foil packet next to the money, as if by magic. The hashish.

Take it or taste it, he grunted.

Without for a second letting go of the knife, I picked up the foil packet and set it down closer to myself. I peeled off one section, saw the brown-green brick, picked at a corner of it with my thumb and index fingernails, and tasted it. Sweet. Musky. Strong.

The money was gone from the bench.

I took another tiny piece off another side of the hashish, ate it, then pocketed the foil packet in my right boot.

The old man was back with his Swiss army knife, carving his fingernails.

I thought if I move slowly and can get out of the house . . .

"Ciao!" I said, got up and walked out, expecting to be attacked any second. I cautiously moved past any doorway, open or closed, until I'd gotten to what I remembered was the front door. Still no one. In fact, the room where the dozen smoking men had been was empty too. Would they be waiting outside?

I opened the door and let myself out. It was still raining so hard, I thought they could be hiding anywhere in the alley to jump me. But the parti-colored Vauxhall was still waiting. I braced myself to walk slowly, like Gary Cooper in *High Noon.* I wouldn't go down squirming. I took one step and heard a voice behind me. I spun around and dropped to my knee reaching for the knife in my boot.

It was the old woman. She held out something wrapped in cloth. Offering it to me with one hand while the other held closed the scarf over her face.

When I didn't move, she used her veil hand to subtly lift the cloth off the package. I don't know what horror I expected to see. What I saw was pastry.

I stood up and she pushed it into my hand and ran inside.

Abashed, I walked to the cab, no longer paying attention to a dozen possible lurking assassins. I came up behind where the cabbie was still reading the comic book. When I tried the back door, it was locked. I rapped on his window and through the rain-soaked glass I could see him hurriedly button his fly beneath the protection of the comic and reach around to lift the lock on the back door. I got in and told him to drive back to the hotel.

Once we were in a place in Galata I recognized, I offered him some of the nut-filled baklava. He ate it using the same hand he steered with and took his fares with and masturbated with behind a comic book. Later on, I also ate the baklava. It was scrumptious.

So you see, I couldn't just *leave* the hashish, or throw it away. But what could I possibly do? I knew U.S. Customs searched like crazy, even more so than British Customs, and that they liked nothing better than to find young people—

even clean-cut ones—"carrying," and give them stiff prison sentences. Within Europe it was bad enough. I'd heard tales of students caught with a stick of grass who were moldering away for decades to come in jails from Madrid to Athens. I'd brought the hash to England through the Dover port wrapped in a particularly pungent group of dirty socks—the approved Provo method of carrying—but my bags were packed now, and anyway, I didn't have any dirty socks.

I was so jangled by this sudden new problem that I immediately knocked a piece off the slab of hashish and placed it upon the glowing ember of my cigarette—a "quick pick-me-up" I'd seen frequently practiced in the darker corners of a gay disco in Amsterdam called the D.O.K. It wasn't enough to calm me down. I knocked off and smoked another chunkette and another and another. I felt somewhat better!

My taxi arrived too quickly. The landlady of my lodgings was rapping on my door. I said I was coming. I hastily rewrapped the hash, shoved it into an empty box of Dunhills, added a few cigarettes and slipped the box into the inner breast pocket of my Harris tweed jacket. Then I ran down to the cab taking me to Victoria Station.

Once there, the bus to take me to Heathrow Airport was just pulling out and I had to run to catch it. The bus connected almost instantly to my flight—a rather crowded flight, even though it was at night, probably because it was cheaper. Passengers were already being called into the plane by seat numbers in groups of tens and wouldn't you know my seat was called the instant I arrived in the lobby. I hurriedly checked my bags, held on to only a largish bar of Cadbury's chocolate and a small India-paper edition of *Bleak House*, which I'd planned to begin on the plane—then quietly but totally panicked. Sure, I wouldn't have to worry about the hashish next to my heart until I landed, but suddenly the Atlantic was too tiny an ocean to cross, six hours but a brief Beckettian moment. I was boarding the plane: I was in serious Dutch.

I have to admit I managed to forget about the hash at isolated moments during the first few hours of the flight, although it ran a constant counter theme throughout the meal, through my attempts at reading Dickens, through my wanderings around the plane. Once the meal had been cleared away and the lights put out, however, I found I wasn't at all tired. No, I was lost in thought—how could I not be? The hashish glowed in my breast pocket like a glowing ingot. I had to do *something*.

I decided to leave it under the seat when I disembarked. The hell with it! So I wouldn't have hashish—my all-time favorite high—once I landed. So I would have lost two hundred dollars. So what? At least I'd be out of jail.

Then I thought about what awaited me in Manhattan.

Not much. I did have an apartment. A small studio in the West Village that I'd been panicked into renting when I'd left for Europe a year and a half before, my East Tenth Street apartment having been burgled so regularly by junkies that I'd been able to move west in someone's car, having little clothing or furniture or anything unstolen really to transport but a few books and records. I'd grown up in big houses, had enjoyed the three sunny rooms of East Tenth Street with its sagging parquet floors and chipped French doors between the living room and bedroom. In Rome I'd lived in a huge suite at the Hassler, in Paris in a duplex I was "watching" for some Americans; even in Chelsea my lodgings had been large and bright—with central heating yet! This hole-in-the-wall on Jane Street with a kitchenette and two windows was going to be a coop. While I'd been away, I'd sublet it to newlywed friends who'd written me that it was almost impossibly close, even as a honeymoon nest. I would need some serious "inner space" to make up for the lack of external area. What better way than a smoke and a Supremes record?

Another problem was that I had no job awaiting me and didn't even know what kind of job I wanted. I knew one thing: I had no interest in ever being a social worker again.

It might take weeks, even months, to find work that brought in money. No job—and limited resources. Just a few weeks before, I'd gone on a shopping spree to replace my clothing stolen from Tenth Street. I could ill afford to throw away several hundred dollars worth of anything.

A third problem I didn't even want to think about was that I was socially adrift. In the two years or so after college graduation, before I'd gone to Europe, I'd still been surrounded by friends from college who'd also lived on the Lower East Side, and later by friends I'd made at the social-work agency. Now my college chums were all gone— Phil and Barbara in Palo Alto, Kenny and Christa down at Penn State, Ruth and Tom in Princeton, Barbara in Gainesville, Matthew in Berkeley—most of them going for their master's degrees. I, too, had been accepted at schools for further education: Columbia for English Literature and the Iowa Writing Program. But I would have gone on a diet of ground glass and cyanide before returning to school. Nor did I want, really, to see the people still left at the East End Welfare Center. I'd gone to Europe to change my life, and I *had* changed my life. I was starting fresh—once again— whatever that might entail. I knew I would be alone a great deal until I met new people—I wondered if I ever would meet new people.

By this time in the transatlantic flight, the mild high I'd gotten in my digs was long gone. Three hours had passed, I'd snacked and eaten a full BOAC dinner. I decided on another tack. I wouldn't throw away *all* of the hashish. I'd smoke as much of it as I could in the airplane john, keeping the ventilator on high, and flushing the toilet often to get rid of the smoke.

Mad, you say? Quite mad. But I was desperate. I waited until all the other passengers around me seemed to be asleep, until even the stewards were settled in their seats with magazines and soft drinks, then I pounced. Selecting the john farthest from my seat, I shut myself in and began to smoke a cigarette and to pick off chunks of hash and to keep the ventilator going and to flush the toilet. Anyone listening outside would conclude that I'd contracted serious dysentery—and hopefully stay away.

It worked! At least the john never got that smoky.

I don't recall exactly at what moment I realized that I'd been sitting on a closed toilet seat in a jet filled with sleeping people thirty thousand feet above the Atlantic Ocean fervently smoking hash for twenty minutes, but I did—quite suddenly—and I managed to reach the following conclusions:

1) I was making very little progress on the sizable chunk of hashish. In fact, I'd barely picked one edge to a quite lovely ruffle. In fact, it seemed more than likely that I would have to sit here smoking and flushing for the next week before I came close to finishing it off;

2) I was already so bombed that if I continued smoking the hash another minute, never mind till we landed, they'd have to carry me off the plane;

3) I'd never noticed before what odd wallpaper was inside BOAC jet johns; and

4) I no longer cared *what* happened to the hash or to me.

I returned to my seat and promptly fell into a series of De Quincyean hallucinations that ended in my falling asleep.

"Sir! Sir!!" I could barely get my eyes open. "Sir, we've landed. You'll have to wake up, sir!"

The stewardess moved down the aisle and I struggled to look around. Most of the passengers from my section of the plane were gone. I was alone, amidst magazines scattered on seats and chatting airline staff. Hurrying, I grabbed my carry-on bag, stuffed my Dickens into it, put on my jacket and disembarked into a cool and starlit April night. As I half stumbled across the tarmac into the International Arrivals Building I realized that I was still stoned: I felt as though I were moving in slow motion, gravity rising to defy me with every step.

After wandering around a bit as if in a dream, I located the right luggage carousel and there was my bag, virtually alone. Someone from the airline urged me to join the rest of the passengers in the customs shed. The minute I got into the big room, new confusion faced me. There were four lines of people at long tables with two customs inspectors per table. The lines were alphabetically divided by last names and I finally found O–S with only a few people ahead of me. I lifted my bag onto the table as I'd seen others do, and the first customs man gestured to me with his fingers several times until I realized he meant for me to open it.

He and his partner were middle-aged fellows in very official-looking uniforms. One wore what I guessed to be a perpetual professional visage of bored, cynical indifference. The other inspector had sharper and more peppery features. He even looked like a ferret and he seemed to enjoy harassing people. At that moment he was hassling a well-dressed woman about her clothing, asking where she had bought various items and how much she was going to declare in customs duty.

"Surely you don't think I travel without undergarments," she sniffed at him. "I'll certainly not declare those."

"Look, lady, did you buy them in England or not? Anything you bought there has to be tallied into the accounting. Liquor, perfume, jewelry, clothing!" he spat out as he rummaged through another one of her many open suitcases in front of him.

Oh, my God! I thought. Virtually everything I had in my suitcase was bought in London: shirts, ties, slacks, socks— even my underwear! I was going to have to pay duty on all of it!

"Well, if you can't find your receipts," he was saying to her, "you'll have to step aside and look for them."

"Why can't I just tell you how much they cost?"

"All right!" He pulled a heavy calculator out from under the table, and she began to roll off prices as he continually interrupted and questioned her.

This was awful. I'd paid cash for my clothing and I hadn't kept a single receipt. How much was this going to cost me?

"You must be completely out of your mind!" the woman shouted.

"Look, lady, either we do it my way or—"

"I'll report you to your superior. Who do you think you are? The Russian Police? I'll have my attorney . . ."

I looked at my open suitcase and began to calculate what my clothing had cost me. Despite being in London a longish time, I'd never quite gotten the exchange rate straight in my head. I had managed to figure out British prices among themselves, which was how I knew something was expensive or cheap. But in dollars? Was it two dollars to one pound sterling? That meant . . .

"Look, lady, there are other people here. You're going to have to wait until I'm done with them."

"What do you mean I have to wait? I want this straightened out now! Now!"

He moved away from her and her half dozen open suitcases, and he and his partner began rummaging through the open bags of the next person, an elderly woman, asking mechanically, "Any liquor, perfume, jewelry or clothing to declare?"

I was next! Let's see. The Harris tweed was the most expensive item. Then the shoes. That equaled . . .

"I did get this lovely little handkerchief set for my granddaughter," the elderly woman simpered. "It cost one and four."

"Next!" they said, and they were suddenly at my suitcase.

"Any liquor, perfume, jewelry or clothing to declare?" Mr. Ferret demanded, all the while rummaging through my bag with two gloved hands.

I stood there unable to say anything.

"Looks clean, Gord," the other one said, and moved down to a couple who'd just arrived late behind me.

"Wait a minute!" Mr. Ferret had grabbed something at the bottom of my suitcase beneath my socks and underwear. "What's this?"

What had he found? I looked and saw two small flexible pebble-covered and bound Collins's Classics.

"Books!" I said, I thought self-evidently.

"Yes!" he replied, his face becoming more vulpine every second. "But what *kind* of books?"

I was so startled by his attitude that I replied, "Just books!"

"Let's see," he said, and began thumbing through *Framley Parsonage,* looking for I couldn't think what. "Books written by trollops . . ." he muttered.

"That's Trollope! Anthony Trollope. A famous British novelist," I said, defending myself.

"Fun-ny name for a writer," he insinuated, dropped the book on top of my shirts, and began looking through the second volume, saying in a confidential voice to me, "Don't think we don't get a lot of people coming through here and claiming they're students and then bringing in all sorts of smut." He dropped *Daniel Deronda* onto my shirts and picked up the third volume. "And here!" he exulted, "is a perfect example of what I'm talking about, young man."

He held the volume so I couldn't see what it was. For the life of me I couldn't remember what it might be. I'd bought the four of them months ago, as they were inexpensive and would look good in my otherwise paperback and college-text library. "You see," he intimated, "they bind them as though they were real books. But I know better. That's my job." He was looking through the book. "Pictures too!" He all but glowed with satisfaction for an instant, then darkened and thumbed on, evidently looking for other pictures.

"What book is that?" I asked, totally befuddled.

"A bad one! I can tell."

"I didn't bring in any bad ones," I declared. "What's its title?"

He wasn't liking the pictures he'd found and had turned to reading the text a sentence or two at a time every few pages. I was now both confused and humiliated by the many people looking on at our little scene and I was beginning to get angry. He wasn't liking what he was reading, either, and moved from page to page, searching for who knew what.

"What *are* you doing?" I demanded.

"Looking!" he said, and mumbled, "Got to be here somewhere!"

"What are you looking for?"

Without stopping his searching, he said, "The scenes! The scenes! The whips, the torture scenes . . . you know what."

"Whips," I fairly shouted. "Torture" causing even more people to look at us.

"Give me that." I grabbed the book out of his hands. "It can't be anything I brought . . ."

I turned to the title page. Jane Austen. *Persuasion.*

"This is Jane Austen, for chrissake! What does Jane Austen have to do with whips and chains? Thirteen-year-old girls read this book in school. I know you people aren't educated. But to so openly show your ignorance and to do it in so embarrassing a manner to a perfectly innocent person like myself is completely unforgivable!" I was now shouting at the top of my voice. "Jane Austen! You dolt! You ignoramus! You blithering idiot!"

He shut my suitcase and threw it onto the floor and moved on to the next person.

"Did you hear that?" I shouted to the assembled passengers. "He thought Jane Austen wrote about torture and bondage. That's the quality of the employees here! That's who you're paying with your hard-earned taxes!"

Two large customs police emerged from out of nowhere and immediately surrounded me. They said they would escort me out of the room. As I was still waving the book around, one of them took my arm, another my other elbow; they even picked up my suitcase and carry-on bag for me.

In half a minute I found myself out of the terminal and being pushed into a taxi. They closed the door on me, shook their heads and, having narrowly averted a revolution, returned indoors.

I sat back in the taxi, gave my address and lit a cigarette.

I fumed more than my Salem until we arrived at the Midtown Tunnel when it struck me what had just happened back there. He'd been looking for smut and he'd found a book titled *Persuasion*. I began to laugh, and as I did, the incident got funnier and funnier and funnier. When the cab reached Jane Street my ribs hurt from so much laughter. The cabbie must have been sure I was completely certifiable.

That evening I was telling the story to Barbara on the telephone when she asked, "But what happened to the hashish?"

I stopped. During all the farandole at the customs shed I'd never once—not for an instant—thought about it. I'd completely forgotten it.

I grabbed my jacket, which I'd thrown over a chair back as I'd come in, and there it was in my breast pocket.

"I'm holding it in my hot little hand," I reported.

"Welcome back to the States."

TWO

The Jane Street Girls

Out of the crooked timber of humanity no straight thing was ever made.

—Immanuel Kant

Within forty-eight hours of my arrival back in the U.S., I was in a new apartment, with a new job, a new boy-friend and, through him, a new group of friends. It would be years before I saw anyone from my social-work days again, and only as they jogged past, or recognized me going into a movie theater. I'd gone to Europe to change my life and I'd succeeded more completely than I'd dreamed. Only a few friends from college days—in and out of the city as they came home from grad school on holidays—remained as a link.

In later years my friend Arnie described me to his first wife by saying, "He'll burn that bridge when he gets to it." She looked surprised. "When he's crossed it, you mean?" Arnie shook his head. "No, when he gets to it."

This hadn't always been my philosophy of life, but in the early fall of 1967, it became as good as any other and remained true for the next dozen years, even though I usually attributed most of my successes and failures, my fuck-ups and sublimities to the simple acronym TMD (Too Many Drugs). And why not? Look what happened.

I'd arrived in New York in the evening, dropped my bags, called Barbara, chatted, discovered the hash, smoked some, looked in the fridge, found nothing enticing, went out to the local deli, got a sandwich and coffee, came home, ate it, looked at the day's *Times* and saw that Fellini's *Guilietta of the Spirits* was playing at a local cinema, starting in an hour.

Now I'd never seen *Guilietta,* even though I was a major

Fellini fan, and the film had played while I was living in
Rome. In fact, Djanko and I were supposed to go to it.
Supposed to. We didn't. We stayed at the Hassler and
fought and made up and made love instead. *Guilietta* was
still running in some ciné on the Champs Elysees when I was
in Paris, not subtitled but in French, and the idea of hearing
Fellini's finely honed ultra-Italian spoken in French with
Gallic inflections gave me the creeps. *Guilietta* was also
playing in London, dubbed into English. I figured I'd wait.
And here it was, in New York, in Italian, with subtitles. So
I went.

The theater on Twenty-third Street is now two film houses,
one of which consists entirely of what used to be the upstairs
lounge. In between these incarnations, it was a legitimate
theater. But in the sixties it was a large movie house with a
half-empty upper loge where I could hang my legs over the
seat in front of me and puff away to my heart's content on
American cigarettes and watch Fellini and listen to Italian
spoken in the Roman dialect I'd come to know and—because
of the romantic connotations—loathe. Did I mention that
I'd broken my regular glasses a few days before in London
and was using my dark ones?

About an hour into the movie I became aware that this
rather pleasant-looking man in the row behind was doing
something with his knees against the back of my seat. I
turned around to tell him to cut it out and he said, "I've
been wondering, why are you wearing dark glasses for what's
been promoted as the most colorful film extravaganza in
decades?" I began to tell him, and the few other people in
the area began to shush us, at which he hopped over the
seat next to me, where I finished whispering my story.

Ten minutes later I became aware of his arm creeping
around the chair back, and twelve minutes later it was
square on my shoulder. I guess I was surprised by his
forwardness. But, on the other hand, I also didn't think too
much of it. After all, I'd been in England a while and there
even the Mods and Rockers I hung around with admitted

that British homos were uptight. Whenever I wanted action in London, I'd avoid (*eschew* was the Brit term) the dreary and uptight Kings Road bar scene and instead drive my motorcycle across the Thames to Southwark where I'd hang out in one of the biker bars until someone I was interested in either challenged me to a "fists-up" brawl or asked me how much I cost for the night. That had been Olde England, right? This was America. Homo of the Free!

I let Bob—that was his name—walk me home, and it turned out he lived on the same block, same side of the street, only three doors down. Why didn't I come in for a drink? he asked.

Bob unlocked two doors and led me through the narrow hallway of his elderly brownstone, a tenement similar to many scattered through the more prevalent Federal style town houses of the Village. We ascended a flight of stairs into a suite of small but well laid out rooms. He gave me Scotch, let me try his new stereo equipment—the best I'd ever heard—gave me more Scotch, undressed me and by the next morning insisted I was to return that evening at eight o'clock sharp to join him and some friends to watch *Star Trek* on his color television.

In Europe, I'd heard about both *Star Trek* and color TV but had seen neither. So I said, sure, why not. Naturally Bob assumed I'd sleep over that second night too. Bob said he wanted to see me a lot before he had to travel again. He worked for a medical journal and traveled all over the country. Naturally that wasn't what Bob *really* did. Didn't I know? No one in Manhattan earned money doing what they *really* did? Bob was a playwright. A pretty good one, he admitted. He'd gotten grant money and the Eugene O'Neill Foundation was mounting his new play the following spring. Of course, I would come up to Connecticut as his special guest for the premiere.

The next morning Bob dressed for work and saw me out. I returned to my still unslept-in apartment with another deli-bought sandwich, coffee and a *Times,* determined to

look in the classified section for a job, even though it was a
gorgeous autumn morning and what I really wanted to do
was take a walk through my new neighborhood.

Briefly I thought about this man I'd just met, just spent
the night with. Bob Herron combined a strong down-home
charm with a contrastingly urbane sensuality, all of it over-
laid with a sharp yet quirky intelligence. He also seemed to
possess other definable qualities. To begin with, he was
opinionated. So much so that when I told him my name, he
immediately said, "That'll never do! That's too girlish. And
you're hardly girlish. No, we'll call you Phil!" For the next
year, in vain, I tried on and off to convince him that I liked
my name, that it fit me and that I fit it—or soon would fit it.
He never budged an inch. To this day to my embarrassment, I still sometimes encounter people I met through Bob
who still call me Phil.

Then there was the way he walked, his soles then his
heels quite high off the ground with every step, as though he
were creeping through a forest. Indeed, Bob told me he'd
learned to walk that way—which he insisted was Cherokee
Indian fashion—growing up in Covington, Kentucky, which
I later learned was across the Ohio River from and considered a rural suburb of Cincinnati.

Most of all, I was impressed by Bob's astonishing confidence, probably because it contrasted so completely with
Djanko's tortuous European sense of nihilism and incapabil-
ity. Bob exuded the belief that he had life by the nuts, and
by Jimmy he wasn't letting it go until he'd gotten whatever
he could out of it. He certainly seemed to have what he
wanted. In his mid-thirties, even with thinning hair, Bob
was quite attractive, with a body worked out moderately
with weights, a Southern manner designed to make friends
and influence strangers and an almost tangible lust for whomever the object of his attention might be. His job, his
apartment, his avocation all seemed to be on key. He appeared to have sufficient cash and ego gratification. Moreover, he had a goal in life and was working his way toward

that goal. He also had interesting friends. Bob could have been—in fact, he more than once suggested I should take him as—a role model. But though I liked him and liked his sexual technique and passion even more, by that first morning I thought I'd already had one older man trying to shape me toward his own ends. I'd continue to see Bob as long as it was comfortable; but I'd play it loose and easy.

"Writer-editor" the dozens of small and larger ads read in the classified section. I concentrated upon "No experience. Will train. B.A. required." Most of these ads were for technical magazines and journals, i.e., nothing that interested me. But one larger box contained a score of open positions and it tempted me as much by the vagueness of the description of the jobs available as by its name and location. It was the Joe Namath (yes, the Jet quarterback!) Employment Agency and was located in the Chrysler Building, which I'd never been in beyond the lobby. I telephoned.

The young woman who took my call from the receptionist listened to my work experience and asked if I could come in immediately. Wait a minute, I thought, this is happening too quickly! I explained that I'd just arrived from England and didn't even know if I had an ironed shirt. "Well, iron one!" she commanded. "Be here at two!"

The ornate Deco elevator rattled its long way up to the eighty-sixth floor. I was given applications to fill out, and before I was done with them, I was escorted to the very busy desk of a very busy young lady who grasped my file and read it over while sipping coffee, talking on the telephone, putting on lipstick, asking me questions and smoking a cigarette.

"This means we get your first week's pay. Sign here!" she said, and before I was able to, she'd handed me an index card with an address typed on it. "You get ten tries. All of these are *ace* jobs! What are you waiting for? Go! He's expecting you!"

I walked the half dozen blocks across to Forty-fourth

Street between Fifth and Sixth Avenues, wondering if somehow, somewhere in Europe over the past year or so I had
lost something: Manhattan *ooomph!* After all, I was willing
to take a few weeks to find a good job. What was the hurry?

The address on the card was located next to the Harvard
Club, and even in early afternoon the building appeared to
be a huge hive of printing companies and ad agencies,
magazines and journals, among them the prestigious *New
Yorker*. The floor I sought, however, was below that one,
and the European-sounding name of the company suggested—
well, I didn't know exactly what it suggested: something
quieter, perhaps a little dowdy.

No, rather chic, after all. At least the outer lounge was
chic, new Italian furniture, huge blowups of the magazine's
cover—*Graphique*—on the walls. Some years later, entering the ultramodern office of a film producer, I quipped,
"Before we do anything, you must tell me exactly what
here's a ashtray and what's a chair!" Had I possessed the
same poise a decade earlier, I might have said the same in
this lounge.

The editorial offices themselves were far more conven-
tional, I realized, once I was led into them by the busty
red-haired receptionist: lots of old woodwork, several giant
freestanding oaken cabinets with tiny windows, huge chests
with very narrow long drawers, cedar and pine and mahog-
any desks and chairs. Even though it was a bit of a labyrinth,
the excess of solid and well-aged wood in this area made me
feel immediately more comfortable.

"Have a seat," said the man who was to interview me. I
noted that he couldn't help but glance at the paperback I
placed atop my *Times* on the desk: Fitzgerald's *Tender
Is the Night*. He introduced himself as the magazine's editor
and asked, "You studied art in college?"

"It was my major."

"But English too?"

"Literature. They called it Comparative Literature."

"Any writing classes?"

"Required ones. For the lit classes I wrote scads of essays and papers. Especially for the seminars."

"You wrote for the college newspaper?"

I saw no point in lying about it. "No."

"The college magazine?"

"No."

"The paper or magazine in high school?"

"No."

"A story? A poem? Anything?"

I wasn't about to bring up the ill-fated short story that had blighted my early adolescence. "No."

"What's your experience, then?" he said, not at all sharply. In fact, he seemed quite sympathetic. I felt he was rooting for me.

"Well, I wrote up elaborate case histories when I was a social worker. The department used one of my cases in a training manual. And," I added in a small voice, "I wrote some movies."

"Movies!" His pale brown and very Irish eyes were more than smiling.

"In Italy. Rome. Cinecittá. First I did translations. Then I worked on some . . . scripts. I'm sure you never saw any of them," I quickly added.

"Movies! Jesus! Would I ever love to write for the movies!"

"It's not all it's cracked up to be," I quickly said.

"I wrote a few short stories that appeared in little magazines. But movies! Which movies?" he asked.

"I'm certain you never saw . . . *Creatures from Rigel VII, Jason and the Argonauts.*"

"Jesus, you wrote them?"

"Parts of them. They were written by committee. Quite different than—"

"Roberta! Come here!" he shouted over a wall of cabinets. "Roberta's my assistant," he explained.

Roberta appeared, a well-dressed, well-coiffed, not very attractive young woman my age with pencils crossed in her Jackie Kennedy hairdo. The editor introduced us and immediately added, "Our news editor! He wrote movies, for chrissakes! In Europe. You know? Gladiator pictures and sci-fi."

"And phony Westerns," I added. Roberta's sneer grew and grew until her largish nose almost filled out the room. Finally she managed to shape her face into a wan smile and vanished.

"Movies! Jesus! Imagine!" he went on, then looked over my résumé a bit more as I inspected him.

Physically Will Drummond was what is usually called unprepossessing. Even sitting in his huge, curved-arm chair, he passed as smaller than medium height. His brown suit seemed less businesslike than chosen to play down the paleness of his pale complexion and to draw attention to the redder glints in his fine, straight hair. His shirt wasn't all-business white but a pale yellow, and I thought his tie wider than executive, with a pattern in reds and forest green that wouldn't have been out of place on a pair of argyle socks. I also noticed that his socks picked up that same shade of green and that his shoes were a sort of brogan, brown not black. Will's apparel, his long Galway nose and thin lips and intelligent eyes all suggested not a graphic-arts magazine editor but an English lit professor at some small, over-ivied, well-endowed New England college for women.

What he didn't know was that he'd already passed my first test as a person by not asking me anything about my unusual first name, despite the fact that he'd pronounced it correctly—i.e., not in the Italian manner. He'd also passed my first test for an employer by expressing what seemed a real interest in literature and my second test by revealing that he himself wrote. That meant he would understand—even if he didn't always agree with—any excesses of artistic temperament I might have.

His perusal of my résumé complete, he looked up and said, "You start tomorrow. There will be about a week of training. Then . . . But after what you've done, this should be small potatoes, I'm sure. They told you the salary."

"Yes."

"Let me explain what your job will be."

Ten minutes later I got up and staggered out the door, employed.

Roberta met me at the elevator and handed me my paperback and newspaper, which I'd forgotten.

"Will's just nuts about Fitzgerald," she said. "He's been looking for someone for months. He's desperate because Camille is leaving next Friday." I already had met Camille, the news editor I was replacing. "And you're on trial, anyway," Roberta added, and smiled her homely smile again.

"And with a little luck," I added sweetly, "I'll be struck down by a passing taxi when I leave the building." I almost told her right then and there to shove the job, even though I just promised to report there at nine the following morning and was now on my way back to the Joe Namath Employment Agency. But the elevator arrived, distracting me, and Roberta walked away.

A tall, hulking, badly shaven, devastatingly handsome man wearing an ill-pressed suit and a loosened tie stepped out of the elevator, edged his way past me and I heard his liquor-coarsened voice yell out, "Berta! Hold the door!" Roberta waited for him to approach, and I could see her acknowledge him in the second before he, too, vanished into that ultramodern lounge.

The elevator doors began to close and I caught them, got into the empty car, pressed the down button and descended to the street, remembering his long, thick dirty blond hair and bloodshot deep green eyes, his wild, reddish mustache and his general sense of unregenerate dishevelment. I knew deep in my heart that he was an alcoholic and a liar and if at all sexual, then probably missionary-position straight: exactly the kind of trouble I didn't need.

Besides Bob and myself, there were five watching *Star Trek* that evening—the usual crowd. Among them were two neighbors from the building, Ken and Joan Estoup.

Joan arrived with a tall, frosty glass of V-8 juice, complete with decorative carrot and celery sticks, but despite this potable she seemed in ghastly health. Her eyes were huge, watery, ink-black and what my New England relatives used to call moon eyes, protruding far beyond their sockets. An overly large, Poesque brow, a thin beak of a nose and an almost careless slash of carmine-outlined lips completed her wan, gaunt but not entirely unattractive face: I kept thinking she'd missed her calling: she belonged on *The Munsters*. Joan wore her long brown straight hair cut into bangs and in varying, beatniklike angles on the sides and back. She was rail-thin and dressed in either dark sweaters and skirts or flouncy outfits, both of which accentuated her pallor and skinniness. She hailed from some minuscule, hurricane-threatened hamlet on the Gulf Coast where her mother—a Christian Scientist preacher of some local repute—still resided; they spoke by phone twice a day. Joan moved through the world with all the liquidity and languor of a Southern belle and spoke with a Mobile accent so thick, I used to listen to it only half comprehending—as though she were singing lieder.

Ken was utterly different and more to my instant appreciation. A Midwestern native, he'd met Bob at college in Cincinnati and they'd been friends and sexual rivals ever since. An architect by profession, a sophisticated cynic by avocation, Ken dressed, spoke and acted as though Oxford and Cambridge Universities were hick aggie schools; he'd picked up a few good pointers from the Brits—their sartorial taste for splendid tweeds, fine ties and expensive shoes; a slight accent; even a few of the more *louche* Anglo-Saxon attitudes—and had discarded all the rest. Despite this incipient effeteness, Ken possessed a square, powerful build and wore his long blond hair in a cut popularized by John Kennedy: a combination geometrically increasing his attractiveness. I would learn soon enough that Ken's taste in young men centered around postgrads but that he liked his preppies a bit exotic—preferably Jewish, tortured by their homosexuality, and too sensitive for life as we know it. What I didn't find out for years was that Ken mistakenly thought I filled the bill to perfection—save for my oversight in being born in the wrong racial group.

Ken sailed into the apartment, headed for and perched himself on the wide arm of Bob's favorite reading chair, threw back his head so his hair would sit just right and gruffly commanded, "Herron! Martinis! And don't use the cheap gin!" He turned to me—sitting Buddha-style on the sofa—and quickly evaluating me, purred, "What do we have here!" When I didn't answer immediately, he bellowed out to Bob in the kitchen, "Where did you pick up the decoration?"

Bob emerged from the kitchen shaking a pitcher of martinis and said to me, "Kenny's read far too many Compton MacKenzie novels. This"—handing Ken the pitcher and glass and sitting next to me—"is Phil. My new boyfriend. Hands off, Ken. And I mean it."

"Daahling!" Ken bawled in his best Tallulah imitation. "If you'll recall, *you're* the one always bird-dogging *my* numbers!"

"Consider yourself warned!" Bob insisted, and the downstairs bell rang, signaling others beginning to arrive. First Douglas and his current beau, then Joan, then finally Miss Sherry Jackson, nee David, but Douglas assured me during introductions that "no one calls him anything but Miss Sherry."

Like most of what Douglas Brashears said, this was not precisely true. David's parents and his many siblings naturally called him Dave; and when he'd hit on a particularly good joint of Mizoachan grass, his close friend George sometimes called him all sorts of names—including Christine, after Christine Keeler, one of the high-class hookers involved in the much-publicized Profumo affair, which had not too long before brought down the Tory government in England.

Looking at David, one would never think to attach a drag

name to him, never mind so detailed a one. He was so . . . so completely ordinary! Dark hair, dark eyes, good-looking in a Waspy American manner, with a slender body, except for his hirsuteness (not revealed until he was undressed) and his iffy sexual tastes (not revealed until much later), at first and even at tenth glance, David was the young man your parents would want your sister to go to the prom with and eventually marry, the young man ancient women asked directions of, not to mention an arm to lean on while crossing an icy street. During TV commercials I found myself thinking that the name was something Douglas had made up.

Douglas, who like David was my age, called everyone Miss. Even his very masculine boyfriend, even his two male dogs. Douglas was infected with "Miss-ness." He called inaminate objects Miss: Miss Sink, Miss Taxi, Miss Cigarettes, Miss Wallpaper, Miss Subway. I once even heard him go up to a traffic cop and say, "Excuse me, Miss Policeman, but that bum is barfing all over my car." The cop didn't seem to notice the appellation; it tripped out of Douglas's mouth so easily, so naturally, so part of the unending flood of chatter and gossip and dish defining him and warning one of his coming a block away, punctuated as it was quite often by his braying, astonishingly loud laugh. Often at his own bad jokes. Example: The cops are raiding the trucks (a spot where "unliberated" homosexuals used to have nighttime public sex) and one calls out, "Run, Mary, it's the cops!" "Puleeze," another icily replies, "no names!"

It turned out that I was wrong. Douglas had not made up David's name, he'd garnered it himself one week after he'd arrived in Manhattan a few years ago. George Sampson had been there at the time and later told me how it had happened.

The concept of a dirty old man is so ingrained in our lives that when we meet a real one we're taken by surprise. A relatively obscure theater actor who in the seventies became a household name as the beloved grandfather on a TV prime-time series was one of the Village's most notable dirty old men during the late sixties. At that time he was merely at retirement age and had done well enough as a character actor on and off Broadway to have bought a huge old loft across Sixth Avenue from the Women's House of Detention. Here he lived, amid a carnival of theater memorabilia, a circus of weird pals, and an ever-changing harem of teenage boys and young men. He picked them up sometimes two at a time during his daily constitutional along Eighth Street down to Washington Square, brought them back to the loft, plied them with talk, grass and beer, had sex with them and let them hang out as long as there was enough food and space—and as long as they continued to put out.

David had been one such pickup, but unlike the others, David's sense of organization, neatness and above all his willingness to clean up and cook made him a welcome live-in guest for months on end. One early evening, George, on leave from Fort Dix, was approached by said dirty old man and, tempted more by the offer of grass than by that of a blow job, he returned with the old actor to the loft. There, after sex, George told me, the dirty old man had left the two of them and gone uptown to act. Some ten minutes later the phone rang. David picked it up and said, "Sure. Uh-huh. Okay, if you say so," reporting to George, "Some friends of his are coming by. Let them in, will you?"

A half hour later a threesome of transvestites in full drag arrived and, after snorting several lines of amphetamine, kicked off their sling-back pumps, pushed off their boas and fake-fur chubbies and settled on a rug in the center of the loft to hold a séance.

Picture the scene: George—young with an almost shaved head from a basic training tonsorial—seated in a rocking chair smoking grass. David, ensconced upon the huge central bed with its Pennsylvania Dutch comforters and dozens of pillows, eating chocolate bonbons and reading *Sense and Sensibility*. And these three extremely stoned drag queens splayed out on the floor amid lighted candles and purses spilling out cosmetics and hypodermic needles, laughing and screaming and trying to hush each other long enough to hold their séance.

The purpose of the séance was to raise the spirit of their colleague—an infamous black drag queen who'd been found murdered a few days ago, her body crumpled into a urinal in the 125th Street subway station toilet, the IND line. Not only to raise her spirit but to ask her spirit what precisely had happened to the ninety-dollar platinum-blond Dynel wig she had purchased just that afternoon. Her name: Miss Sherry Jackson.

Finally the three settled down long enough to realize they needed incense and a "medium" to go into a trance so that Miss Sherry could speak from the grave. At this point George was stoned enough and amused enough to agree to join them, but Miss Capella, a Brazilian hooker with huge tits—compliments of an adoring plastic surgeon on Central Park South—declared with what in retrospect seems perfect instincts that George was already far too corrupted to do. He might, however, join the séance. They made room for him on the floor and their eyes all turned to the four-poster, where David lay chortling quietly over some delicious little Janeism.

"That's the one!" Miss Animal Farm immediately said what all four were thinking, and over his demurrals, protestations and finally attempts to escape, they jumped David, tied him hand and foot with used nylons, fake pearl chokers and Miss Tamara's "works" strap and plopped him onto the floor amidst themselves, where they stuffed his nose with crystal meth, dropped the lights and began to chant, "Miss Sherry. Miss Sherry Jackson. Can you hear us?"

Unused to any, never mind sizable, quantities of amphetamines, David fell over and began mumbling. Convinced he'd fallen into a trance, the three drag queens grabbed at him, trying to hear what he was saying, asking questions of him, demanding he fess up to what he'd done with the wig, until David had had enough. He suddenly sat straight up and in a deep voice—Miss Capella swore it was the very tones of the real Miss Sherry herself!—told them all they were cheap sluts and gave lousy head and were infected with crotch lice and she'd never, never, never, never let any of them ever touch her fabulous wig.

The smashed trio was momentarily stunned by this performance but still somewhat disbelieving until, touched by genius, David concluded, "As for my wig, the fuck who killed me took it home to his bimbo, who threw it out the window into the Hudson River. It should be somewhere near Governor's Island by now." At which all three queens jumped up, gathered their things and decamped so rapidly, their skirts knocked over the incense and snuffed out the candles—George assumed on their way to catch the Statue of Liberty ferry.

Which is how Miss Sherry got her name.

The following day I began work at *Graphique* and discovered three things. First, the name of the man who'd excited me so much was Ron Mallory. He was thirty-three, divorced and worked as a sales rep for the magazine, mostly traveling around the country: a job he'd held for close to six months, despite various fuck-ups. All this from Tonia Caputo, a gossipy, ultra-efficient, busty little fussbudget of an office manager. Second, the magazine's main office was in Zurich, where the publisher lived, which explained why his office in this building was usually closed. However, he was due into New York next week, and naturally he wanted to meet me. Third, I immediately decided I'd applied for and been hired for the wrong job.

Camille Desarzens, the woman I was to replace, seemed to be a double of the job-agency woman who'd sent me out. Camille was tall, dark-haired and all business. She'd been at *Graphique* for two years and in that time had stretched the job from simple news editor to doing feature articles, an irregular column on film, and whatever else she could contrive to get out of the office—and Roberta—in the way of interviews and research. She'd left a largish amount of this material behind for the next three monthly issues, but she assured me that the job was "what you choose to make of it," and made clear her tacit belief that I'd make little enough of it.

If her initial assessment of my skills was pretty low, it was with good reason: this was the last kind of writing I'd ever considered doing. The main brunt of the job was to fill out three pages of the magazine with "news"—appointments, promotions, firings and hirings of personnel in the "creative" departments of the city's larger ad agencies and magazines; announcements of new products or techniques that should interest art directors, graphic artists and photographers—the basic readership of *Graphique*. These fillers were to be devised from "in-house" ad-agency publicity releases and various promotional materials that crossed the editor's desk twice a day in a huge pile of mail. Will sorted through this mess, threw most away, and marked some to be "done up." My job was to reduce to three sentences of fact two pages of hype some publicity department had spent days puffing out. Camille had already perfected this art and she taught me how to do it with the most ruthless blue pencil I've encountered before or since.

"This is the lowest form of journalism," Camille assured me as she looked over my work while putting on her lipstick, and being "held" on the phone with her new employer. "Who, what, when, where. Why, only if absolutely necessary. By the way," she added, "I counted three adjectives and two adverbs in your copy. Get rid of them."

"All of them?"

"Every single one of them. Hello," she said into the phone, dismissing me as though I were in another county, not two feet away in the same cubbyhole.

And later on she said, "If you have a question about anything at all in a press release, call and ask."

This struck me as a fantastically adult way of doing things and I admitted I found talking to strangers difficult.

"Are you kidding?" Camille insisted. "Once they hear

who you are and what's it for, they'll bend your ear for an hour. Just make sure you get the facts."

During that day two important executives of a huge ad agency happened to announce that they were leaving the company and setting up their own agency. They had lured away two very lucrative clients with enormous annual billings. "This is a big story!" Camille said. "If I had any sense, I wouldn't let you touch it." Nevertheless, she insisted I contact one of the executives by phone and get the real dope on why they were leaving—and, more importantly, how they'd managed to inveigle a major airline and American Motors to go with them.

The executive turned out to be a Madison Avenue whiz-kid copywriter who'd worked closely with David Ogilvy, but he couldn't have been nicer to me. "Why not come by," he suggested. "The offices are half bare, but we'll sit on crates." Before I could find an excuse, Camille covered over the mouthpiece of my receiver and said, "Tell him you'll be there after lunch." A minute before I left the office for the interview, she told me all the questions I should ask him, then added, "This is the second creative branch-off in a month. If it's a real trend, you'll be on the ground floor for a feature article. Suggest it to Will the moment you hand in this copy. As soon as Roberta lays eyes on it, she'll try to jump you."

The interview with Stu Green went well. His new partner, Mary Wells, came into the nearly bare office while we were talking, and she was even nicer—and more filled with information and opinions. It was she more than Green whom I quoted when—a few weeks later—the editor gave me the go-ahead for the feature story about the small, creative new ad agencies which in the following decade were to dazzle Madison Avenue and scare the hell out of the giant companies, stealing away their clients and garnering vast amounts of publicity, truck loads of awards and huge incomes with their daring and witty new TV commercials.

As for me, willy-nilly I'd gotten in on the beginning of

this ground swell. By the time the second issue of *Graphique* with my name on the masthead was published, executives, secretaries and sometimes even the ad-agency cleaning ladies (with access to unshredded memos) were calling me with tips, gossip and rumors. Within a few months personnel managers on the Avenue were known to go into convulsions whenever they heard I was on the phone asking to confirm a personnel change. By the time I left, reporters from *Advertising Age* and *The Wall Street Journal*'s advertising department were cornering me in restaurant men's rooms, begging for news. It was a strange sort of power: stock prices rose and fell with some of my items, but I never really appreciated any of it at the time. To me it was all "business" —something to be utterly forgotten the minute I left the office.

I was far more interested in Ron Mallory, whom, for the time being, was back "out on the road" again, and who scarcely knew I existed.

I had promised myself in the airplane that I would disdain the truth as much as was practically possible upon my return to the States, and for the most part I was able to keep to that promise. And now that I was on my own, amidst an entirely new group of people, it was certainly easy enough to tell people anything I wanted about myself and my past. The refreshingly curious thing was that not too many people ever asked. Certainly not my coevals. But both Bob and Ken seemed to have an almost obscene interest in people's backgrounds—I supposed then as a result of their growing up in small towns in the Midwest—and so they, and especially Bob, drew information out of me and ended up being the major repositories of my newly invented self.

I offered nothing. When pressed to the wall, I allowed them to believe that I came from a wealthy family still living on Long Island, but I said that I was on the outs with them. This was understandable enough; like most of the British homosexuals I'd met, although American, Bob and Ken were completely closeted about it.

It was easy enough for me too. For two summers of my adolescence my father had rented as a family summer house a huge old pile in Locust Valley—Scott Fitzgerald's Gold Coast in *Gatsby*—a house owned by a business colleague of his, a house so huge that few millionaires could afford to staff it, never mind heat it during the winter.

Our family had lived in the wing of this pile closest to the kitchen and large backyard swimming pool. On rainy days my siblings and I roller-skated through the top floor's curving hallways and investigated mostly empty rooms. Suddenly opened wardrobe doors emitted the still lingering odor of Mitsuoko from women's wraps hung there during parties held decades before, and we might happen upon a pair of initialed suspenders or a black sequin brooch with its pin broken or a pair of torn tickets stuffed inside a much-folded program to that night's performance of *Faust* at the Metropolitan Opera starring Geraldine Farrar and Fyodor Chaliapin.

The rocky beach was a bicycle ride away. What there was of the town itself was equally distant in the opposite direction. As was anything else of interest in the area.

Our few friends at Locust Valley were grandchildren of those industrial moguls still in summer residence. There were so few teenagers that anyone halfway attractive or not apparently brain-damaged was included. We became part of this small, fairly close-knit group. Who else was there to take to the movies and to sunset beach parties and to outdoor barbecues? Thus I was neither lying nor boasting when I told Bob that I'd dated an Astor girl, or that I'd joined Tommy Harcourt in stealing and riding around Oyster Bay most of one night in a limousine belonging to one of his father's friends.

Nor was I lying when I said I'd lived in the Hassler in Rome, nor when I told them I'd house-sat for a famous American tennis player in his Sloan Square digs: a situation I'd more or less fallen into a few months after I arrived in

London, when at a dinner party I somewhat tipsily declared I'd sell my soul to the devil if only he'd provide central heating and a real shower. I was immediately assured by my dinner neighbor, the owner of the Chelsea town house, that I could have what I craved without any such bargain, as long as I didn't throw large parties or cause breakage.

For consistency's sake, I did fudge facts about the size, extent and precise nature of my father's business, which struck me as boring beyond words; and I lied outright about where I'd first gone to college; although I did say that once I'd broken with my family, I'd lived in dire impecuniousness in the East Village and been forced to attend one of the tuition-free city colleges on a small state scholarship, which was quite true—and which made me somewhat admirable in their eyes.

The rapidity with which I'd gotten a fairly good job and the speed with which I was promoted at the magazine in the next few months also helped to substantiate my story, suggestive as it all was of good connections and "pull."

What Bob never really understood and what Ken only later came to realize was that much of what they took for granted socially was dog doody to me. Only a decade older than I was, they were of what has since been dubbed the "silent generation"—I suppose to distinguish it from my own far noisier generation. They'd come of age during those same Eisenhower-placid fifties in which I and my cohorts were already rebelling.

Bob and Ken still pretty much believed what so-called authorities told them: that the wealthy were better than the poor; that an Ivy League college was the best place for a good education; that Negroes all carried knives and smelled funny; that marijuana use led irrevocably to heroin, incest, and murder.

Whereas circumstances had flung me from Queens to Locust Valley to the Lower East Side, from the slums of Spanish Harlem to a suite on the Via Veneto and thence to Kings Road—with various stops in between—by the time I was twenty-three and living on Jane Street, I didn't have to be brilliant, merely awake and aware, to realize that it was all pretty much the same.

Nowhere was this gap larger than in our basic attitudes toward homosexuality, and secondarily in the important issue of how to entertain ourselves. If the older men I came to know characterized myself and my younger group first as beatniks and later as hippies, their group was perfectly characterized by the term "the Gin and Judy Set."

In my short life I'd already been part of the first student strike against a university—in 1962. I'd joined SNCC that same year and had been arrested for integration sit-ins in three states. Someone once joked on the steps of the college library, "Hey! someone from HUAC (The House Un-American Activities Committee) was here looking for you." Big joke. Later on, the first year of my first real job, I'd become a leader in the Social Workers Union's illegal strike against New York City in 1966, as the real union leaders were arrested three at a time, level by level, in an attempt to end the walkout. And all that was merely the documented nonconformity I could be accused of.

Now, suddenly, here were two rational, intelligent people telling me that I "couldn't do" certain things: couldn't kiss a man in public, couldn't take hallucinogenic drugs in my own apartment, couldn't call myself a faggot and bash in the face of anyone else who called me the same name.

As I got to know him, I came to realize that while Bob was certainly bright and original and could be freethinking when it advanced his own interests, he'd accepted these tenets as a method of showing his rise from the farming class of Covington, Kentucky, into the middle class of college-educated Cincinnatians. His success—so far—in life had been based upon a structure he'd agreed upon, accepted.

I found that touching. In fact, I found very moving indeed the way Bob and I would lie in bed on those mornings we didn't have to go to work and he would talk about growing up the third—or was it the fourth?—child in a poor family of eleven—or was it twelve?—in a time and place where the Great Depression was still vividly recalled and daily remembered amid amber waves of grain in the heartland of this great nation. Really! I did.

Ken was a bit more comprehensible to me. Probably because he'd come from a middle-class family more like my own and had read his Sinclair Lewis while still an overbright junior-high student. He was certainly willing to criticize, to satirize, to make fun of politicians, social mores, commonly held beliefs. But he did so with a true satirist's credo: to make them better, to make them work more efficiently. Ken had his own Pantheon, consisting mostly of writers like Lytton Strachey, Anthony Powell and Evelyn Waugh, all of whom had fallen outside the range of the twentieth-century lit classes I'd taken in college. And Ken took his serious matters very seriously indeed.

One example of the first time I felt completely excluded in their company: A new book had just been published on the Whittaker Chambers case during the winter of 1967. Ken bought it the day it came out, and he and Bob avidly read it and discussed it for days afterward.

Now I remember coming home from elementary school at lunchtime, years before, and seeing—if not understanding—the McCarthy-Army trials on our little black-and-white GE television. And I remember that one day before sending me back to school, my mother pointed out Joe McCarthy to me and said, "Look at that man! He doesn't look very different from the other men, does he? But he is. He's an evil man! Look at him!" I looked and at the age of six or so saw my first evil man.

Even so, the complications of the hearings and the Communist witch-hunts and especially the Whittaker Chambers case naturally eluded me as a child, and more importantly continued to elude me later on, despite hours of explication by Bob and Ken. So I sat and listened to them arguing, Ken sometimes taking the devil's advocate role. And I realized

that I could read all about Chambers et al., could look at all
the photos and study up, but no matter how much I studied
the issue, these people I'd barely heard of would never be as
vivid to me, as full of significance for me, as say John
Kennedy and Malcom X and Herbert Marcuse. So I discovered one of the truths of experience: It limits you.

Yet for all the differences between the two generations,
we shared one important thing in common: romance. Not
just sex. We could get plenty of that from people our own
age. No, it seemed as though the differences between these
two generations and the concomitant misunderstandings and
confusion were somehow necessary in making them attractive to us, and we to them.

However, several young "dirty old men" of Bob and
Ken's age group had established their own sort of youth
reach-out program, operating out of Julius's, the first openly
gay bar in New York—possibly in the country. Ken liked
Julius's and it was nearby, so we used to stop in for a beer
or burger after work and run into Douglas or Miss Sherry
and various friends of theirs, so it became our hangout too.
Naturally it was crowded at times, and loud, with this sort of
black, dry cobwebby stuff dripping from the ceiling about
which Ken quipped, "That's where all the queeniest lisps
collect." But I was young and in the midst of friends and it
was easy to meet and be with people. Especially when they
were in search of such golden preppy youths as myself and
my buddies. Even so, Julius's was far too public a scene for
their (hopefully) more nefarious purposes. For that they
needed privacy, and thus they threw private parties.

It was at one such party, held in someone's Greenwich
Village duplex, that I met Arnie Deerson, who would later
become my closest friend, and it was at the same party that
I first—finally!—laid eyes on the much-talked-about George
Sampson.

Douglas and his current beau, a grumpily handsome youth
who was into S and M and not so paradoxically penned
rather Hopkinesque Catholic poetry and even had a poem

accepted for the *Oxford Book of Religious Verse,* took us to the party following one *Star Trek* viewing. As soon as they mentioned it, Bob Herron immediately announced that he refused to go along, saying, "Grass and things are smoked there." Which certainly piqued my interest.

"Oh, come on, Miss Bob," Douglas insisted. "There'll be plenty of young dick there! Oops! I forgot!" Douglas quickly added, always making a point and at the same time a joke out of his tactlessness. "You've got a boyfriend already."

"You can go if you want," Bob said to me, managing to sound both aggrieved and yet not in the least sacrificial about it.

"Fine," I said. "But I wish you'd come too."

"*I'll* go along as chaperon," Ken said. He'd also been piqued by Douglas's description of the party, although I thought not by the same details as interested me.

Directly west of Washington Square is a series of narrow town houses built in the same mid-nineteenth-century decade and with similarly tilting staircases above the third floor. We entered an edifice painted a particularly putrid green and climbed and climbed until we'd reached the top landing, where as we stepped over them we couldn't help but notice two youths necking with total abandon. The apartment door was thrown open momentarily from within and I instantly perceived a swirl of garish lights and the sound of Frankie Valle's falsetto screaming, "She-he-he-reee!" before the door slammed shut again. It looked like a definite party to me.

Inside that door was another staircase leading up to the top floor of the duplex where the more public aspects of the party were being held, and at the top of that staircase, leaning against a wall, swirling a snifter of brandy and observing the goings-on with the objectivity of Turgenev at the Opéra Comique, was George.

I'd already heard much about George. About how beautiful he was. So beautiful that famous film directors from two continents were after him for both professional and personal reasons. So beautiful that when a leading lady of a hit TV series George had guested on found out that he was completely uninterested in women, she'd seriously inquired about the efficacy of a sex-change operation. I'd also heard about how talented an actor George was, even at his young age. So talented, he'd taken over Christopher Plummer's role in *Royal Hunt of the Sun* shortly into its Broadway run. So talented, Franco Zeffirelli was doing a film version of *Romeo and Juliet* just so George could be in it. I'd heard about how intelligent, how clever and "satirical" George could be—and for that reason how feared and adored he was. Above all, I'd heard from both the exaggerating Douglas and the more even-keeled Miss Sherry how completely *George* George always was in every way, and would always be, world without end. Douglas and Sherry and even several older people spoke of George with that hint of awe in their voice that suggested that they were saving up every morsel for future reference so they might not only later say, but say in excruciating detail, that they'd known George when; he was so evidently slated for stardom.

Months after this party, George would admit he'd been irritated that evening by an unfortunate incident with another guest a minute before we arrived, and although he never went into specifics, I soon gathered that he'd just been forced to reject someone's advances, an almost hourly travail in his life, yet one which never failed to sadden him. This might have explained his mood.

As we ascended the stairs, George slurred, "Hel-lo big boy" at Douglas, nodded and slurred out, "Sher" at David, and as the rest of us rose into his purview, he looked us over with a mixture of disdain and surprise so intense, he might have been auditioning for Lady Bracknell.

Oblivious to the near brush-off, Douglas blared, "Mandy Rice!"—Davies, after the other harlot in the Profumo affair. A bit more sensitive, David introduced George to me, but George merely waved his snifter over me as though in vague benediction and looked at some passing number. I decided on the spot that I could live very well without knowing George Sampson, thank you very much. Grabbing Ken, I demanded he squire me into the party room and dance with me to the following four identical-sounding Four Seasons songs. For the next few hours I smoked grass; met people, most of whose names I instantly forgot; drank beer; flirted with strangers; danced with various members of the quartet I'd arrived with; and in general had a great time frittering the night away.

George did swing into view several times during the night, but I don't remember much more of him until we were all leaving the party, headed variously for home, one of the gay "Bird" bars, which under the then current mayor were owned by the mob and raided with depressing regularity, or for the meat rack.

Greenwich Village was a quite different place then. Not that it has physically changed much in two decades. But its homosexual geography was utterly different. As today, Eighth Street was the sleazy Broadway of the area, and one paraded along its narrow sidewalks on display all hours of the day or night. Indeed, while I was still a senior in high school and had cut class to come into Manhattan to see Alain Resnais's film *Hiroshima Mon Amour,* I'd left the theater, walked a half block to the subway and arrived at Sixth Avenue just at the time people were coming home from work. Two enormously tall drag queens swept across the avenue in their Lord and Taylor outfits, parting around me, and it was clear that they were at home, on their turf, in full array.

After dark the pipe railing fence on the western side of Washington Square Park became a meeting place for homosexuals looking for a quick pickup. Thus the northwest fence area became the area where—failing to make a pickup by midnight—they met hustlers and other such lowlifes. This was the first meat rack I ever heard of.

In truth, at night during these years, the cruisiest street in the Village was Greenwich Avenue, arising out of the hub of Eighth Street, Sixth Avenue, and Christopher Street. After dark, along its mostly closed shopfronts, one might find a lesbian bar open—Paula's, which shut its doors only recently—and a very gay late-night restaurant inexplicably named Mama's Chicken Rib, with passable if cheap food and only a merest hint of table service. Mama's catered to slender, no-longer-young men with peroxided hair who flaunted their Broadway dancer legs in tights and Capezio shoes. They wore fluffy, pastel-hued mohair sweaters virtually year-round—in the summer the sweaters were replaced by striped boat-neck shirts—and they all seemed to possess a genetic inability to recognize the male pronoun or to address anyone except as Mary—or at odd times—Virginia.

During the sixties, any place significantly west of this axis was homosexual no-man's-land. One could walk along Hudson or Christopher Street for hours, encountering no one but an occasional bum or an infrequent man walking an overpampered poodle. The one bar along the riverfront—Keller's, located in the street floor of the Keller's Hotel—was about as rough and lowlife as a person could get.

So picture our group leaving the party, half tumbling, half walking down the flight of stairs out of the Waverly Place duplex, when Ken bawled in his party-loud voice, "Now what exactly is this hash stuff?" to me. Suddenly, from out of nowhere, George's arm was thrust into mine as he obviously accompanied me through the tiny lobby out onto Sixth Avenue and headed up to Eighth Street.

"Yes, Phil," George said, sounding unexpectedly sober and trying not to sound like the drug viper I immediately assumed him to be. "What *about* this hash stuff?"

In my usual cordial though not overfriendly manner (the Arctic Princess, Arnie later dubbed me, adding, "Ice cubes wouldn't melt halfway up his large intestine!"), I allowed as how I indeed possessed a smidgen of hashish, although naturally I refrained from saying how much of it I had and the details of how I'd obtained it. George carefully walked me across Sixth Avenue, keeping us somewhat behind the others, looking thoughtful and far more intelligent than I'd assessed him to be at the party. He took a while before he wistfully said, "I haven't had hashish in months. Not since I was in Brussels. Turkish hash is my favorite."

Ken dropped back to us and said, "Hey, Phil! Why not pick it up and bring it to my place. I'm not through partying yet." Before I could protest, Ken leapt ahead to the others, saying, "Hey, you guys! I've got a great idea!"

So we all ended up in Ken's digs—quietly creeping up the stairs so as not to waken Joan, whose door was at the first-floor landing, or Bob, whose door was at the second-floor landing. While the others began smoking grass and drinking Scotch and inhaling amyl nitrate in Ken's stylishly bare-bones living room, George and I sat, rather more sedately, at the kitchen table, looking through Ken's architecture books, smoking hashish.

Through the ajar door, we would hear silence as the record was changed or as everyone began to get off on the amyl nitrate. Then there would be a general sigh of wows, followed by laughter from one person, which quickly moved to another and another, until it burst out all at once, peaked with someone yelling out an incomprehensible word the others instantly took up and repeated, causing a general hubbub that died down slowly to near silence again.

George would toke on the hash and utter, "But if it's vintage Thackeray you're after, forget the novels and go straight for *The Four Georges*. It's brilliant." Or "When asked in the King's presence by a foreign admirer what she thought of living at Versailles with its astonishing architectural symmetry and its resulting draughtiness, Madame de Maintenon was witty yet honest enough to quip, 'Ah, yes, M'sieur, the symmetry! Yet, like the schoolboy, one could perish from too much geometry.' "

"What are you two doing?" Douglas brayed as he burst into the room. "Something both immoral and illegal, I hope!"

George looked at him with a gaze that would wither a sequoia.

"Mandy," Douglas demanded, "do 'The Countess Receives'!" He offered round a popper, which George waved away as though it were a slightly off dish of Dover sole. David seconded the demand for "The Countess Receives," and even though I had no idea what they were asking for, I told them to go away, we were talking.

"Conversing, you mean," Douglas said snootily, before taking a hit off the top of the amber vial.

"Discussing," David explained, and also took a hit of popper.

"Discoursing, rather," Douglas said, his voice rising as the amyl began to take effect.

"Confabbing," David added, also feeling its effects.

"Disconfabulating," Douglas explained.

"Condisulating," David corrected.

"Disfabulating."

"Condiscufabulating."

George shut the door on them and turned to the photo book. "On the other hand, Palladio is always in style. Don't you think this villa is both charming and symmetrical?"

Although I certainly looked at George a great deal that evening and admired his lean torso and strong, long legs, his excellent taste in dress, his long chestnut hair and his Nureyev-like face, I found to my surprise that I didn't think him beautiful, and moreover that I wasn't in the least bit sexually excited by him.

On the other hand, I thought that I did like what he'd revealed of his mind and his range of interests. Thus began what I thought for years was a friendship. Not an easy friendship by any means: George was prone to impulse, to sudden comings and goings; he was mysterious about where he went and what he did and he was completely unreliable about times and places. But it certainly seemed to be nothing more than an intruiging and often comfortable friendship.

What a fool I was!

*   *   *

Although over a month had gone by since I'd returned to
New York, I'd not slept in my apartment a single night—
because I was sleeping over at Bob's every night, awakening
with him and leaving when he was showered and dressed for
work. I'd slip on my sweater, denims, sneakers and jacket,
pick up a *Times* and a cup of coffee at the local deli and go
back to my place. There I'd also dress for work. It was
comfortable, convenient and easy.

One night, after we'd made love and were about to go to
sleep, Bob said, "Now, I don't want you to become upset
over what I'm about to tell you."

He said it in such a way, I thought he was telling me he
had a brain tumor. "What?"

"I've told you before that I sometimes have to travel on
my job, going around the country and interviewing doctors
and pharmaceutical companies. Well, I've got to leave for a
week."

Was that all? "Okay," I said.

"I don't *want* to go. I *have* to go."

I said I understood, thinking I'd finally get a chance to
sleep at home, wake up late, not have to dash out into
increasingly chilly mornings.

"This doesn't mean I don't love you," Bob insisted.

I wouldn't even begin to address that subject.

"I'll be gone a week. But I'll be moving around. From
Rochester, Wisconsin, to Chicago to Kansas City, so I can't
leave you a phone number. But I'll check in. And of course
you'll have a key in case you want to listen to my stereo
(Bob had tons of classical records) and naturally you can
come here Thursday for *Star Trek*."

It took me ten minutes then, and another ten minutes the
next morning, to persuade Bob that I didn't mind, wouldn't
esteem him less, wouldn't run away to Timbuktu in a snit,
etc. Even so, I had to wonder if it was mere consideration
that made him go through such a rigmarole. Or what.

I was scarcely home from work the day that Bob flew off

to the Midwest when Ken phoned me. "Phil, what are you doing for dinner?"

"Actually I thought I'd stay home and use my kitchen."

"Joan wants us to go there. Say yes!"

"Is her cooking that bad?"

"Her cooking's great if you like Gulf style. But I don't want to be alone with her. She'll chew my ear off about her boss and work and Christian Science and all that other twaddle."

"Well, I guess I—"

"Great! I'll call and tell her we're three. She won't mind. Be at my place at seven-thirty for a drink."

Although the layout of Joan's place was the same as Bob's by now familiar apartment, the walls were painted almost black, the floors were equally dark and bare of carpets. Despite Joan's older and far more delicate furniture, her tiny fragile *objets,* her lacy antimacassars and frilled brasswork lamps, the apartment seemed smaller. The room off the living room, which Bob and Ken used as a study, was in Joan's apartment a dining room.

Joan seemed unusually gaunt and even somewhat in pain. When Ken and I walked in the door, I sensed instant resentment aimed at me but decided I was being oversensitive. Ken and I sat sipping the martinis he'd fixed upstairs, and Joan perched now here now there around the living room as though afraid of being glued down if she should settle for more than a minute. All the while she talked to Ken about—as he'd feared—her work at the occult bookstore, some of her more eccentric customers, the man with whom she was having a most unsatisfactory love affair, and eventually her mother—the Christian Science Queen of Mobile, Alabama, and environs.

I couldn't help but notice two things: Joan was utterly unhappy, and every time she popped into the little kitchen to check dinner she emerged with a refilled glass of wine, which didn't strike me as terribly Christian Scientific. Whenever she was gone from the room, Ken pretended we were alone and would pick up a conversation that Joan's return immediately shattered.

Dinner was eventually served, and as I sat down I happened to look behind me at a corner of the little dining room where I noticed even in the dark something odd. I took advantage of Ken and Joan talking to look closer. Cockroaches. Dead ones. Mere shells, carapaces. White ones too. Albinos! A little row of albino cockroach carapaces! Odd, as the place seemed otherwise spotless.

We ate some sort of jambalaya—or at least Ken and I ate—Joan touched fork to plate, reconsidered and drank more wine. The salad was a bayou speciality—chicory and dandelions and endive in a balsamic vinegar dressing; dessert, a key lime pie she'd made herself. It was all delicious and I ate with what I thought was obvious gusto.

Ken disappeared into the bedroom to make a phone call while coffee was brewing, and Joan, who hadn't until this moment addressed a word to me, looked at me while fondling her wineglass and said in her most theatrical voice, "You know, of course, I was fully prepared to hate you."

"Oh? Why?"

"You see! That's why I can't. Because you don't have a clue why."

I thought, Ohmigod! She and Bob were lovers. But wait, weren't she and some guy at work lovers?

"It's not what you think." She sighed. "It's just that until you came along, I got all the attention. Now no one pays any attention to me."

I decided she was drunk and feeling sorry for herself.

"This pie is great. What's it called again?" I asked.

"Key lime pie." She served me another slice. "But I'll tell you something else. I feel better now, because I know you won't last. And I'll still be here when you're gone."

"Why is it called that?"

"It's supposed to be made from Key West limes. They're smaller and juicier than the others. But I used regular

Jamaica limes. You know why you won't last? Because Ken and Bob will fight over you. That's why."

Nonsense, I thought. "I've never been to Key West," I said, then, "Your kettle's whistling."

Coffee was New Orleans style—flavored with chicory—and Joan insisted on giving me some in a little packet to take home.

Ken returned from his phone call—a young man he was interested in—and in minutes Joan became maudlin over her wine about how ghastly her life was and finally burst out screaming. "You all hate me because I'm a woman. You're all jealous of me. You all treat me like shit!" This startled me, but not Ken, who calmly got up and slapped her face until she stopped, gaped at us, and broke into hysterical tears. Ken put her to bed while I remained in the dining room trying not to look at those roach shells or eat all of the pie. We left the apartment with Ken suggesting a short hop to Julius's for a nightcap.

"I knew that would happen," he said with great sangfroid.

I asked about the albino roaches.

"Her graveyard. Christian Scientists don't believe in killing anything."

Once in the packed, noisy bar, Ken pulled me over past new acquaintances to the back of the place where a side door opened to a jukebox abutting three tiny tables with ice cream parlor chairs, where he introduced me to a giraffe of a man coiffed like Paul McCartney on the *It's The Beatles* album cover, dressed à la Mod, and with a South African accent. This man proved to be Jonathan, and with him was his lover, Oliver, almost as tall but a great deal more restrained, a handsome sphinx to Jonathan's overexcitement.

I discovered they, too, were neighbors of mine, living a mere block away on Jane Street, that Jonathan was a photographer and Oliver an actor. I also discovered that they'd met Bob and Ken during the time I'd known them but where or how was never clarified. Despite his very British affectations (very chic in those days), Jonathan hadn't lived in

England much, although Oliver had, and he and I ended up talking about London. Despite the fact that they were lovers, Jonathan chattered on and on to Ken about a new man he'd been photographing, whom he described as classically beautiful, although he was from somewhere in Texas. I wondered exactly what sort of relationship Jonathan and Oliver had.

The young architect Ken was interested in never showed up at Julius's that night, and Ken escorted me home. Over the next days, Ken insisted on taking me to a play—the closing night of Albee's adaptation of Purdy's *Malcolm*—to dinner with the young architect and his lover, a striking Greek-American philosophy professor at Princeton who resembled photos of the young Robert Oppenheimer, to two parties, three dinners, *and* he insisted upon cohosting the regular Thursday night *Star Trek* viewing at Bob's apartment.

Despite Ken's and Bob's well-known rivalry and Joan's prediction, Ken didn't choose the opportunity to make a pass at me, and even in his most convivial moments, he never placed more than a friendly arm over my shoulder. By the end of the week when Bob returned, I'd concluded that Joan had been way off base. I also came to another conclusion: Ken had been "watching" me for Bob, making sure I didn't have a chance to go out alone.

I didn't know whether to be irritated or flattered. But I did know better than to bring up the subject.

Meanwhile, at work, my career was on the move. I'd managed to put together several months worth of news articles and the feature article on new agencies in only a few weeks and I already felt settled in.

It was an odd place to work, mostly because it seemed so very quiet. The editorial office was in one good-sized wing, divided between Will's larger space, defended as it was by head-high filing cabinets and three smaller partitioned-off spaces—only two of them in use, by Roberta and myself. All three of us were quiet workers. The sound of an electric typewriter or a telephone ringing was the loudest noise I had to put up with all day. Nor were any of us very social, either with each other or anyone else. True, Will would have some visitor almost daily—an art director or photographer he'd contacted who was planning an essay for a future issue. Very occasionally an attractive young woman would come in and sit at Will's desk. He always dressed extra spiffily those mornings, so that after a while one might predict their arrival. And of course both Judy, the busty receptionist, and Tonia, our equally chestsome office manager, would come sit with Will, discussing some detail of administration or production, and he'd always emerge from these little sessions with a particular glint in his eye, suggesting satisfaction.

All three of us were so private that after months at the magazine I discovered I knew very little about my coworkers. Roberta had been there three years before me, commuted from New Rochelle, and some weeks after I arrived, she became engaged to someone named Thomas. Will had been in the Korean War where he'd taken shrapnel in both legs. He walked with a slight limp and was sometimes in pain. He was married and had a child. Age, names unknown, unasked for, unoffered. Will's typing was most often done as the rest of us were leaving for the day, and I assumed it wasn't work-related so much as the war novel he'd once blurted out that he'd been working on for the past five years.

I don't know what they knew of me and my life. I never said much. I would arrive at nine, drink coffee, eat some kind of take-out breakfast and read the *Times* until nine-thirty. Then I'd scan the trade mags relevant to work, go through my mail and whatever Will or Roberta had dropped on my desk. Any business phone calls or appointments were all done around eleven A.M. Then I'd write up whatever news stories I had ready and go to lunch around one—after Roberta, before Will. Back in the office, I'd work up more items, make more phone calls, go out on any appointments, until about four. After that the day was more or less our own, and I'd read, make personal phone calls, or just hang around the other offices—with Tonia in the more central administrative office or in the large, interesting studio of Corbin, the art director, where bit by bit I picked up the essentials of layout, pasteup, and making up the mechanical of the "book," i.e., each current issue.

My initial attempts to meet Ron Mallory had all gone astray in one dumb way or another. Although we spent whatever days he was in the city less than sixty feet away from each other, he might have been on the moon for all the contact I was able to establish. I could tell if he was in his office every time I came or went in through the ultra-modern lounge: a glimpse of a messy desk, the sight of his trench coat hung from the wall hook, sometimes even a portion of his body as he leaned forward across his desk attempting to be persuasive to whoever was on the other end of the telephone. That was it. My job was to write news copy, his job was to sell advertising space in the magazine. There was no reason for us to speak.

During those weeks when our publisher was in Switzerland and his office door closed, I felt more comfortable about spending a few minutes at Tonia's desk, chatting her up, but even that took some doing. Finally I said to Will, "You know I'll bring stuff out to the office, if you want."

He looked at me curiously and said, "She's married, you know."

"Come on, Will. I mean, if your legs are bothering you."

"Her husband's about twice your size."

"Forget I offered, Will."

"But she does have great knockers," he allowed. "Okay."

It was around this time that I came up with an idea for a second important feature article. Each month we gathered together and selected what we considered was best in print, graphics, illustration, film and TV commercials. This beautiful color section of the magazine, simply titled "What's Best," had grown under Roberta's nurturing from a few pages into a striking and quite influential monthly declaration of our tastes as well as any trends we spotted. Few book covers, TV commercials or magazine spreads that hadn't been in "What's Best" were even considered for the yearly spate of awards culminating in the posh, prestigious Art Directors Club Award ceremonies. In fact, committees for each category of awards to be nominated usually began their process by going through the past year of our magazine.

I'd become slowly aware of this, as I'd become aware that an inordinate number of covers from *Harper's Bazaar* were appearing in the section. When I brought up this fact, Roberta merely shrugged, explaining, "They've got the best photographers. Kitaro. Arthur Penn. Skrebneski."

"They've had great photographers from the beginning," Will said, and went on to name Stieglitz and Cartier-Bresson, Platt-Lynes and other names I'd never heard before.

A few days later Roberta handed me her newest issue of the magazine to look at. In her editorial page, Diana Vreeland mentioned that the journal would soon be celebrating its hundredth birthday.

Showing him the editorial, I said to Will, "Why don't I do something with this?"

"Go ahead. But let me know what you get. You'll have to go to Conde Nast's offices and speak to them and go through their files."

"*Good* luck!" Roberta sneered. "I've tried to get in there for three years on one story or another. Vreeland is a monster."

It looked pretty bad, and I put off calling the magazine day after day until finally Will got after me and insisted I follow through.

The first three women I spoke to at the magazine had no idea what I was talking about. They weren't even certain who I should be speaking to. The art director? "Yes, him too. Eventually," I admitted, but I thought I needed someone who knew the history of the magazine. "Let me see," they would say, and the following day I'd be phoned back by someone else equally in the dark about my purpose and intent. Finally I said to one youngish-sounding woman, "Look, I don't want anything from you people. I'm not selling anything. I'm writing history. Got that? The history of your magazine. It may not help your magazine much, but it sure as hell can't hurt it!"

She pondered that statement long enough to put me on hold. The next voice was a man, I thought at first, probably the current art director. "Diana Vreeland here. Now what's this all about, young man?"

I explained myself in great detail, and she asked all the right questions, including some I wasn't prepared to answer, such as how many pages of copy we'd give the article and how many photos we'd use. She admitted they had tons of stuff in one room or another, and I could look through it all if I was willing to come over there and spend the time.

Remembering Camille's injunction, I said, "I can be there in ten minutes."

"Tomorrow will do," she said with a hint of amusement in her deep voice. "I'll have someone arrange to see you."

As we were leaving the office that day, I casually said to Roberta in the elevator, "I'm going to Conde Nast tomorrow."

Roberta looked skeptical, then said, "Better dress up."

Our little magazine was so dreary once you made it past the lobby and publisher's office, and even the warren of rooms and hallways that formed the offices of *The New Yorker* several floors above us were so very strange, almost Dickensian the one time I visited, that I really wasn't prepared for the elegance that greeted me the next morning at Conde Nast. I walked through what looked like model showrooms and fin de siècle parlors. The offices were like someone's living room with quaint little curtains and tea trolleys, windowed by Federal-style dormers. Desks and chairs were utilized only after rolls of incredible silks and brocades had been shifted aside. Puffs of Florentine lace, drapery, rainbows of satin ribbons, yards of chintz lay everywhere I turned. Every employee seemed to be twenty-two, female, educated at private school, dressed beautifully and in a genteel hurry about something.

One of these creatures managed to find a minute to lead me up a tiny, rickety lift into what seemed to be a sort of atelier, where she left me with yards and yards of photos of magazine covers, photo spreads and illustrations. When she remembered me hours later, long enough to come for me, I was goggle-eyed from all I'd sifted through and almost unable to speak. I had managed to piece together for myself a sketchy but fairly accurate aesthetic history of the magazine from its inception to the present, and I held a thick sheaf of photos I wanted to select from for my article.

She took me back down to a floor I'd not been on before and ushered me into what looked like someone's private study tucked into an unused corner of the building.

"Well?" the sharp-faced, middle-aged woman asked. Even in the single word I recognized La Vreeland's voice.

I held out the portfolio and said, "I think I can write up something."

"Do you like this?" she said, holding up blue material with tiny pale flowers on it.

I nodded, not knowing what she was asking.

"Your tie is boring. Catherine," she said in a normal tone of voice, and seconds later, a young woman was inside the office. "Have Eunice turn this into a tie. Oxford width."

"You don't mind, do you?" La Vreeland asked as Catherine vanished with the material. "I knew you'd want to ask me a few questions about what you'd seen."

"Yes."

"And we do have to eat something!" she said. "And you are otherwise completely presentable. So I thought we'd hop over to Lutece. You don't mind French cooking?"

The material made into a tie arrived that minute via Catherine, and she held my jacket and La Vreeland watched while I knotted it.

"A perfect four-in-hand!" La Vreeland said as I tied it in what I'd always been told was a Windsor knot. "My father could make a perfect bow tie, even when he had a disastrous hangover, even when he was on his deathbed. The Mysteries of the Masculine! Catherine! Don't *ever* marry a man who can't knot a tie as good as that. Leave those." She referred to my folio. "I'll messenger them over."

She was dressed and ready, and we took the tiny private lift down to the street where a cab was waiting to take us the few blocks to the restaurant. The maître d' was holding a table, and all the rest of the afternoon we talked, lunched and she alternately dished other diners, erroneously introduced me to ladies who stopped by as "the brilliant young editor of *Graphique*," picked at her food, flirted, answered my questions and—inadvertently?—touched my leg with her nyloned foot.

I returned back to work five minutes to five, drunk, with a new tie and in a great mood.

Roberta darkly said that a package had arrived for me from Conde Nast. And did her best not to ask where I'd been all day or what had happened.

Not Will. "Where the hell have you been all day!" he asked.

"Diana Vreeland took me to lunch at Lutece."

"I thought she was such a monster." Will turned to Roberta. Then, to me, "Just be careful. Unless you want a career as a gigolo."

"If it's anything like today, I'll take it!"

Will looked shocked. "What about writing? Literature?"

"Fuck literature!" I swore, and in my gesture spilled an entire bag of jelly beans on the floor.

"Now, Phil," Bob said to me, once again beginning to lecture me on why I should avoid using marijuana, "I work for a medical journal, and studies show that it's terrifically dangerous. Not only can smoking that stuff lead to other drug use, but more importantly, it can cause all sorts of chromosomal damage and who knows what kind of brain damage."

"You and your friends use far more alcohol than I use grass. What do the medical studies say about liver damage and brain damage from alcohol?"

"That's not the subject."

He went on to pontificate for another five minutes before I said, "I've been smoking the stuff since college and I don't see any damage."

"What do you mean?" He was clearly horrified.

"In fact, the first grass I ever smoked was in high school. Or to be more exact, at a pool party given by Dave Breslau in our senior year. I just thought they were regular cigarettes and smoked two of them."

"Listen to what I'm saying," Bob insisted. We were walking along West Thirteenth Street on this sunny if chilly afternoon from Sunday brunch to visit some friends or other of his. "I know all about this."

Sure, Bob, I thought, and about everything else too. I changed the subject.

Once inside the apartment, Bob acted entirely different toward me. No lectures, no irritation. He stayed close to me as I was introduced to a half dozen people in various states of relaxation induced by what seemed to me to be the excessive imbibing of post-brunch Bloody Marys and Mimosas. I vaguely felt as though I were being shown off. I found a beer in the fridge and managed to extricate myself from Bob long enough to look around the apartment. I wandered back into the largest room, perched upon the arm of a sofa, and immediately felt Bob at my side.

Two languorous young men lying side by side upon an ornate Victorian divan introduced themselves as Michael and Joseph. Both were slender and elegant, but I instantly and unreasonably decided I didn't like Michael—whose features seemed far too large for his face—but that I very much liked Joseph, especially when he made clever, snippy remarks in the most ultra-polite of manners and in a Southern accent.

"What ever happened," Joseph asked Bob out of nowhere, "to Tom? Or was his name Herb? Such an attractive and pleasant fellow. We met on the corner of Greenwich and Perry Streets. You were on your way to—"

"I remember where we were," Bob said quickly, interrupting. "Tom. A guest from out of town."

"Odd," Joseph mused, "that I came away with the impression that you two were lovers."

"We were not and have never been lovers," Bob declared. "I met Tom on one of my trips and mentioned that he should look me up if he were ever in the city. He did."

"Of course, I might have been mistaken," Joseph said, in a way that suggested he couldn't possibly have been mistaken. "Such a wonderful body," he continued to muse. "Those white chinos he wore couldn't have been more revealing if he'd dressed himself in Saran Wrap."

"Tom's someone I met on one of my trips for the magazine. He means nothing," Bob said, defending himself for my sake.

"Really?" I said, although in fact I didn't give a damn who Tom was and was getting a kick out of Bob's discomfort at Joseph's continual needling.

"I'm getting a drink," Bob said. "Why don't you come too?"

Anything to get out of that room. But I said I'd remain, thank you, and instead Michael pried himself out of the divan and joined Bob.

Joseph waited until they were out of earshot, then leaned forward and said, "It was an honest mistake. I didn't know you two were together."

"Don't worry about it."

"Anyway, I'm making a great deal more out of it than was really there," Joseph added so contritely that I liked him even more. "And after all, Tom was blond and you know how quickly blonds go to pieces after thirty."

"Ah! But *until* thirty . . ." I said.

"They can be stunning," Joseph admitted, and lay back on the divan, once again musing.

We talked more and I discovered that Joseph was about to move to Jane Street also, or at any rate right around the corner from our block, to an apartment on Hudson Street. Would I come visit?

"With or without Bob Herron?"

"That's entirely up to you," Joseph insinuated, although I felt it was more out of a desire to keep in flirting practice than out of any real sexual interest.

"Did I hear my name taken in vain?" Bob queried from the doorway.

"Vain, indeed," Joseph murmured sotto voce. Then, louder, "No, dear! We were talking about . . . what were we talking about? Ah, yes! Jean Dixon's yearly predictions."

Bob and I soon left the party and went to two or three more soirees that day, until I'd been exhibited to his satisfaction.

"Are you ever going to hand in that article on *Harper's Bazaar*?" Will asked me at work one morning.

"Sure," I said. It was a week and a half after the lunch with La Vreeland and I hadn't even looked at the photos and notes.

"I need it in a week," Will said, not in his usual placid mood.

"Okay," I replied, wondering how I would ever sort through all that stuff. Not to mention my notes, half of them surreptitiously taken down on an envelope against the soft, uneven surface of a Lutece banquette.

"If I don't get it by then, I'll have to put in Roberta's other article," Will added.

"Okay!" I was thinking how I could select through those scores of photos to come up with about six. If I was even allowed that much space. Maybe if I took a single page for the artwork and devised it like a gallery of some sort and called it something: "Changing Photographic Design over a Century Reflects the Growth of Fashion." It sounded terrible. I'd have to do better.

"I can't guarantee that we'll be able to fit it into a later issue," Will added.

What was with him, anyway?

"I'll *have* it for you," I said, tightening the noose around my neck for him.

"By Monday."

"By Monday," I assured Will, and mentally canceled all weekend plans.

Will grunted with some semblance of satisfaction, but the way he continued to frown suggested that he was dubious that he'd see my article in a week or in a month. As far as I was concerned, his belief seemed completely justified.

Because he worked nights when he was working and like most actors wasn't working or rehearsing for varying stretches of time, George had developed the habit of going around town and "dropping in" on people he knew during the afternoon.

The first time he did this to me, we were both surprised I was in. I'd awakened with a brain-stunning sinus headache that morning and as usual (before I learned how to prevent them in advance) it had taken me most of the day to get rid of the headache and clear my mind. It was close to three P.M. when George rang my bell and I looked out one of the two windows onto Jane Street down four floors to see George waving up, with the kind of expansive gesture Mercutio might make just before taking a bow and/or thrusting a foil into an opponent's heart.

"The Sherpas abandoned me somewhere below in the foothills" was George's comment on the long walk up the stairs as he sailed into my tiny studio, took in what there was of furniture and decor in a glance, parked himself on my rocking chair and pulled out a small pipe that he immediately filled with marijuana. "Since you are at home, I thought we'd have a smoke and a walk over to Fourth Avenue to look through the secondhand bookstores."

Since part of my therapy for sinus headaches has always

been large amounts of caffeine, by this time I was quite jazzed up and restless enough that this seemed like a good idea. I flaked some of my hashish onto his grass, and this "cocktail" was enough to induce a mild buzz which in turn helped propel us out of the building and into the Village streets.

I don't remember our conversation except to recall that it more or less picked up from where we'd left off at our first meeting. George had thought Palladio might have built outside of Italy and wanted to prove or disprove it for himself. Also, he loved the musty old bookstores I was unfamiliar with and simply wanted to hunt through them for the hell of it. I do remember that as we walked, George referred to people and places we passed as though they were old acquaintances, seeming very sophisticated to me, and that he mentioned that he'd studied at HB Studios on Bank Street, not far from my apartment, with Bill Hickey, whom George assured me was "one of the best unknown actors of our generation." Hickey has since made a name for himself playing character parts in Hollywood films, garnering praise and awards, and justifying George's evaluation.

In those days, from Fourteenth Street down to Cooper Union, dozens of secondhand bookstores of various shapes and sizes abounded. A few were mere holes-in-the-wall, others storefronts that could adequately house delis or flower shops. But several of these bookstores had been rather grand in their day a century before, with upstairs balconies curving around two- and sometimes three-story open courts, reached by now perilously dilapidated stairways.

No matter their size or pretentions to past glory, every inch of these shops appeared to be covered with books of various ages and of even more varied literary quality. Some were arranged more or less by subject, others simply tossed in heaps onto huge, rickety trestle tables that were carried out to the sidewalk on sunny days; still others had been stacked who knew how many years ago into tall, tottering piles in corners; and even more were still packed in the same dusty cardboard boxes they'd been shipped in from someone's basement or library.

George said he'd spent many an afternoon in these bookstores and had found books on arcane topics—*French Carriages of the Seventeenth and Eighteenth Centuries*; *The Gardens at Nymphemburg*; *Atlantis, The Antediluvian World*; *Secrets of the Babylonian Necromancers*; etc. Since the books ranged in price anywhere from a quarter to ten dollars (for the glossiest and most arcane of art and picture books) I found that I, too, could afford to lurk in these musty book-filled alcoves hours at a time on rainy afternoons and manage to find inexpensive hardcover books to begin to build a real library.

That afternoon, however, we were both too restless to spend more than fifteen minutes per shop or to buy much—I located a first edition of Conrad's *Mirror of the Sea* for a dollar—and we ended up on St. Mark's Place in search of a café specializing in a type of Viennese coffee—"With a dollop of *Schlag* sprinkled with grated nutmeg, a virtual Nectar and Ambrosia in one!"—which George swore was the best he'd ever tasted.

Somehow or other we missed the café, or passed it, or it was no longer in business. We'd just turned around and were in the middle of the block, about to cross the street and ask a likely-looking neighborhood type when a flower-pot containing a rather large and gangly-looking geranium fell between us, its pot shattering on the sidewalk.

"Oh, my Gawd!" we heard directly above us. We turned to look up to the second floor where an astonishing head was peering out a window over a small parapet down at us. "I hope I haven't *kill*ed anyone."

"What," I asked George, "is that?"

"That," George answered sotto voce, "is a British Auntie of a certain age and of indeterminate gender."

"You're quite quite *cert*ain neither of you two de*light*ful young men aren't in *some* way injured?" the possessor of the remarkable head asked.

"We're fine."

"Your geranium looks fatally injured," George replied.

"I feel *simply awful*," the Auntie insisted. "I might have *dashed* your brains out."

George and I looked at each other.

"It speaks in blank verse," I said.

"As the Chimera was said to do," George replied.

"Might *I*?"—all the while the Auntie was shouting. "Might I *right* things a*gain* by the offer of a *cup* of *tea*?"

"No thanks," I called up, but George pulled my arm.

"This might be fun."

"Fun?" I asked.

"Cultural fun, high-toned fun." George then called up, "Yes, thanks. We'll bring up your plant. What's left of it."

"Oh, good," the Auntie said, and disappeared from the window.

The stairway turned several times, each tiny landing at a wildly different cant to the last. We arrived in a small foyer of one of the oddest, most overfilled and disorderly apartments I'd ever seen.

The Auntie, it turned out, was male, and was garbed in overlarge worn corduroy trousers of the palest blue, cinched by a makeshift belt of two knotted neckties. His wide torso was sheathed in a summery short-sleeved shirt with a haphazard pattern of scarlet biplanes against a background once ivory, now grimy gray. On his veinous feet he wore a pair of beat-up canvas slip-ons, called espadrilles in Essex.

But if his costume was curious and the apartment a horror, the man himself—only partly glimpsed from a steep angle forty feet below—was something to behold. He possessed the largest head I'd ever seen on a human, an almost perfect cube topped by a mop of graying reddish-brown hair. His face exposed its features slowly—puffy lips, bulbous nose, eyes hidden below fleshy overslants—because of its enormous and wrinkled surface.

His voice on the other hand was smart and bright, if slightly querulous.

"Poor *loves*. And you *are* a pair, aren't you?" he gushed. "I doubt that two such young *love*lies have been between these sad walls in *de*cades. Yes, yes, *just* what Mother needed as a *pick*-me-*up* today." He all but spun around in pleasure and enthusiasm, ended up facing George, who held out part of the geranium and its former domicile. "*Dash* the geranium! But of course it's already suf*fi*ciently dashed, isn't it?" he added. "Now for a *nice* pot of *tea*?"

The Auntie pointed vaguely to what we took to be a living room/study: chairs and a table littered with papers and books of various decreptitude and a cracked-frame love seat missing two clawed legs. Before we could say a word, he vanished into the kitchen.

We knew it must be the kitchen because we soon heard crashes and bangs and sudden clatterings indicative of tea being prepared.

George and I found a month-old *Times Literary Supplement* and dropped what was left of the plant on it, then looked at each other.

"You're certain about this?" I asked George.

He shrugged.

"*Dar*jeeling!" our host announced, and arrived a minute later, balancing a battered, once-painted and now much-chipped metal tea tray, a sufficient number of unmatched cups sans saucers, several cake plates, assorted pieces of silverware, a creamer, lemon slices and a sugar bowl almost as large as the lovely old Wedgewood teapot. A package of Peek-Freans had been torn asunder, its butter biscuits artfully dominoed out. George and I moved a variety of objects off the love seat and settled in.

"I'll be *Mo*ther," the Auntie said, pouring, "but then I'm *always* Mother."

Between sips and bites we answered a barrage of questions: did George know that type of leather vest was called a jerkin (he did); did we think that wearing tight denims caused sterility as some people said, or instead, did they caress the genitals and cause lubricity (the latter, we opined);

we were so attractive, were we actors (one of us)? Did we ever go to the Electric Circus on the next block? (George had.) Did we use large amounts of hallucinogenics? Did we object to being called beatniks or were we merely individualists? Were we interested in politics or had we given up on all that? Did we think Socialism was utterly passé? Had we ever been to Europe? California? Bali? Did we have group sex often? With each other? Might an older, non-participating stranger be invited? Was that Conrad I was reading? Did we think Conrad was a repressed queen, so many sailor-writer types were, like Melville and his marinated boyfriends, and Jack London, that old bestialist. Or did we think Conrad was merely dying to out-dickens Dickens?

We attempted to answer his questions as well as we could. In return he told us virtually nothing of himself over two pots of Darjeeling in what might have been two hours. But we felt comfortable with him and were amused by his interest, his obvious attempts to refrain from touching us. His general air of being either incisively probing or utterly confused, although in his own apartment and his constant referral to himself in the third person, usually as Mother, tickled us. He was definitely a character.

When George asked about the café we'd been searching for, the Auntie told us it shut some months ago, then he waxed rhapsodic about Vienna, his favorite city in the world, and mentioned in passing that Iceland was the newest country on earth: "Did you know that Iceland grows *five yards* a day? It does. Because of tectonic activity," he assured us in perfectly enunciated dactyls, and took five minutes to locate and show us some rather technical-looking tomes in German on the subject of North Atlantic topology.

Finally we said we had to leave; it was already dark outside and George had a performance that night.

The Auntie said we'd been the nicest thing that had happened to him in months, and perhaps we'd come visit again. Or should he simply toss geraniums down at attractive youths on the sidewalk? And couldn't we stay only a min—

Oh, but he was late himself for a dinner appointment. He stood there, short and squat in his espadrilles, face wrinkled like a Sherpa, and shook our hands and said we'd been *so* kind and *so* good-looking and so very *int*eresting to talk to.

George waited until we were across Fifth Avenue and safely on home turf before he said, "There! Wasn't that different?"

"I've got to do rewrites on the play for the production at the Eugene O'Neill," Bob told me one morning as we were leaving his apartment. "So perhaps you should come over later. Say, eleven?"

Which meant to fuck and sleep. Again.

"Maybe I shouldn't. This way you won't feel you have to stop work just because I'm coming over," I suggested. Actually I wouldn't have minded having a night to myself.

"Now, Phil," Bob began in that same lecture-about-to-begin voice. "Don't take it like that. You know I've got to do these rewrites. This production is . . ."

I could have repeated the words verbatim by now. The production was Bob's big chance, possibly his only chance. He'd been writing plays for ten years, had one tiny production of a full-length play six years ago and not a bite since.

". . . doesn't mean you're not as important as my play, but . . ."

This new play was in an entirely new mode, which Bob called a "stereo-play," which while not as radical as Bob made it out to be, with its overlapping speeches and spot-lighted monologues (what else were most opera ensembles?), was nevertheless unique enough to require more rehearsal than usual, not to mention extra care in the writing . . .

"So I'll see you at eleven?"

"At eleven," I replied.

But the next night I insisted *I* had a writing deadline—which Bob completely understood—and thus I was given off two of the next four nights to sort through the stacks of photos and drawings I'd brought home, to once more attempt to decipher my notes and draw some meaning out of them, to decry my own lack of alertness while at Conde-Nast, my general stupidity in taking on the project, and to recall all too well that whom the gods would punish they first drive mad with hubris.

Despite all this, I did manage to put together some sort of outline, and the following Sunday night, in the true panic-stricken cramming-for-finals and writing-term-papers-at-the-last-minute style that had gotten me through four years of college—I did cancel my moviegoing with Bob (he was annoyed dontcha know, and settled for going with Ken) and actually typed out an article and arranged the artwork and finished it by three in the morning.

I didn't hand it in that morning. Will came by my desk three or four different times on different trivial errands, and each time I made certain that I was on the phone or otherwise undisturbable. I waited until he'd gone out to lunch, then dumped it on Will's desk and ran out of the office, pleading an interview.

Obviously I didn't want to be around for his response.

I was back at the office of *Graphique* by five but Will wasn't at his desk, and I noticed he hadn't even touched my article. Or had he glanced at it and thrown up his hands?

He finally limped back, growling and unhappy, gathered up his things (my piece included) and left the office without so much as a good-bye. I got up the nerve to go ask Roberta what was up. She said there had been phone calls all day between Zurich and New York, i.e., between our publisher and Will.

"By the way," Roberta said, "we have a new employee."

Here it is, I thought. *I've been replaced.*

"He's going to be working this end of subscriptions and sales. You know, sort of helping Ron Mallory," she added.

Roberta took me out to Tonia's desk where I looked in Ron's office—no trench coat hung on his coatrack—and to the next office, where Budd Singleton was sitting behind a large and quite littered desk, looking as though he'd that moment been dropped into a pit of boiling tar.

Budd was slender and fair-haired and while probably thirty-five had one of those boylike faces and childlike bodies that defy age until senility sets in. He was wearing a perfectly tailored gray suit, sparkling white shirt ironed till it hurt, and a deep pink necktie. He was bright and cheery and he definitely welcomed our interruption. When we left his office, Tonia assured me that although he'd only been there three days, Budd had already considerably lightened the general gloom in the office; she characterized him as "funny and fun!"

A late phone call kept me at my desk long after everyone else had left the office. When I walked out to punch the down button for the elevator, the halls were empty, all sounds behind the doors of the other offices on the floor stilled.

I was surprised to see Budd step out of the men's room, neat as a pin, as fresh as though it were nine in the morning. We stood together waiting for one bank or another of elevators to provide us with transportation. Finally an empty car arrived, and I gestured for Budd to get in first.

There's no other way to describe it: Budd Singleton actually pirouetted into the elevator, ending up in a full-toothed smile, hands-out gesture that Vera Zorina would have been proud of—even with his attaché case in hand. In that moment I saw him in a pink tutu with a frilled gauze puff skirt.

I was so astonished that minutes later, as we walked to the subway, I only half made sense of what he was saying about Ron Mallory. I did catch the following.

"*It* is a morose queen if I've ever seen one," Budd was chattering on. "And *It*'s completely unable to admit the fact. But that doesn't mean that *It*'s not makeable."

"Oh, come on," I said. "I doubt that's true about Ron."

"What? That *It*'s *comme ça*? Or that *It*'s makeable?"

"Both."

"Trust me, lovey. Many a morose young man has lost all

taste for alcohol and depression through the many delights of Buddwina's boudoir."

"Well, good luck," I said. We'd now arrived at the stairs of my station.

"No! No! No! I've got to work with *It*. I don't want to have any more than that to do with *It*. *It*'s for someone else to do," Budd said. And when I remained silent, he added, "*It*'s makeable. Believe me, *It*'s distinctively and definitely makeable."

That night Bob was busy doing rewrites and I stayed at home playing the Supremes' *Holland-Dozier-Holland* album until my downstairs neighbor phoned to complain. I thought about my job—if I still had one—about the article I'd written—it couldn't be *that* bad—about my relationship with Bob: all of that boring stuff.

And I remembered the Taystee Bread Man.

I don't know about you, but in my life people seem to fall into two basic types: either they are unprecedented or they are variations on someone I've already known. Naturally, when I was a child, everyone I met was unprecedented. As were most of the people I encountered in my teens and twenties. Djanko, for example. Or Angel. As were most of the people I was now meeting from knowing Bob Herron and living on Jane Street. As I've gotten older, surviving where other hardier types have fallen from accident, war and disease, I've noticed certain almost archetypical figures return again and again under different names years later. One such figure I call the Central European Over-cultured Gentleman. Another is the Seductive Young Blond Beauty, which can be of either gender. A definite third is the Taystee Bread Man. If I were ever to arrive at completely believing in the Buddhist doctrines of reincarnation and "working out one's Karma" from past lives, this return of certain types of people in my life would be considerable substantiation.

Only a month after being at work at *Graphique,* while listening to Diana, Flo and Mary singing "That Boy" in my apartment one night, I suddenly realized that although I knew him only to speak to, and thus not very well, Ron Mallory seemed to possess more than a small physical resemblance to and might indeed be considered a variation on someone I'd known as a child: my first love, in fact, although I was unaware of it at the time—the Taystee Bread Man.

That's what I called him. I never knew his real name.

Before my father's business had expanded and become specialized in wholesale produce selling bulk only to airlines, hospitals and smaller food stores, it was a small super-market in Richmond Hill, a long edifice abutting the service road of the newly constructed Van Wyck Expressway. Outside and in, wooden stands held fresh produce. Indoors was a grocery store and small delicatessen. From the age of eight or nine on, during the summer and on Saturday afternoons almost all year round, my older brother and I "worked" for my father.

Ostensibly this was to teach us how to be good bourgeois as well as to prepare us for the day in which Picano's would become Picano & Sons—a day that never arrived. The bulk of our work consisted of trivial odd jobs none of the clerks wanted to do, and chief among these was the repacking into their proper wooden flats of empty soda and beer bottles that had been returned for deposit all week, which would then be picked up by trucks delivering Coca-Cola, White Rock, Yoo Hoo, NeHi and other local bottlers.

It wasn't hard work, and our other jobs—stacking empty crates, sweeping up—were equally easy. We were usually done in an hour or so and could hang around the store, or go out to the nearby park and play. A side benefit was that we got to drink all the soda and eat all the snacks we wanted.

In the back of the store, just past a huge old wooden refrigerator with dozens of beveled glass windows on four tiers, a small office had been set up with most of the required trappings: desk, telephone, easy chair, filing cabinet.

Here my father napped after lunch, and here I would hide out if I'd had another fight with my brother, or simply stay in out of the sun on hotter days, reading my newest comic book, or playing with my latest toy purchased at Krantzler's Candy Store at the end of the block.

Others used the office, including a few of the deliverymen. They would get a beer and sandwich made up front, then come back to the office to eat and read the newspaper. I never discovered who got selected—probably the most easy-going and most likable of the multitude of canned goods, soda and pastry men who delivered all morning and half the afternoon. But one of them was the man who delivered Taystee Bread, a company that had begun an enormously popular TV and print-ad campaign and was thus currently very successful.

The Taystee Bread Man first arrived while I was reading the Classic Comics version of *The Man in the Iron Mask* in the office, and he said I should remain in the easy chair, he'd sit on the ottoman, a Naugahyde seat removed from someone's van. I'd been raised well, however, and immediately got up and gave him the bigger chair. As he ate and scanned the sports pages of the *Daily Mirror,* I looked over at him above the pages of my comic book.

The TBM was tall and broad-shouldered, wide-bodied yet slender, and he looked lithe and yet strong in the two-piece dark green uniform with its touches of carmine, which all the company's deliverymen wore. He had what in memory I'd have to call an ugly-pretty face: not immediately hand-some or model-perfect, but once you really looked at it, devastatingly sexy: skin a bit rough yet not really scarred from acne, large warm hazel-brown eyes, a generous mouth with a lower lip fuller than the top. His hair was light brown, iron-straight and full: unlike my own curly hair, his grew out and down from the middle of his head, like a living cap, and it must have been a cinch to cut. At the time he couldn't have been more than twenty-three or twenty-four and he wore a wedding ring.

Unlike most adults who made a point of ignoring me, the first time the TBM came into the back office, sat down and checked the local teams' stats in the paper, he asked what I was reading. More, he listened to what I said, he looked at what I considered the more spectacular drawings in the comic and he even admitted he'd not read the book it was based on. I said he could borrow the comic, and after I'd insisted, he did borrow it, promising to return it and to bring other comics.

Again, unlike most adults, who never remembered, never mind kept their promises to children, the next Saturday the TBM was back with the comic as well as two other Classic Comics: *The Deerslayer* and *Twenty Thousand Leagues Under the Sea.* We talked about *The Man in the Iron Mask,* discussing the characters and their motivations. He was patient and interested and when I asked him about the Verne comic, he really opened up. He told me that he'd been in the Navy and knew all about the ocean and being a sailor.

The following Saturday, the TBM showed me some of his Navy mementos and brought more Classic Comics. I'd anticipated his arrival as I would a friend. And why not? He never condescended to me, never lied to me, never made a promise he didn't keep.

It was summertime, when the clerks would sit outside the store in the fresh air under long awnings and my father would drive home for longer naps, when I began to see the TBM more often. Not every day. He delivered Tuesday, Thursday and Saturday. He began to let me sit on his lap, and he would casually put his arm around me as we read through a comic together. One time he fell asleep with us like that. I don't know if he was ever sexually aroused; sometimes I did wiggle around until I found a comfortable spot, and he never seemed to mind or told me to stop squirming.

Recalling it, I'm surprised to find myself thinking that either he was completely naïve and had no idea what he was doing, or if he did know, he was a terrifically cool customer.

He never touched me where he shouldn't have, but he would scoop me into his lap in an instant and keep me there until it was time for him to leave. I'm certain that had he done anything in the least bit sexual I would have gone along without any hesitation, and not for those reasons the so-called child-abuse experts give—out of innocent trust and caring. No! I would have done it because he excited me; whenever I was with him, I was in a constant state of mental and probably also physical arousal.

Our friendship lasted throughout summer and into early fall, when our meetings were curtailed to Saturday only by my return to school. My father saw us sitting together several times and I think felt a bit guilty that he seldom held me in his lap like that or found the time to share my interests. He was probably a little proud of me, too, of the fact that I was bright and interesting enough at nine years old for another adult to take such an interest in me. Whatever he thought, my father never said a word about it.

One Saturday before Halloween there was a new deliveryman on the van. I asked week after week for my TBM, but I never found out from his replacement where my friend had gone or why he'd left the company. I was upset for a while; disappointed; then I forgot about him. Several years later, when I was a relatively grown-up twelve-year-old, his replacement's replacement told me that he'd known my friend, and that my Taystee Bread Man had suddenly left his wife— they had no children—and reenlisted in the Navy.

That's all there was to it. Except that Ron Mallory was my childhood friend with a mustache and green rather than hazel eyes. He was more unkempt, too, less sociable and he had a drinking problem. And, of course, I'd never sat in his lap. Yet.

My friend Barbara returned to the city from Gainesville where she was at the University of Florida, and we took advantage of the holiday season to party. This was made somewhat easier by the fact that Bob Herron was now deeply involved in rewrites of *Arrangement for Children,* and I slept over only two nights at the beginning of Thanksgiving week. In fact, Bob now took up my earlier suggestion and said he was busy at the magazine during the day and working so long each night on the play, perhaps I'd better not sleep over until he'd gotten it in shape. Fine, I said.

This may be a good time to explain exactly who Barbara was, and the nature of our relationship.

By my junior year in college I'd fallen in with three brilliant, creative and, to me—two years younger than any of them—sophisticated young men: Barry, Alan and Steve. Together we became known as the Hellfire Club, terrorizing professors with four-pronged attacks on their lack of preparation for class, their vague and generalized statements and indeed any statements they made which we considered to be of literary or social inanity. Together the four of us discussed books, politics and most intensely, film, with that total commitment and rapacity toward ideas and authors and fictional characters which only the young possess. Despite how spectacularly well read they were, all three believed that film—not the novel—was the art form of our time, and they all fully intended upon becoming filmmakers. Naturally we saw every foreign film that opened in a hundred-mile radius, sometimes driving to Westchester or down to D.C. for showings of Mizoguchi or Eisenstein rarities.

Also, all four of us partied together, usually with our dates, although by our senior year Barry was serious with Beverly, Alan and the very attractive Helene were hot and heavy, and Steve had been going out for several years with Barbara: a situation disliked by both her mother and father, who were divorced and apart and agreed on almost nothing else.

When he graduated college, Steve—like all of us—decided to avoid the draft by going into the Peace Corps. Although we'd all spoken of doing it and I'd accompanied Steve to take the entrance test and passed it along with him, we were amazed that he actually went through with it. A few weeks into the summer, we got letters from Steve at the Peace Corps training camp in Puerto Rico. One mentioned that he was shipping out to Brazil for the next two years. That was the last any of us saw of Steve for years; for me it was the last time for fifteen years.

The Hellfire Club ended. We went our own ways, Alan to graduate school, where little by little his fiancée talked him into taking enough education courses so he might teach high school to support himself until his film career could get started. Barry and Beverly married, and although they remained in the city and Barry also attended graduate school, they fell out of sight. Some years later they moved to the West Village, and I would see them on weekends filming with a hand-held camera stuff like "Bright Yellow Objects" and "Things With Patterns." They moved West.

Unaccountably, Barbara left New York, to complete college in Florida. She was younger than us, and when I was working for *Graphique,* my third job in three years, she was in her senior year at school.

I don't recall precisely how she and I got together after I graduated from college. Possibly it began with phone calls between us checking up on Steve's whereabouts. At the time I was a social worker, part of the Vista program, a sort of urban Peace Corps. I do know that Barbara and I shared a taste for good marijuana, and that we enjoyed each other's company.

There was also some sexual tension between us that was never completely worked out. Possibly Barbara's own natural sensuality and attraction was responsible for much of it, as I was in a state of complete sexual confusion at the time.

Barbara and I ended up in bed together twice, and as it seemed both natural and a pleasant way to pass the time, we began to make love. The first time we actually arrived at the point of intercourse was in my old apartment on the Lower East Side, and Barbara looked up and her dreamy mood suddenly shattered. "That ceiling is cracked. It's going to fall on us," she said in a voice tinged with hysteria. I ignored her and continued what I was doing. But instant and total paranoia had gotten hold of her; she refused to remain on the bed, in the bedroom, or even in the apartment, convinced we would end up with plaster and broken roof beams athwart our lifeless bodies. Naturally all thought of sex had vanished.

The second time we ended up in bed together was in her own bedroom at her mother's apartment—no chance of being done in by a cracked ceiling, I thought. But here, too, she stopped me at the last minute. Just as I was about to adminster the *coup de foutre*, she asked rather breathily, "Are you safe?" meaning was I wearing a contraceptive.

Hell, no, I wasn't "safe." I'd never met a girl of my generation who wasn't on the pill and/or using a diaphragm. Barbara and Steve had lived together for close to a year. She couldn't be naïve. So I asked if she had a condom. She claimed she didn't. Claimed she wasn't on the pill—which might have been true, as I knew she'd had health problems in that area of her body—and that she didn't have a diaphragm. I naturally thought this was a particularly dirty trick on her part, turned around and, without saying another word, went to sleep.

Thinking it over the next day, I concluded that since Barbara wasn't a bitch, something else must be going on. More than likely, in her mind I was too connected to Steve. After all, he *had* been my closest friend in college, and after all, he *had* ended their love affair—her first, begun when she was sixteen!—and broken her heart. It would take years for Barbara to be able to get past that. Until then we'd never be more than friends. That settled in my mind, I relaxed, and she relaxed. We still went out occasionally, still flirted. Easily, as we both knew it would lead to nothing.

Quite by accident one evening, Barbara and George met at my studio apartment, and given our history together, I found it intriguing to watch the two of them size each other up mentally, physically and even sexually.

That night we went out as a trio to the Electric Circus and

danced in twos and threes throughout the night to live music played by Country Joe and the Fish. We ended up at Max's Kansas City about one A.M. and were shown into the large back room with its red laser "sculpture." I was surprised to see that I knew one of the waiters—Marty Brennan—and though he wasn't serving our table, he noticed me, waved and, a few minutes later, came by holding a red cloth napkin folded to stand up as though for a formal dinner setting.

I was about to introduce him to the others when Marty placed the napkin under my nose and whispered, "Breathe deeply."

I did, and took in a hit of fresh amyl nitrate. George and Barbara also got off on the popper. Before I could recover from the total instant high, Marty said, "Now what were you going to say?" We all laughed and took another hit off the popper.

The following day was Thanksgiving, and because George had been working for a daytime television program that shot "live," he wasn't able to get enough time off to go back to Plymouth, Massachusetts, to be with his family for the holiday. I was once again in contact with my own family, following years of separation during college and a *rapprochement* at my parents' thirtieth wedding anniversary, which had required the intervention of several friends and siblings over a period of months, and negotiations in diplomacy that dwarfed the Paris Peace Talks to end the U.S. involvement in Vietnam. Since my mother had continually insisted I bring friends home to meet them, I suggested that George help take the boredom out of my holiday by joining me at my parents' house for dinner. To my surprise, he agreed.

As we walked in the front door, my mother took one look at George and said, "You *bastard!*"

"You know each other?" I asked.

"I know him!" my mother said, then blushed, the first time I'd ever seen her do it.

"From the soap," George explained with what I thought

was incredible coolness as he sat himself down in the living room. My mother, I noted, had perched herself on a chair across from him and was now apologizing. I formally introduced them.

It all came out: On the daytime serial George played the role of the sheriff's son, a very bad egg who was not only the local drug dealer but also made a habit of seducing every female teenager in town and, when they became pregnant, of knocking them unconscious and leaving their bodies in burning automobiles. He hadn't told me about the program because as he later explained, "It's too ridiculous!" He'd also not told me that although he'd been on the soap only three months, he was already a star: an evil-sex figure. He received tons of fan mail, most of it indecent proposals. He always had women waiting for him outside the building where the show was produced, and got provocative phone calls at three A.M. until he changed his phone number.

My mother managed to calm down and believe me that George was nothing like his character on the soap, then dinner preparation called her away. I was terrifically embarrassed for his sake and dragged George out and across the narrow road to the little park and adjoining pond where throughout my teens I used to hide out and read Dostoyevski in the summer and ice-skate after school during the winter.

I'm not certain I ever really persuaded my mother that George wasn't a dope-dealing, murdering parasite, but dinner was pleasant and we drove back to Manhattan as soon as was politely possible afterward. Not, however, before George provided my mother—and two neighborhood women friends of hers who just happened to drop by—with autographs.

As we'd planned earlier, we stopped at Barbara's mother's apartment on East Seventy-second Street, smoked some grass in Barbara's large bedroom and when we were good and high went to the movies to see Warhol's *Chelsea Girls*. Once again we ended up in Max's—this time upstairs where groups performed in a small space to a dining-car setup of customers in booths. The two of them wanted to go up to

Harlem to a cabaret George knew of, but I flaked out early and cabbed home.

I thought I might ring Bob Herron's bell and see if he wanted overnight company. In fact, I was standing in the outside foyer of his building, about to ring his bell, when I saw a young man come down the stairs, turn at the landing and speak to someone directly above him. The person he was speaking to could only be standing in Bob's doorway. Who was this young man and what was he doing there past midnight? He didn't seem to be shy—no, he seemed very pleased with himself and with life in general. He even blew up a goodnight kiss.

I went out to the stoop and waited there, watching him walk out of the building so I could get a better look at him. A few years older than I, definitely cute, with dark curly hair, possibly of Lebanese or Greek origin. He bounced away from the stairs as though walking on air.

Working on the play all night, huh? I thought. Gotcha, Bob. I rang his bell and was let in.

If Bob was surprised to see me, he sure did a good job of concealing it. He certainly was pleased to see the pumpkin pie wrapped in aluminum foil that I'd brought from the dinner at my parents'. Bob said he'd just finished working— Sure, Bob!—and was starving, a fact proved by how quickly he scomped up the entire pastry. He said he was glad I decided to drop by, after all. He was scarcely done with the pie, then he began taking my clothing off and pushing me into the bedroom. He was as affectionate and lusty as usual, and he went to sleep immediately afterward. I remained awake a while longer, still trying to figure out what was happening.

Over a week had passed and the editor still hadn't said a word about my article on *Harper's Bazaar,* written in such a burst of energy. Nor did I find time to ask him about it, as our publisher had arrived in New York and was at the office day in and out: a time of excitement for everyone on staff except myself. Will seemed to be in the publisher's office or in our art director's studio far more than he was at his own desk. And when he wasn't in either of those places, he was out having lunch with the publisher or with one or another of the magazine's regular columnists or with our distributor or with virtually anyone. Roberta, who was usually bovinely placid, was also on edge. She seemed to leap up from her desk at all times of the day to make a beeline for the publisher's office with some file or folder or artwork. At least I assumed that's where she was going. I had my own work to do, which kept me busy, and as I was going out almost every night to Julius's or the Electric Circus or to Christmas parties and nursing hangovers the following morning, just getting through each workday was about as much as I could accomplish.

One particularly hung-over morning, exacerbated by my sinus condition acting up, led to a lunch period in which I sat in my cubbyhole and stared at an egg salad sandwich wondering what on earth it was supposed to be *for* when Roberta skipped over to my desk and blithely announced that Mr. Boelmann wanted to see me.

Boelmann, as in Klaus Boelmann, I reminded myself, owner and publisher of *Graphique,* New York and Zurich.

I was feeling so ghastly that day, I assumed something bad would happen. Uh-oh, I thought, here it is. Will had read my article and it stank. Nice guy that he was, Will couldn't bring himself to fire me; he'd let this guy I'd never met before do it.

I fought down my nausea walking the short corridor that separated the editorial from administrative sections of our company, I smiled wanly at Tonia, whose jaunty nipples in her sea-green turtleneck hurt me to even look at, and I went to my doom.

Boelmann was a large Teutonic gentleman with a Wehrmacht commander's taut-skinned face and battleship-gray hair worn in what I assumed was a regulation Gestapo cut. His blue eyes were almost transparent, and he appeared to wear a great many rings on his sausagelike fingers. From a first glance I guessed that he would not only fire me but also have me horsewhipped without blinking.

He sat back from his desk as I entered, so I could see his entire well-muscled girth in his pin-striped suit. Next to him, poor Will, although not small, seemed a ten-year-old boy. Let's get it over with, I said to myself.

Boelmann didn't say anything. Will introduced us, and the publisher reached across the desk to shake my hand in a relaxed grip. "Will tells me that you've absorbed your duties quite easily," he said with a hint of an accent.

This was nothing like what I'd been expecting.

I was so surprised that I mumbled some inanity: "I guess" or "I'm still learning the ropes."

"Will also told me that you are interested in motion picture and television techniques!" Boelmann immediately added, coming to some point or other.

I was hardly that. I suppose what Boelmann meant was that the only real—if much abbreviated—conversation I'd had with Will in the past week had been about Warhol's film *Chelsea Girls,* which among its sleazier and fruitier aspects had presented a split-screen, double-action and real-time narration. I'd thought those elements important enough in a feature-length film—even if it wasn't made by Paramount—for us to mention it somewhere in the magazine and said so to Will. He had listened anxiously, put up several dumb arguments, then relented, muttering, "Short review. Three hundred words. Focus on innovations"—which I had done.

So I told Boelmann yes, I guess I was interested in film and TV techniques, meaning I was interested compared to Tonia or Budd or the janitor.

"Good! There is a new television medium called video-tape. It is said to work like recording tape. At some studios it is believed to be replacing Kinescope for storing television programs. It may provide a breakthrough of some importance. Investigate this videotape and write an article about its benefits, its drawbacks, its future uses. Everything! Will has a list of people you will talk to."

I was dismissed.

Not a word about my article. And I was stuck with a subject I knew nothing about and wanted to know nothing about. What was I doing working here?

I went back to my cubicle, threw my egg sandwich in the trash, took another three aspirin and wished I were dead.

Bob finished the rewrites on his play and sent them to the director at the Eugene O'Neill Foundation. If he was in any way nervous about them, he certainly didn't show it. He phoned me at work one afternoon while I was trying to sort out some of the very technical notes I'd taken at top speed from one of the people at NBC whom I'd interviewed about videotape, and in spirits even higher than usual Bob suggested I come by for dinner that night to celebrate the completion of the play.

Although I didn't want to be around anyone in such a good mood, I'd do anything to keep myself from staying at home in my studio apartment as I'd done for the past few evenings looking outside at the gray, unusually warm and rainy mid-December weather and wondering how I could possibly pull this article out of thin air, when I understood only every third word I'd been told. So I said yes.

Joan was there when I arrived, draped over one side of Bob's sofa, and looking overly made-up and overdressed for the occasion. I'd never before understood the phrase *forced gaiety* until I saw Joan on that occasion. She laughed, she drank, she made bad jokes, she tried to be seductive and glamorous and at the same time to be one of the boys. In turn, I tried not to be too embarrassed for her.

"I thought Ken was coming," I asked Bob as he arranged our dinner plates around his large cherrywood coffee table.

"You know Kenny! He's off sniffing after that young architect fellow," Bob said, not concealing his distaste. "Sometimes Kenny reminds me of a hound dog. It'll take twenty minutes to lift a leg against a tree. Unless another hound's already been there. Then it dashes to the spot."

I don't recall what dinner was, or how it tasted, except that as usual, with Bob cooking, it was oversalted. But Joan managed to settle down and Bob couldn't wait for the main course to be done before he showed me his new purchase.

Bob Herron was one of the first electronics addicts I ever met. In the days in which I was satisfied to do without television and to listen to Beethoven and the Temptations through my Webcor one-box-holds-amplifier-speaker-and-turntable, which had been a high-school graduation present, Bob owned an expensive stereo receiver, a separate turntable, speakers half my height and more than my weight each, plus the first nineteen-inch color television I'd seen, with an elaborate antenna.

He'd arranged his living room so that from one seat—"The Magic Chair"—he could receive perfectly spread stereophonic sound and be able to watch the television screen. Arranged and rearranged it, I should add, since Bob went through constant readjustments, sometimes based on some new purchase—an equalizer, a highly receptive new turntable cartridge, an extension speaker—and at other times merely upon whim. I've never seen anyone fuss so with an antenna during a TV program. Nor have I ever met anyone so unsatisfied with his sound.

"Sit in the Magic Chair"—Bob vacated it for me—"and close your eyes."

I felt something go over my ears and heard with astonishing depth and clarity the strains of an all-male voice chorus singing something spectacular from *Lohengrin* through a pair of expensive stereo headphones Bob had just bought. It was glorious, wonderful, and I sat listening for the next half hour, oblivious to the unheard, seemingly mimed, yet heartfelt conversation between Joan and Bob as he served coffee and dessert.

I also resolved in that half hour that I must upgrade my music system. I still had cash in my savings account. I'd go tomorrow to look at a new one, with, of course, earphones, so I could play the Supremes as loudly as I wanted and not bother my neighbors.

Ken arrived, after all, and with him wasn't the architect but a tall, stately blond man of about thirty, who was introduced as Orlan Foxx. Besides being quite good-looking and just a bit haughty, Orlan was the first person I ever met socially who was wearing a motorcyclist's leather jacket. And a white T-shirt, and black leather pants, and engineer's boots.

Joan left. Bob said she was expecting a "gentleman caller," which somewhat explained her giddy mood all night. During the conversation among us I casually mentioned the fact that I'd driven a Ducati Scrambler when I lived in London, a fact which I thought a cyclist such as Orlan would pick up on. He didn't. Instead he ignored me even more pointedly.

Later on, after they'd gone and Bob and I were cuddling on his sofa and watching the Late Show, Bob explained to me that Orlan didn't *own* a motorcycle; he dressed like that because he was into "the leather scene."

"What's that?"

"Nothing you'd be interested in," Bob assured me. "It's all a lot of dress-up and pose."

Ken popped in again about an hour later—following drinks at Julius's—and was even more caustic.

"Did you check the getup on Orlan?" he asked me out of the side of his mouth. "That outfit cost three hundred dollars!" It seemed that Ken had met Orlan some months before and that Orlan had taken Ken to a leather bar. "You should have seen the place!" Ken said. "It's right on the riverfront down at the end of Christopher Street on the first floor of this flophouse hotel. Inside were all these queens covered in dead cow, thumping about like Gary Cooper. Some of them were so old, it's a wonder they're not swaybacked from all the chains and belts on them. I wanted to yell out 'Fire!' just to see how fast they could move."

Despite this and despite Orlan's small affectation, Ken and Bob assured me that he was a great guy. Bob added, with no little awe in his voice, that Orlan was amanuensis to the famous poet W. H. Auden and had promised to let them meet the great bard soon. Auden was working on a new book, Orlan had assured them, and so was not to be bothered. But as soon as he was done, Orlan would arrange a small get-together.

"If you promise to behave," Bob told me, "you can come too."

"In fact, Bob," Ken clarified, "Orlan specifically said that Auden would like to meet a few guys Phil's age."

"*If* he behaves," Bob insisted.

I went into the bedroom and fell asleep while they continued to dish.

I've been to worse office Christmas parties since, but the one at *Graphique* was my first. And it was an odd affair. Only ten of us, once the publisher left, to begin with. And as assorted a group as one could find. The doddering art director and his wary young black assistant; Roberta, myself and Will—still in a dark mood—representing editorial; Tonia, Judy, the receptionist, Mrs. Krafft, another chesty although near retirement age woman whose exact job I never did discover; Budd Singleton and Ron Mallory in administration.

Klaus Boelmann gathered us in his office and opened a bottle of champagne and toasted "another productive and innovative year for the magazine!" Then he left.

I'd already had a morning and afternoon of much irritation and no little anguish going over my article on videotape, first with Will, who seemed to find a problem in every paragraph and who demanded that I phone back some of my sources to clarify points, and then with Boelmann, who wanted me to make some sort of concluding statement about the new medium, which I felt completely unable to do. At that time videotape was still on large, unwieldy reels—not in handy cassettes—and it required large, expensive hardware both to shoot the original stock and to reproduce it. Forced by Boelmann, I finally appended a paragraph to my piece saying that while videotape provided an undeniably superior finished product to Kinescope, until it could be streamlined and made less expensive, it would remain for industrial use only.

I admit I didn't have the foresight in December of 1967 to see how far videotape would develop, but then Marshall McLuhan and Buckminster Fuller—the techno-philosophers of the day—didn't even see fit to mention magnetic tape in their grand scenarios for our future society. At any rate, the publisher seemed satisfied with my coda and the article was sent out to be typeset.

Meanwhile my article on *Harper's Bazaar* had been type-set, laid out in columns and was dropped onto my desk for proofreading that same day, with "Rush" written on top. I'd gone through it quickly, noting that it was almost unaltered and that captions for almost as many photos as I'd asked for had been typeset. I should have felt pleased. Instead—because of what I saw as a debacle surrounding the other feature—I felt like a phony.

Which was probably why, as the Christmas party slowly dragged on with lots of drinking and little cheer, I got up the nerve to interrupt Will in what looked like a very personal conversation with our ordinarily standoffish receptionist.

"You never said anything about my article, Will."

"We spent an hour going over it," he replied, evidently anxious to get away.

"I meant the one with Vreeland."

Will wasn't even looking at me. His eyes were following Judy, who'd decided to get another drink. With difficulty he sidled past me, saying to her as she opened another bottle of champagne, "I'll have some of that too!"

"Will!" I demanded, grabbing his arm.

"What?" he held his glass up to show her he was on his way.

"My article!"

"Come on! You know it was a tour de force. Coming!" he said to her, and left me there wondering what in the hell he could mean.

Before I could reach a conclusion, I heard, "Not very social, are we?" Budd Singleton was circling me. "Someone wants to meet you!" he added, taking my arm and guiding me over to the far end of the room where Ron Mallory was half perched on a desk, scowling into his glass.

"And here!" Budd said, "is our resident literary genius!"

"We've met," Ron said curtly. I noticed that he'd eschewed the champagne and was drinking what looked like whiskey. Ron noticed me noticing. "Want some?" he asked.

"Thanks. That other stuff makes me thirstier."

He poured a stiff drink for me, and more for himself. We drank in silence.

"I don't see you around here much," I said, stupidly trying to make small talk with someone who seemed to be interested only in his whiskey. "I guess you're on the road a lot. What's that like?"

"Could be worse. At least I'm not stuck in an office."

"I guess you hear a lot of traveling salesman jokes," I said, even more stupidly.

"Whaddaya think? Old Will trying to put the squeeze on the receptionist?"

"Looks like it," I opined.

"First week here, I coulda had her. After that she became as bitchy as the rest of 'em. You're not married, are you? Well, don't *get* married. Ever. Like a cement straitjacket. Want more?"

I demurred; he poured more for himself.

"Notice something about all the women who work here?" Ron asked.

"They're not very pretty and they all have big tits!"

"You got it!" he said, and almost fell off his perch, righted himself and asked, "Now, Budd here, although he's a complete fruitcake, says that's because old Boelmann wants to be mothered. What do you think?"

I was so busy looking at him and wondering precisely what he meant by "fruitcake" that I shrugged.

"I don't know, either," he said, and this time he made what looked like a half dive for the floor. Instead he managed to get into a chair and he slumped there and remained slumped for the remaining twenty minutes of the party, which was dull enough for me to tie on a light alcohol buzz and notice that Will and Judy had disappeared.

When it was clear that seven P.M. had come and gone and the Christmas party was over, Budd Singleton came over and said, "We'd better move this one." We managed to get Ron into his raincoat and into the elevator before he came to in any significant way. He slumped again as we walked him out to the elevator, came to once more on the street long enough to bawl out for a cab, then slumped again as a taxi stopped for us.

Budd got in and pulled Ron next to him. "Get in!" Budd insisted as he gave directions to the driver for what I assumed was Ron's address.

"I've got to get home."

"Get in!" Budd insisted.

I got in.

On the next corner, Budd jumped out of the cab, yelling, "Have fun!"

He was through the traffic and down the subway entrance before I could say a word. What the hell was I supposed to do now? Ron Mallory lay half slumped over me, one leg half across my lap, his oddly sweet breath—considering his alcoholic consumption—regularly wafting across my cheek. I could picture me trying to get him inside and up to his apartment by myself.

I didn't have to. As the taxi pulled up to the building, the doorman recognized Ron, and recognized the situation, which must have been familiar to him. He stepped out of the lobby, said to me, "Thanks! I'll handle this," pulled Ron out, propped him up and dragged him into the building.

About three hours later, after I'd showered, eaten and sobered up, the phone rang.

"Well? Was It wonderful?"

"Budd? Where are you?" It sounded like he was in Times Square at five minutes to twelve on New Year's Eve.

"A bar. A party. Well? Was It fabu?"

"His doorman took him out of the taxi."

"Rats! Better luck next time."

"Come on. In that condition, what could he have possibly done?"

"*It* wouldn't have done anything. *You* could have done plenty. Got to go," Budd added, and hung up before I could sputter out, "I'd never do anything like that!"

The next day was a Saturday, bleak, unpromising weather outside, and not much to do inside, either. I was about to dress for the outdoors to go do my wash at the local Laundromat, the only chore grim enough for that steel-gray, pre-sleet early afternoon, when my downstairs bell rang: George. I buzzed him up, and as he came into my apartment I admitted that I'd just been saved by the bell.

George sat at my little table—metal and from the thirties although it pretended to be wood with all sorts of trompe l'oeil effects including "distressed" grain across the top—he rolled a joint and smoked it, sipped reheated coffee and opened out his lovely leather satchel, which contained a giant pad of drawing paper and colored pencils.

"Depressing as the day is," George said, "this might be a good time to take a trip."

I knew he wasn't talking about traveling. Since we'd met, George and I had discussed LSD, which I'd taken once and which he said he'd taken twice. We'd agreed several times that it might be fun to "trip" together, as we found each other's company both pleasant and stimulating.

These were still the early days of the drug, and what was known about it was completely "underground." It would be another six months before the state of California made its possession illegal, and so thrust it into the spotlight of the media's ever-watchful eyes, another year before the Beatles released "Strawberry Fields Forever," dressed à la New Delhi. My first "trip" had been at Ocean Beach on Fire Island where I'd had a share in a summer house with a half dozen men and women I'd worked with at the Department of Social Services: it had been a stunning mental and physical journey in comfortable, beautiful circumstances with people I knew and liked, an experience that had completely changed my life, in the way that my first orgasm at age eleven or so had changed my life, and several years later the experience of writing my first novel would change my life.

What we knew about LSD was that there were "good trips" and "bad trips" and that these depended completely upon "set and setting." Set represented your own mental attitude toward taking the drug at the time, and any fears, hang-ups or neuroses you might bring to the experience. Setting was the people around you at the time—and your relationship to them—as well as the actual physical setting. Timothy Leary, the guru of LSD, made a great deal about these elements having to be at optimum for the best trips, and of always having a guide present during trips—i.e., someone you liked and trusted who'd already taken the drug, who was not taking it with you, and who would be able to cope with you and with the world in case anything went amiss. All of these factors were so well known and so accepted by me and the people I knew that I asked George who our guide would be.

"Miss Sherry. He can be here in an hour or so."

Set, setting and guide were now established for the trip. Unable to hide my excitement, I said, "All I have is one Hoffman"—a barrel-shaped tablet of LSD from the Hoffman lab which I'd picked up during my last days in London.

George went into his leather bag, drew out a battered-looking Navajo silver pill box decorated with a chunk of turquoise, opened it, and within lay two minuscule orange-yellow tablets I instantly recognized as Sunshine, the best-known American-made LSD, supposedly manufactured at Owlsey's own lab on the West Coast and distributed by the Brotherhood—whoever those mysterious and benevolent people might be.

"You're certain you want to?" I asked.

"Why not?" George said, always soigné.

Trembling with anticipation, I took one Sunshine and washed it down with coffee. George took his and filled up the pipe with more grass. I added a little hashish so we could slide into our trip, and we smoked and chatted while George continued to draw with the colored pencils.

I began to tell him what had happened at the Christmas party and afterward with Budd and Ron Mallory.

When I was done, George said, "I, myself"—he paused, searching for the precise words he wanted—"have been known to possess men who were in a less than fully conscious state."

"You're kidding! Drunk?"

"Stoned. Drunk. Name it. In fact," George added, "I've been known to possess gentlemen of the Bowery, right on the Bowery."

"Now you must be kidding!"

"Well, in an abandoned parking lot, amid rubber tires and garbage."

"Ooooooh! What was that like?"

"Surprisingly tender," George said, then dialed Miss Sherry's number, talked to him a few minutes, hung up, continued to draw and added, "It's a fact that the more bruised by life we become, the more appreciative we also become."

Some twenty minutes had passed since we'd dropped the Sunshine and George finally said, "I don't think these are working."

"Let's wait a while. Sometimes they take longer if you've had breakfast." We compared our breakfasts, both of which had been light. Then George said, "Perhaps we need a booster to kick them in."

"My tab?"

"Why not?"

I got my Hoffman and we carefully split it with a sharp knife, and each took a half. It was right at that moment that I happened to look at what George was drawing. The latest page began at the left side, with a three-quarter profile view of a road, picket fence, a few clumps of flowers, a pointed wooden sign reading WHILOM? MILES. But the carefully drawn cobbles of the road had begun to elongate as he'd drawn on, the picket fence became a series of what looked to be intertwined limbs, and the next clump of bushes that grew alongside the fence was transformed into a Rococo ornament that threatened to take over the page, and possibly the entire tabletop.

"I have news for you, George," I said, much amused. "You're already completely *smashed*!"

"Really!" He didn't dispute me.

"Look at what you've drawn!"

"I would. If I could focus my eyes."

I began to laugh and somehow or other executed a minute movement of my body to the left—and watched in amazement as the entire apartment appeared to swing around me three hundred degrees.

"Geo—rge! Guess what?"

"What!" he finally asked, still busily drawing away.

"We didn't *need* that booster," I said as I stumbled back, watching the floor beneath me curve downward at a variety of unlikely yet highly diverting angles. "And I don't know about you. But my acid just hit!"

"Really?"

"Really!" I said, and decided that I would be safest on my daybed with its large, supportive bolsters, and so fell onto it.

George finally gave up trying to draw and warily stood up. He looked at me, looked at the sofa placed catty-corner to the daybed and began to walk toward it as though he were swimming through Jell-O. He seemed to take forever to get there, although the distance couldn't have been more than six feet. At last he lay back with a barely audible "Whew!"

In front of me the floor he'd just vacated had turned into an abyss and whirlpool.

"I . . . should . . . tell . . . you . . . some . . . thing!" George managed to utter.

I peered over the daybed, looking far down into the enormous maelstrom where my studio floor had been. "What?"

"Miss . . . Sherry . . . will . . . be . . . late!"

"Okay." I was sure that Miss Sherry had never tripped before, and guessed he wouldn't be of much help when he did arrive.

"And . . ." George looked at me with wildly glazed eyes. "I've . . . never . . . done . . . this . . . before!"

"Never did *what* before?" I asked, already suspecting the answer.

"Never . . . taken . . . L . . . S . . . D!"

The walls were melting away, leaving a vast, eerie light, and I felt as though George and I were upon the only two safe floatable rafts in the immense and perilous Pre-Cambrian ocean we'd found ourselves in. I had a moment of total panic. What if George freaked out? I was too far gone to do anything.

"Don't worry!" I was able to say in a falsely calm voice, before the booster tablet we'd split struck me with a sudden light show. I was able to add, "Just let go!" before I took my own counsel and had my ego blown away as I'd experienced it only once before, my self splattered to the ends of space, nothing left but a single speck of consciousness floating up, up into a region of whirling galaxies where it met other specks of consciousness, all of them headed toward the terminuslike heart of a huge, comforting, intensely white star.

Several hours later both of us returned to earth and were able to sit up, and even able to converse, although hesitantly and in fractured phrases we were instantly able to complete for each other.

Miss Sherry called to cancel altogether. But he wasn't needed, and while George still wasn't together enough to speak on the phone, I was, and I laughed a great deal at Miss Sherry's explanation of why he couldn't come and at his extremely concerned tone of voice and especially at his final assessment of my condition, which he defined as "beyond hysteria."

That amused George and when he felt able to stand up, he made it back to the table, grabbed the pad, and began to draw his interpretation of the land we now inhabited.

An hour—and much fun later—Barbara called, heard with envy that we were tripping, drove by and watched us with mingled respect, amusement and finally annoyance that she couldn't share in the experience with us. She was easy to be with, however, even useful: she cooked us omelets and toast and sat to watch us eat—always a bizarre experience under the influence of the drug. When we ended up playing with, building with and designing with the eggs instead of eating them, Barbara had enough and left.

We had dropped the LSD around noon. Sometime after nightfall, George suddenly remembered he was supposed to meet some people at a local restaurant for dinner. When I suggested he call and cancel, George said he couldn't possibly: it was the director Franco Zeffirelli, who wanted George to star in a new film. George *had* to make an appearance.

The two of us got on our street clothing and I walked George the five blocks or so to his apartment in an old tenement opposite the Sixth Precinct. There, I watched him change clothing for the business dinner. At one point George got cold feet, phoned Zeffirelli's hotel suite to cancel but didn't get any response, and tried the restaurant. There, Zeffirelli's secretary, a young British woman named Anne, took the call, and while she was understanding about George's "stomach problem"—the excuse he made up—she persuaded him to try to stop by, anyway.

I walked George the few blocks over to the restaurant for moral support, and by the time we reached Casey's, he'd regained his self-confidence. He could handle the situation, he said. We shook hands. George went in, I walked home, picked up a Sunday *Times* and read and listened to music.

The next morning George phoned me. His going to the restaurant had been a mistake. There had been a half dozen of the director's hangers-on present, as well as several other "business types," and Franco himself had been too busy to pay much attention to George. Naturally George couldn't eat a thing. And when he spilled a bit of champagne on the tablecloth, he'd become fascinated by how it reacted with the cloth, and ended up pouring more and more and watching it through candlelight, until the noisy table of people had been silenced, watching him. George had managed to regroup and say something vaguely indicative of his scientific interest in such phenomena, and conversation had resumed around him. Then he'd become intrigued by the melting wax of the candles and had ended up playing with the table candles with such complete fascination that even Anne finally suggested that George wasn't feeling well and he should probably go home. More than a mere mistake, George said, the evening had been close to disaster. "I doubt that Franco will ever speak to me again, never mind want me to be in his film," he concluded soberly. "But the truth is, that candlewax *was* more interesting than anyone at the table."

"Who is that?" I asked Ken, and nodded in the direction of the small foyer where a movie-star-handsome man had just entered and was taking off his coat and scarf, being effusively greeted by Jonathan, our host. The stranger was about six foot one, with broad shoulders and a muscular build. He had coal-black straight hair curling slightly at the tips where it grew long in back, a trimmed black beard and large dark eyes set in one of those Celtic faces of perfectly complected, fair—almost white—skin that looked copied out of some anatomy textbook.

"I don't know," Ken said. "Oh, wait! That must be Luke Harms. Jonathan was raving about him at Julius's."

Oliver had joined them, and typically was being equally welcoming to the new guest, although by no means as effusive as Jonathan.

"What's his story?" I asked.

"I assume he's as queer as anyone else here," Ken said out of the side of his mouth. "And knowing Jonathan, Luke's probably already been photographed, thoroughly investigated and a substantial file on him prepared and stuffed in Jon's 'trick' file."

"Are they a triad?" I asked, using the current word for a ménage à trois popularized by the Byrds' recent hit.

"Got me!" Ken said. "But if they aren't now, you can bet it's in the works." Ken spotted someone he was interested in, and went to follow his destiny.

The setting was Jonathan and Oliver's top-floor apartment on the corner of Jane and Greenwich Streets. The occasion was a New Year's Eve party. And Ken hadn't been as exact as he usually was in saying that everyone present was gay. For example, Jonathan's mother was present, a tall, horse-faced, maternal woman given to oddly patterned handmade dresses, curious handicraft jewelry and large amounts of straight gin. Also present were several young women of varying attractiveness and interest, most of them sounding "terribly British" and somehow connected up with Carnaby Street–clad young men, ostensibly straight, friends or colleagues of either Jonathan or Oliver. Also present were most of what I'd come to think of as the Jane Street Girls—Joan, Ken, Bob, Douglas, Miss Sherry Jackson, along with assorted boyfriends, lovers, past seductions and about-to-be seductions. Under some circumstances the mixture might have been explosive, and at the least it ought to have been stimulating. But I was bored and irritated. Or had been until Luke entered.

One reason I was irritated could be seen if I turned my head and looked right some eight feet away where Bob Herron was holding forth on some subject or other with increasing fervor to several straight couples, who looked—variously—unconvinced, amused, indifferent and trapped by his rhodomontade. From the rising pitch of his voice, I knew that: 1) Bob had drunk too much—i.e., anything over one glassful; 2) surrounded by an audience, he felt completely in his element; and 3) he actually thought he'd won our earlier argument.

I can't recall precisely what that argument had been about. Of late, it required virtually any subject to set one off between us. Partly my fault, I admit. I'd gotten so very tired of Bob always knowing more than anyone alive on any subject, of always being willing to parade that knowledge—spurious as I knew it to be at times—in front of me, and of using it to batter me into my place: an undefined spot but definitely beneath Bob, if not altogether beneath contempt.

Why did someone as intelligent as Bob, who claimed to care for me—and after all was affectionate and loving—why did he also need so much to play out these nonsensical old-fashioned games of I'm better than you, I know more than you? Wasn't inborn equality one of the main points about same-sex relationships in the first place? Lacking the centuries-long cultural accumulation surrounding male-female love and marriage, wasn't homosexual romance free to discover new ways of people relating to each other? *I* thought so. Bob didn't even think about it, and in fact failed to understand what I was even talking about whenever I attempted to broach the subject—equating it with séances and astrology and "all that other hokum!"

So I sat alone amidst a pretty successful party and simmered, and I remembered more incidents like today's, more arguments we'd had, and I knew what was bound to happen in the next half hour. Bob would lecture until his audience appeared convinced or fell away, then he would come over to where I was sitting, make a fumbling, affectionate gesture and say, "Why don't we go home?" Once again we'd be doing what he wanted, when he wanted; not what I wanted, when I wanted—whatever that might be.

"Someone doesn't like parties very much," I heard someone drawl near me and looked up and saw Luke Harms. Great, I thought. I've made a wonderful first impression. Oliver was there, too, and introduced us. I shook hands with Luke—big, warm palms—then sat back and continued to sulk. A minute later Oliver was called away to do something hostlike and Luke pulled over a hassock and sat down near me. "I'm not crazy about parties, either," he said, and I realized that his drawl wasn't any of the Southern ones I was familiar with. So naturally I asked where he was from, and he told me the name of a small town in the Texas panhandle.

Slowly and quietly we talked for another half hour or so until I noticed that Jonathan was making great swooping arcs around us, trying to get Luke's attention without appearing to actually do so. Finally Jonathan disappeared into the kitchen and a minute later his ambassador, Oliver, came out and forthrightly said, "Luke, Jon will have a conniption if he can't speak to you immediately." Luke and I exchanged glances and he got up to leave. We'd had a good conversation—background, work, a few likes and dislikes—and I was a great deal more charmed than I'd been expected to be by Luke's modesty, given his looks and his seemingly genuine interest in me.

Bob Herron appeared at my side instantly and began nuzzling me—proving he'd been drinking, he was never that open in public—and said, "Let's go home."

I said no.

He tried to convince me.

I said I was still pissed off at him from earlier.

He tried to defend his earlier action and—tactical error of the grossest sort—he said that whatever he did was out of love and concern for me.

I said he could go home if he wanted to. I was going to another party.

He said I was being completely unreasonable.

I said if he was so horny, he should go fuck himself. I got up, pulled my coat out of the pile of outer clothing stacked on the bed, refused to listen to further explanations and left.

Actually I did have another party to attend, one George had invited me to, and I began to walk along Hudson Street, looking for a taxi to take me uptown. It was sleeting out, a needlelike frozen rain, and at a quarter past one in the morning there wasn't a cab to be had on Hudson Street even though a dispatching garage was located a few blocks away on Perry Street. Undaunted, I strode down Hudson Street, annoyed at myself, completely pissed off at Bob, seeing no taxis and in fact hardly any traffic at all until I'd reached the taxi garage. Inside, I was told that all the cars were out. I could wait around if I wanted to.

I did wait around for a while, my irritation and anger coming to a slow boil, then I gave up and decided to walk back up Hudson Street to Fourteenth. I reasoned that between these two major traffic arteries I should find one cab willing to take me uptown.

No luck. I walked up and down Hudson Street, now less angry than feeling sorry for myself with my soaking hair and waterlogged jacket and rain-sloshed shoes. I'd found myself on Twelfth Street, a short block from home, and decided the night was to be a complete failure. I might as well admit it. I was about to cross the street when a black limousine pulled up to the traffic light with a screeching halt. Its back wheel sent a six-foot-high splash of dirty puddle water all over me, soaking what of me had not yet been waterlogged.

The back window opened, and inside I saw a tall man not yet thirty years old and strikingly good-looking, dressed in a tuxedo. The oddest thing about him was that he had his fly open and was casually stroking an erection.

"Want a ride?" he asked.

For a moment I wondered whether to be angry or amused.

In that space, I reacted simply. "I live right over there." I pointed.

"Climb in," he said, and I heard the door locks pop open.

"I'm all wet," I protested.

"I have Courvoisier to warm you up."

All of the elements of the night—the argument with Bob, meeting Luke, not finding a cab, getting soaked—seemed to converge at this moment. Without further hesitation I got into the back of the limo and he handed me a white silk scarf to wipe my hair with, a silver flask of brandy to sip from and his cock to play with.

He opened the window to the front and directed the driver to my block. I told the driver to stop in front of my apartment building.

"Invite me in?" the man asked.

"Well . . ."

"I can't stay long, I'm afraid. I'm expected at a party. But they won't miss me for, say, half an hour."

"Better zip up," I said.

In the hallway going up the stairs, his hands were all over me, and when we reached my doorway I hoped no neighbor was peering out of the peephole to see him pull off my wet coat while I fumbled with the keys, to wrap his arms around me, to cover the back of my neck with kisses.

We fell into the studio, tore off our clothing and eventually made it to bed. I guessed that if I'd hesitated for even a second, he would have raped me. No problem, though. His looks, his passion, the pickup, the entire situation, even his new wedding band—all excited me. Later on, in the seventies, as their number and exotic settings and situations increased, I would seriously consider doing up a catalog of my "quickies"—i.e., instant, completely unexpected, utterly mindless sex acts with total strangers. To this day the best one remains a blow job I got in the middle of Tenth Avenue at Twenty-first Street in the middle of a snowstorm at four A.M. in January of 1976, while occasional cars swerved around us, flashing their lights and tooting their horns. But on that first day of 1968, I'd only had one such previous encounter, with a Frenchman in Marseilles, and it, too, had come at a crisis in my life. So I enjoyed myself.

When my gentleman had completely exhausted himself and me and had gone into and stepped back out of my little bathroom, all dressed again in his tuxedo, his white tie perfectly reknotted, he pulled me naked to my feet to kiss me good-bye. I wrapped his silk scarf around his neck and kissed him back. What I wanted to do was to thank him, thank him not only for picking me up and making great love to me but for making my life interesting again, and thus worthwhile.

I slept like a well-fed infant and awoke to bright, clear winter sunlight. I still didn't completely believe what had happened the night before until I went into my bathroom to urinate and then I received complete and amazing proof: placed under a worn bar of Ivory soap was a crisp hundred-dollar bill.

You might expect a year that began so intriguingly would continue to be intriguing. You'd be wrong.

At *Graphique*, Roberta took her long-threatened vacation—off to some Caribbean island with her fiancé, a C.P.A. named Thomas—and I wished I were there. Or, in fact, anywhere but at that office.

Not that I had more work to do because of her. Roberta had left plenty of material behind for the next few issues. But because the general situation in the office seemed to be sliding downhill rapidly. Our editor, Will, seemed to clunk about the office banging his cane in an effort to damage every surface and to annoy me. He was more taciturn than ever, scowling all the time he wasn't actually glum. The few work-related conversations we had together were curt to the point of being Delphic. Any possibility of friendship between us which I'd thought likely when I'd been hired because of our shared interests, despite our age difference, was now shown to be a vain and foolish hope. At times I wanted to grab Will by the shoulders and say, "Tell me what's wrong." But I was young and too unsure of myself to be able to do anything but keep out of Will's way.

One probable reason for Will's changed attitude may have been that the publisher was present all the time, which to me at least meant that I couldn't saunter into the other office and chat with Tonia as much as I used to, nor speak to Budd Singleton, who seemed to have become Boelmann's very busy right-hand man in a matter of a few days—nor to peer into Ron Mallory's office to see if he was in or on the road. The one time I managed to accost Tonia by the elevator to ask her if it was usual for Boelmann to stick around so long, she shrugged, then said darkly, "He's making changes." She wouldn't specify what those changes were. Naturally, following that single brief interview about the videotape article, Boelmann never asked to see me.

I discovered one of the changes Tonia mentioned when Will sent me with a batch of material into the art director's studio. I'd always been fascinated by the place, feeling that here, finally, was where the magazine *really* happened. Perhaps because it actually looked as though work were done: so many instruments whose use I didn't know. So many low, wide cabinets covered with artwork and batches of copyproof, the slanted worktables always strewn with cover drawings, the corkboard walls of page-by-page layouts of ads and editorial matter. The elderly art director who'd paid no attention to me on previous meetings looked up from his work when I stepped in and said to his assistant, "Jerry! Show him the fashion stuff."

Jerry, his assistant, an overweight but likable black man about my age, got up from his worktable and said, "I think you're going to like what we did with your idea." I realized he was talking about my proposal for displaying the artwork La Vreeland had given me for the *Harper's Bazaar* article.

The article had been laid out on five pages, the first a recto, the introduction with a large headline—and my byline in letters almost as large—and a single photo dead center.

The second and third pages also had art spots in the midst of copy: the essay itself. The fourth and fifth, however, were also a spread, with photos and drawings at the top, and my article continued at the bottom. It looked great.

"Well?" Corbin asked without turning around.

"It's terrific!" I said.

Jerry began to show me various details of the layout using terms I'd never heard before and which I made him explain. As I looked, I had an idea. There were six main breaks in the copy, each beginning with a period (1922–1935), and as I looked, I thought, and finally said out loud, "What if these years were done in the type of the period? Nouveau, Deco, sans-serif. You know, to convey a sense of time passing."

Jerry's face went strange. I could see his eyes dart over to the art director as though afraid that Corbin had heard me.

"Probably too much trouble," I concluded. I thanked them and headed back to the gloom of the editorial office.

Budd Singleton was just coming out and he grabbed me and pushed me into a little space between two offices and said, "Now that Roberta is away, you should meet with Klaus and propose some new articles. Strike while the iron is hot."

His familiar use of our publisher's given name suggested that Budd himself had taken opportunity by the horns, but I said, "Will has already turned down all the ideas for articles I've come up with lately. They weren't very good, anyway."

"Want me to arrange a meeting with Klaus?"

"I don't think so," I said. Seizing an opportunity was one thing, but going behind Will's back was another. Besides, I felt my job was secure for a while, anyway, and had no other ambition.

"What about *It*"—nodding in the direction of Ron's office. "Want me to arrange a little get-together for us so you can make your move at your leisure?"

"What kind of get-together?"

"You know, an intimate dinner for three in which I suddenly vanish."

"You're kidding. Ron wouldn't fall for that."

"*It* already has," Budd said with what Douglas called "much eyebrows."

"You're welcome to him," I said.

"I told you before, *It*'s not my type."

"What is your type?"

"Right now my type is older, richer, more powerful, and with a distinct foreign accent." Before I could express my astonishment, Budd sashayed off.

That evening as I was leaving for the day, Jerry asked me to step into the studio. His boss was gone. Jerry led me over to the layout for my article where he'd altered each of the years to exactly the type of the appropriate period.

"Does Corbin know you did it?"

"Minute you walked out, he said, 'What are you waiting for? Do what he told you.' "

Jerry seemed so put-upon and so overly humble that I blushed. "I didn't mean to . . . I just thought . . ."

"That's the way Corbin talks," Jerry said. "Anyway, it *was* a good idea. It's about time someone in editorial had visual ideas. We've been on our own since I've been here. And Corbin is so old-fashioned. You know he's planning to retire."

"When?"

"Soon. I hope they give me his job. I could use the money, not to mention . . . I've got all sorts of ideas."

Jerry showed me his portfolio, begun when he was at the School of Visual Arts, which contained far more exciting stuff than anything in our magazine. We talked about the new graphics appearing in underground newspapers and magazines, like *The East Village Other*. We shared a taste for Warhol and Rauchenburg and pop art rather than abstract expressionism. We agreed there was a visual revolution in the making, but that people like Corbin and Will, who didn't buy rock records or read Tolkien and Vonnegut, were missing it. Jerry told me how *he'd* like to lay out the magazine, changing all sorts of things. He sighed, knowing it was a dream.

He'd also given me an idea for an article—on rock-record covers—which he and I could work on together, fusing art and copy as they'd never been done in the magazine before. I doubted that Will would be responsive to it, but I promised Jerry I'd try—bringing in album covers the next day— and that I'd exert whatever influence I had in getting Corbin's job for Jerry.

I'd never heard of him before, but I was assured that Jameson Metcalf was a well-known concert pianist, who, although young, had played all over the country and even in several European capitals. More important than his career, however, was the fact that he was having a party.

"A lease-break party," Joseph explained to me. As promised, Joseph had moved into a flat around the corner, and he'd found me that evening loitering on Bob's stoop—one of only two on the block—catching the last rays of a surprisingly warm sun and reading *Dune*. "It should be fun."

Naïve me, I asked what a lease-break party was.

"Jemima gets tired of apartments before the leases are up. So he throws a party and is invariably asked to leave the building."

Jemima, of course, was Metcalf's drag name among friends, its origins obscure but having something to do with his Southern upbringing and/or his black nanny. The party sounded like fun and I needed fun badly. I asked if some of the other Jane Street Girls might come too.

"I don't see why not," Joseph assured me. "Jemima usually anticipates—nay, Jemima insists upon—reprehensible behavior at these particular *fêtes desengagées*."

So, about nine o'clock of a dreary early January workday night, myself, Douglas and his tortured Catholic boyfriend, Miss Sherry Jackson, George, and Ken presented ourselves at the twentieth-floor apartment door of a well-known Chelsea building, already half tanked and ready to party.

"Joseph invited us," I said to the slender young man who opened the door.

"I wouldn't care if Sophonsiba McQueen invited you," he drunkenly drawled while splashing what looked like a jam jar filled with bourbon all over himself. "Come on in and don't be shy about taking hooch or pussy! Har-de-har! Only six of you? I hope you girls know how to slap it away!"

The phone was ringing as we stepped into the penthouse apartment. We were met by an enormous window with a fabulous view of downtown Manhattan and in front of it a giant white Steinway. Jemima grabbed the phone, which had to be on an extension long enough to wrap the entire building, took a chair in the middle of the room and proceeded to scream into the mouthpiece, "Magnolia Blossom, you slut! I heard you sucked off half of Fort Bragg in a single night! Har-de-har!"

Several people were playing the Steinway at once: two young men and a flame-haired goddess of a woman, in what appeared to be a rendition of *The Sabre Dance*. Meanwhile a phonograph was playing the Supremes belting out "Where Has Our Love Gone?" Several guests had already found comfortable drinking spots where they wouldn't be trampled by the dancers, most of whom were already four sheets to the wind. Under the Steinway itself proved to be the remarkably public necking spot for a long young man and a nubile young lady wearing most of the remnants of a cocktail dress. In one corner, a slim fellow was leaning against the wall, apparently barely conscious, having his erection removed from his trousers and measured by a mixed group of people, each of whom took turns with the ruler. The bar was a tabletop filled with liquor bottles. Ken, wide-eyed as were all of us newcomers, played bartender for the first round, then announced that after that we were on our own.

"Now," he said, "let's see what kind of pickings we have here."

"Panties!" our host shouted into the receiver. "Not those

Frederick's of Hollywood kind with the crotch cut out?"

Surprisingly sober—despite the liquor and hash—George took me out onto an extremely tiny balcony around the corner from the main room where we sipped and looked down at the city.

"Someone I don't exactly want to see is in the other room," George said.

I immediately turned to look at who it could be.

"The big blond at the piano. He's an actor. We used to sort of have a thing," George said.

The big blond was at that moment singing "Swanee" directly into the cleavage of the red-haired woman.

"He's certainly good-looking. An actor?" I asked.

"He's just been picked as the male ingenue in the film version of *Paint Your Wagon,*" George said. "If he speaks to me, I may murder him."

"You'd never get that part, anyway," I said, trying to mollify him.

"Not because of the part," George said, then turned back to the view of the city and sulked.

I began to tell him about my encounter with the man in the limo a few weeks earlier. George listened with no apparent interest, then asked, "Is that the first time you were paid?"

I began to defend myself. "It's hardly the same as hustling for it."

"There's nothing wrong with prostitution," George said, then surprised me by adding, "I've hustled."

"You have?"

"It hasn't always been easy getting roles." George left it at that. "And with Zeffirelli, it's a kind of prostitution, anyway."

"You don't mean . . . ?"

"No! He'd never actually touch me. But as long as I'm around long enough for him to adore me, he'll feel obligated to pay up in some way. The role of Mercutio in his film of *Romeo and Juliet.* That's what I've decided on. For now."

George went on to explain all about the film as Zeffirelli was planning it. He'd put the idea together partly to have George around him in Europe, where he'd be filming. To my surprise George wasn't interested in playing Romeo— although the role had been offered to him. "Both lovers are dimwits, but Mercutio! Now there's a contemporary character!"

Douglas joined us on the minuscule balcony, asking if we'd seen Joseph.

"We're hiding him," George said acidly.

Douglas insisted that someone in the other room had seen Joseph go into the john, he was sure with a young lad. "The door's been locked forever!" Douglas declared. "I just want to take a look."

We made a space for him on the balcony, and Douglas perched up as high as he could on the railing, aiming himself toward a tiny frosted window. George and I had to hold his legs as he leaned forward and knocked.

After a minute or so it opened a fraction, and we heard Joseph ask in an irritated tone of voice, "Yeeeesss. What is it?"

"Miss Joseph, are you doing a boy in there?"

"What I'm doing in here is *my* business," Joseph asserted.

"You *are* doing him. You old suckbucket!"

Joseph slammed the window down, but Douglas insisted on knocking more. When the window opened again, Douglas said, "Peace offering! A popper!"

It seemed that the window was rather to one side and almost as difficult to reach from inside the bathroom as from the outside, so Douglas had to lean all the way over to hand it over. And although we were holding him, Douglas began screaming as he lurched against the wall. Finally he tossed the popper through the window as we hauled him back.

"Thank you," we heard from the window, then it was slammed shut again.

"That girl has better suction than a jet engine!" Douglas

declared as he found his feet and went back into the party.

"I've been thinking," George said to me, as though nothing had happened, "about what you told me about doing a motorcycle tour of Europe."

"France, actually."

"Why not all of Europe? We could each get a bike and plan an itinerary. Begin in England, cross the Channel to the Low Countries, into Germany and Denmark, down to Prague—it's supposed to be a really hip scene there—then over to Austria, into Italy, then up to France."

"Too many mountains on that route," I explained. "Mountains are hell on a motorcycle. You have to downshift all the time. And the curves! I spent two hours after every day's ride in a hot bath trying to keep my kidneys and liver from falling out."

"But you said yourself that it could be marvelous."

Indeed, as George spoke, I recalled a night-time motorcycle ride through the French Maritime Alps. It was as difficult a trip as I'd told George it was, hours long, and my innards had been badly jolted. Enough for me to stop the bike on a tiny shoulder of the road several thousand feet up and to step around a giant boulder to urinate. I unzipped and took it out, but when I looked, I saw through a cleft of silhouetted mountains the city of Cannes strung out on the horizon like a string of pearls. Its lights glittered white against the cobalt sky and were joined by distance or distortion to a paler second string of pearls: its reflection in the Mediterranean. A crescent moon hung above the fairyland city and, nearly within its crescent but brighter and whiter than the entire city, shone Venus, the evening star, radiating like a supernova. It was so unexpected a sight, so utterly beautiful, that I just stood there looking, penis out, for the longest time. When I finally realized what I was supposed to be doing, I also realized I wouldn't be able to right off— I'd gotten a hard-on.

Miss Sherry Jackson came out onto the balcony with a pipe filled with grass, and while George and I puffed on it,

Miss Sherry excitedly described some of the antics going on within the apartment. "These kids sure know how to have a gay time!" he said, taking the pipe back and concluded, "Come on in, you'll miss it all."

George and I allowed ourselves to be talked back inside. He encountered his big blond actor and they disappeared arguing into a room. I found myself back at the bar, being introduced by Miss Sherry to a friend of his, a cute, curly-haired, stocky gentleman in his thirties who smiled a lot and said as I put out a hand to shake his, "Hell, that's no way to greet a lover!" He used my outstretched hand to pull me to him and began to French-kiss me. I'd barely gotten out of that clutch when he pushed me onto a nearby divan and got on top of me, where he began to show me exactly how one did greet a "lover."

At some point during this ravishment I heard George's voice asking, "Where's Phil?" and evidently seeing my arms waving about helplessly under the weight and passion of my new friend, he tapped my new friend's shoulder, then, when that brought forth no response, George pushed him away from me long enough to ask if I wanted another drink.

"Yes, please," I said, trying to detach the animal from my body; a difficult task, he seemed to have more gripping power than an octopus. I finally managed to get him off me and was standing up, buttoning myself back up and fending off his further amorous advances, when I heard the sound of glass breaking. A lot of glass: the picture window. Not difficult to locate the cause of its breaking—one edge of the white Steinway, which several drunken people were attempting to launch out the window with great heaves and much laughter.

"Oh, my!" Jemima danced a little pattern in front of us. "Do you think they'll manage to get it out?" He seemed anxious for them to succeed. "I've never actually heard a piano fall twenty floors. Should we help? Or would that be *too much*!"

I looked at George, George looked at me, and we got out of there, fast.

Down on the street, we saw two police cars pull up, sirens whirling, and four cops rushing into the building. High above us, we could see the broken window and a good portion of the white Steinway sticking out.

Needless to say, the party fulfilled its function. The next time I visited Jameson Metcalf, he was living on Sheridan Square.

Will was out for lunch when Boelmann called me into his office. Uh-oh!

Once again he loomed over me while shaking my hand. Once again he motioned me into a chair as though it were electrified.

"You know that Mr. Corbin is retiring at the end of this month," he began.

I hadn't known when exactly, and said so.

"We're interviewing replacements. But so far, Will and I haven't agreed upon anyone. So for the time being, Jerry will be putting together the magazine. I understand the two of you have worked together."

That was hardly true: I'd made one suggestion about one article. Still, I thought it pretty shady policy to let Jerry think he was in charge when he wasn't, and I said so.

"We have no choice," Boelmann said. "Anyway, Jerry's been apprised of the entire situation. Meanwhile I want you to be in his office a great deal."

Spying? No way, I thought.

"Not to oversee his work but to encourage him. To lead him wherever he goes astray."

I didn't get it. I was a news editor, not an art director. Why me?

"You are possibly wondering why I'm assigning you this duty?" Boelmann said. "*Graphique* is supposed to be in the forefront of design. It has fallen behind in that task. Not far behind, but behind. Naturally one—or even two people—

cannot be expected to recognize all of the fast-moving trends in the field. Which is why we have columnists from different areas—film, type, techniques. I don't know whether it is because you were trained in art or whether it's because you lived in Europe or simply because you're young and have a fresh view, but you seem able to recognize the importance of the new."

This statement based on a few articles and a film review. I didn't get it.

"Roberta will not always be with us," Boelmann added darkly. "She says she will return after she is married, but . . ."

Now it was getting clearer. I was to be primed for her job when and if she left—unlikely, I thought—she had a grip like a barnacle.

"And as you know, Will isn't entirely happy working here. He'd rather be at a more literary publication. Of course, I've known that he would leave for some time. We both have. But we needed someone who could work under direction and under pressure to take over before he could leave."

What? Will leaving?

"So probably by the middle of next month he'll be leaving."

What! Will leaving in three weeks?

"Naturally he will have prepared material for several months ahead. But I want you to prepare the May issue yourself. Make out a proposal for the issue and we'll discuss it. And I'd like you and Jerry to prepare a special cover for the April issue. You know, of course, that *Graphique* will be the catalog for the Twenty-fifth Art Directors Awards Show. I'd like the magazine to somehow reflect the importance of that occasion. That's all for now."

Stunned, I returned to my desk.

I wasn't certain what had happened in his office, but I thought I'd just been promoted over Roberta to be editor of the magazine. No. Couldn't be. Yes. It had to be. No way. It *couldn't* be!

Much later that afternoon, when the administrative office seemed empty, I knocked on Budd Singleton's door.

As usual, he was on the phone.

"C'mon in!" he said brightly. Then, before I could begin to prepare to hesitantly ask his opinion of Boelmann and what our conversation could have meant, Budd covered over the receiver and asked, "So, how's it feel to be crown princess?"

Bob was back in town after two weeks of traveling. He'd phoned me three times from various points in the Midwest where he'd been gathering material for a series of articles for his magazine on heart transplants—and, I suspected, sleeping with a variety of men he'd met on previous trips to St. Paul, Denver and Kansas City. I knew that his phone calls were designed to calm me down, to reassure me of his continued interest, and to ensure that I'd be in a more receptive mood when he returned to town than I'd been the day he'd left: i.e., New Year's morning following the party at Jonathan's, where I'd walked out. To that end, Bob phoned once again, now that he was back in New York, and with much sweet talk he insisted that I stop by his apartment "right after work," which Bob quickly amended to "not during the news."

I hid my irritation. "What time exactly, Bob?"

"You know I can't concentrate upon you and Lyndon Johnson at the same time," he tried to explain.

I was so completely antiwar, antigovernment, even anti-media (since I was certain it was all bought and sold by the military-industrial complex) that I couldn't fathom why any rational human being would wish to follow the day-by-day lies and absurdities they aired. Nevertheless, Bob and I had had that argument too many times already, so I simply repeated, "What time, Bob?"

"Seven."

Hardly after work, which was more like five-twenty.

"Seven," I agreed.

In the few hours between, I attempted to be more rational about the entire situation. After all, I *had* missed Bob while he was away. Missed spending nights with him, missed his good humor and the good sex we had together. If he was sometimes didactic and pretentious, much of the time he could be charming and funny. Like all Geminis, he seemed to contain an entire dressing room of characters, and they would pop out of him at the most unexpected moments. After a good bout of lovemaking he might suddenly be a perfect sprite—high-voiced, trilling, tickling me until I fell off the bed, all the while hilariously imitating the people we knew, as well as various others—"Dame Edith Evans receiving an enema," or "Joan Sutherland with a head cold." At other times Bob would suddenly drop his guard and start talking about his youth—how when he'd first gone to college, he used to masturbate to the accompaniment of "The Corsair's Orgy" from Berlioz's *Harold in Italy*; how ashamed he'd been of his family's poverty when he was in high school and how he used to awaken and do farm chores a half hour early so he could rush to school and use the school showers to wash off the smell of farm animals and manure he was certain clung to him anyway. Bob wasn't a perfect person, not even close, despite what he usually thought of himself, but who was? Compared to Djanko, he was comprehensible at all times, his moods easily explicated and—best of all—usually quickly passing.

Thus I was in a pretty good mood when I arrived at Bob's apartment for dinner that night, expecting we'd have a pleasant reconciliation, which after all was one of the best things about having a fight with a lover.

The minute I got in the door, I knew my plans would be shot apart. Bob was on the kitchen phone, sounding serious, and he barely bussed my face with a kiss before he sent me into the living room, suggesting I listen to his new records with the earphones.

"Joanie's in trouble!" was all that Bob would say when he

got off the telephone and came back into the living room. He looked both annoyed and troubled.

"What kind of trouble?" I asked. The last time I'd spoken to her at any length, Joan had been complaining vociferously and in excruciating detail about some witch, a regular customer of the occult bookstore where she worked, who'd decided to put a curse on Joan, and how Joan had thrown the woman out.

Bob hemmed and hawed, uncertain whether to tell me. The phone rang and this time it was Ken on the phone. Bob said Ken better come downstairs, and returned to me and said, "Well, you're one of us now, so I guess you might as well listen and learn. Who knows," he added (typically and unnecessarily, I thought), "you might even be of some use."

The gist of Joan's "situation," as she was calling it, was her ghastly romantic life. For going on three years she'd been sleeping with a man she worked with at this shop, but although he was eager enough for the romance to continue, his wife definitely wasn't. She'd finally confronted Joan and threatened her with arrest and who knew what else. This had all come to a crisis the same day in late November that Ken and I had had dinner with Joan.

Joan and her lover continued to work together in what couldn't have been a very easy relationship, while Joan looked for another job. Not very seriously, according to Bob and Ken, since they'd given her several great leads for work she'd not done anything about. So, while suffering lovelorn at work, Joan had taken up at home with the delivery boy from Spyros's delicatessen. I'd seen this tall, slender, rather ugly young man around the neighborhood, and while I didn't think he was much to look at, and Bob insisted that he barely spoke English—having come from the Dominican Republic only a few months previous—I also thought, well, good for Joan, at least she's getting laid regularly.

Except that Joan had managed to get herself pregnant by the delivery boy, which was bad enough, as she was unmar-

ried and this was, after all, the late sixties, when this was
not as casually treated as today. In the true fashion of a
weak-willed person, Joan had decided to break off the affair
with the boy and have the baby. Until, that is, she found
out from Spyros that her lover was epileptic and came from
a line of epileptics, and in all likelihood her baby would also
probably suffer from grand mal seizures.

The moment she heard that, Joan's willfulness had
dissipated in realistic visions of a future of being an unmarried mother in Manhattan with no job and a chronically sick
infant. She'd phoned her mother about it, and her mother
had preached that abortion was against the word of the
Lord. Joan's mother promised that a hundred and seventy-
five different Christian Science churches all over the South
would hold some sort of telepathic convocation in which
they would seek out the precise word of the Lord on this
particular topic and decide what Joan should do—hopefully
nothing while the Lord sent some near fatal accident to
settle the matter.

What Joan was doing during our powwow in the apartment above hers was burning candles and trying to keep
herself from committing suicide.

Naturally both Ken and Bob thought she should have an
abortion immediately—and never speak to her lunatic mother
again. But Joan was being adamant. She'd do nothing until
after the "convocation."

I saw I could be of no help since everyone's minds were
already made up, and I also saw that the Bob-and-Me
reconciliation would have to wait. I said I'd see him and
Ken later. I was at the front door, about to step out of the
building, when the first-floor apartment door opened and
Joan looked out. With no makeup on she appeared even
more gaunt than usual, even thinner in her loose-fitting
black robe.

"Hi!" I said.

"I thought you were someone else," she said distantly.

I was about to leave when she suddenly said, "Won't you come in for some elderberry wine?"

I really didn't want to, but I thought, poor woman, maybe she just wants company.

Her small apartment seemed even darker and gloomier than before. I sat on the little love seat and she sat on her little imitation Hepplewhite chair and she poured the wine out of a crystal decanter into matching minuscule cut-crystal glasses and we drank in silence.

"I know they were talking about me," she finally uttered with a sigh.

I kept quiet and sipped.

"Everyone seems to know what I should do but me."

I continued sipping the vile liquid.

"Don't you have an opinion?" she asked.

I shrugged.

"You must have an opinion," she insisted.

I told her that since pregnancy was a situation I couldn't possibly get in myself, I'd never thought about it before and so could offer no opinion.

"What would you do," she asked, "if you were me?"

"I just told you, Joanie, I don't know."

"Say anything. Say what comes into your mind," she insisted.

"Okay. I'd change my name and move to California."

"That's not enough!" She flared. "What about . . . ?" She wouldn't say the word *baby*.

"Truthfully?" I asked.

"Truthfully!"

"Joanie, you're anemic. You're a nervous wreck. You don't eat. You drink too much. I have no idea what pills you take. . . . It would be a miracle if you *didn't* miscarry."

She stared at me and I could see overlapping mascara stains under her eyes from days of tears.

"That's not a very positive thing to say!" she said with irritation.

"You asked."

She calmed down. "I did ask. And you're probably right."

We drank a bit more, and she finally saw me to the door where she kissed me on the cheek. "I was right to stop you. But I won't talk to them!" Meaning Bob and Ken. "Make sure they know that."

"Whatever you say."

The multistate Christian Science "convocation" failed to spontaneously abort Joan's baby. She remained in seclusion a few days, then vanished.

A week went by before Bob said to me quite casually one morning, "Do you think you could possibly get out of your lease at 51 Jane?"

"I don't know. Why?"

"Joanie's returned to Alabama to live with her mother."

"She's going to have the baby?"

"Guess so." Bob didn't sound too happy about it. "Of course the place will need to be painted, not to mention cleaned up. But it's only a little more expensive than your rent now. And it is four rooms."

A key point. My studio had begun to drive me crazy with its limitations. Even the East Side apartment I'd lived in had three rooms. Not big rooms, mind you, but rooms one could move to and be in a somewhat different visual environment. From cozy, my studio had quickly grown to being oppressive. No wonder I was out of it as much as possible. At Bob's, or at Ken's, or at Julius's. I really wouldn't mind staying home a few nights and just reading or listening to music. Bob's—and Joan's—kitchens were too small for anything really but cooking in, and the bedroom was the shape of the interior of a box of cornflakes—its greatest dimension was its height—and so only big enough for a bed. But the living room was sizable and it opened to another room, which both Bob and Ken had turned into small studies. And there was a nonworking fireplace. Seeing what they—especially what Ken—had done to the apartments, I could envision Joan's apartment painted white, with its old wooden floors cleaned up, bright and clean.

"Let me think about it."

"Kenny and I would prefer having someone we know in the building," Bob said. "No sense living in the Village if you don't know your neighbors."

"When do you have to know?"

"Better make it fast. I want to keep the landlord from having strangers come look at the place."

"I'll talk to the super at 51," I said.

Neither Bob nor I bothered to mention the obvious: that by moving into 43 Jane, I'd be only a short staircase away from Bob's apartment. What would that actually mean in terms of our personal relationship? And how would others see it?

Bob went on to talk about how three years before, the building's first two floors had been filled with his friends. Sally had lived in the first-floor front right apartment, Tom in the second-floor front left. Bob, Ken and Joan—then a new tenant—in the back-line three floors. It had been a great time for all of them, he said, with a real sense of community.

When Bob and I separated to go to work that morning, I made a decision—if my landlord gave me any trouble, I wouldn't push it. If he didn't, I'd go ahead and move, even though I had butterflies in my stomach about being that close to Bob—and Ken.

That morning, lying in bed and discussing apartments with Bob, I'd not given much thought to the week ahead of me at work and at first I had no hint of any trouble.

Will didn't come in and I thought nothing much about it. Lately he'd been coming in late, or spending most mornings with Boelmann and/or the art director, sometimes not arriving back at his desk till after lunch.

Roberta, however, was back from her three-week Caribbean vacation with her fiancé and she seemed a changed woman. She actually looked pretty with her café-au-lait tan, her sun-streaked hair not drawn back and up in a bun as usual but loose and flowing. Even her clothing seemed less formal and restrictive than before; no more frilly white blouses and corduroy jumpers; she wore flowery patterned skirts and brightly dyed scarves. And her attitude was a lot different: easier, breezier, almost friendly.

Budd Singleton sized up Roberta as she stepped past us going to lunch—early, saying she'd be back a bit later than usual. Budd turned to me and sighed. "Lunch, my superbly contoured ass! If she touches anything to her lips today, it will be C.P.A.'s dick. It's amazing what a steady lay will do for a woman. God knows this woman"—a finger on his own breastbone—"could use a steady lay!"

"Sure, and you'd sashay around the office in mumus and big wooden earrings."

"Now that Klaus is back in Europe, I may, anyway."

I hadn't heard that our publisher had returned to Europe. I felt somewhat panicky. "What about Corbin? What about Will? What about . . . ?"

"Will's gone, of course," Budd said. "You mean you didn't know? I thought Klaus told you."

"He said in a few weeks."

"That *sly* puss, Klaus! Now calm down, honey," Budd expostulated. I was clutching my chest, certain I'd developed instant angina, as well as a burst appendix and a fatal ulcer attack. "Everything'll work out fine," Budd said, not able to hide his amusement at my predicament. "You just let me and Tonia help if you've got any problems. In fact, we've already set up an appointment for you to interview someone for your old job this afternoon."

"This afternoon?"

"Right after lunch. Gotta start sometime."

"This is insane."

"Now out with you!" Budd got up from the desk and began to shoo me out of the office.

"But I can't run this magazine with a dick-crazy assistant editor and an inexperienced art director and an untrained news editor!" I lamented.

"I don't see why not. Will did!"

I stared in shock and sheer terror.

"Out! Out! Out!" Budd said, pushing me out of his office and slamming his door on me.

Naturally I couldn't eat lunch, and naturally I panicked all over again when Boelmann called long distance from Zurich and sounded as though he didn't have a care in the world. He explained that Will had left the magazine a bit earlier, so I'd be thrust into the middle of it. Both Will and Boelmann insisted that hiring someone to replace myself would be a good way to begin my reign at *Graphique*. He seemed so calm about it, almost succeeded in calming myself down to a state of merely mild hysteria with accompanying intermittent nausea.

Before he hung up, however, Boelmann said, "About the April issue of the magazine. Have you given thought to what you're doing for the cover?"

Naturally I lied and said I had.

"Make it very special. Very, *very* special!" Boelmann said before hanging up.

Roberta returned from lunch even later than she'd said she'd be, and just as Budd predicted, she looked freshly fucked. She hummed at her desk, made one quite long phone call—obviously to Thomas, the C.P.A.—and did little else.

I saw some of this because I'd moved to Will's desk to interview the young man who'd come to see about becoming news editor. I was as nervous as he was—and a few years younger, too, but I think he didn't notice. He left several pieces for me to look at overnight, and I gave him a few news releases to condense, which he might leave at Judy's desk the next morning. All stalling techniques, of course.

Budd wasn't in when I went to talk to him about the interview.

Unable to remain calm enough to return to Will's—now *my*!—desk, I went into the art director's studio. There Jerry was working hard on layouts, and it was clear that with

Corbin gone and his need to prove himself, Jerry wouldn't be much company and no help in calming me down. So I merely said that I wanted to look at some covers from past Art Director Show issues of the magazine and he pointed them out without moving from his stool.

I felt terrible. I hated most of the previous efforts, finding them either boring or feeble or overly obvious. Yet I had no idea what to do myself, at least nothing very, *very* special, as Boelmann had ordered.

Not only that, but I was distracting Jerry. I decided to leave the studio and return back to editorial to sulk when I noticed a sort of swatch book on the floor.

"What's all this?"

"Things manufacturers send us. Samples."

"Mind if I look through it?" I asked, a child drawn to shiny objects.

"I was about to throw it out."

I took the load of them back to my own—not Will's—desk and looked through them. And there I found my answer. It was brand-new, from a large, reputable paper manufacturer. Quilted aluminum foil bonded directly onto heavy stock and laminated with a double-strength plastic so it wouldn't scratch or peel. It looked festive. It looked silvery. It looked twenty-fifth anniversary. It looked very, *very* special.

I called the paper company rep and asked how long it had been on the market, and where and how it had been used.

His answer: It was due out this month. They'd just set up the machines to run it out. It had been test-pressed and had come out beautifully.

I asked how it could be imprinted.

He said simple: just like embossing. In any combination of colors of ink I wanted. The inking would go between laminations.

I asked if we could buy the first roll off the press—and in return, if he'd hold off manufacturing any more for at least two weeks. I brought Tonia in to tell him the exact size of the paper run we'd need to print all the covers for all the magazines of that issue. They also confabbed about shipping it to our bindery, which it turned out was located in the same industrial park. I then asked him to send samples to our bindery and had Tonia call there and ask them to try it out, using overrun past copies of the magazine.

While all the phoning back and forth between them was going on, I went into Jerry's studio, dropped the quilted foil sampler on his desk and said, "What do you think? We print our logo on the spine and back in black, and the Art Director's Club Show logo on the front."

He made a few suggestions—the front logo should be centered in a light benday.

I agreed and Jerry promised me a cover sketch the next day—it shouldn't take longer than an hour.

We now had a cover for the April issue.

The following day I hired the young man I'd interviewed to be news editor: his name was Carl Busch and he proved to be reliable, steady, unimaginative, a solid editor, a pretty good writer, and fascinated by various technical aspects of the field; in short, utterly different than I'd been. He also turned out to be the most boring young man on God's green earth.

To accommodate him, I was forced to move my gear to Will's desk. Once there, I settled down and began to work on ideas for the next batch of issues, contacting our regular contributors, arranging two weeks ahead of lunches and drinks meetings with them to talk about how to update the magazine and make it reflect the graphics revolution Boelmann insisted we were undergoing.

If Roberta noticed any changes at all in the office around her, she gave no indication of it for some time.

As I'd promised Bob, I spoke to the superintendent of my building and he'd been more than a little vague about whether or not I could move out. At the least, he assured me, I'd lose my security deposit on the studio, a loss I could afford now that my salary at *Graphique* was higher.

My questions about moving into 43 Jane Street remained as before. The one time I spoke to George about it, he merely told me to get the longest possible lease when I did move. He was distracted by an impending flight to London, with Zeffirelli and his assistant Anne, where they'd be meeting with financial backers of the new *Romeo and Juliet* film, as well as where Franco hoped to audition and pick the rest of the cast.

Ken naturally thought my moving was a great idea, and like the architect he was, he visited and immediately spread out the floor plans he'd drawn up for his own, nearly identical, apartment when he'd worked on it. He began to make suggestions for how I would redo the place, which came to several thousand dollars more than I had, or had any intention of spending. When I attempted to explain my anxieties, Ken quashed any possible nonfinancial considerations with the single word *ridiculous*.

What really decided me to move was what occurred one misty evening as I lay on my daybed. I'd just been listening to Hindemith's symphony, Mathis Der Maler. This intensely realized piece of music had been one of my favorites since I'd lived on the East Side. At first I'd gone to it merely for its colorful orchestration and soaring climaxes. By repeated listenings, I'd also come to learn a great deal about the mechanics of musical harmony: the movement at differing speeds of blocks of chords through masses of melody, at which Hindemith was a master manipulator. But there was another element to it; like several other of my prized recordings—Landowska's Goldberg Variations, Gagaku Music of Heian Japan, *Duets from India,* certain Mozart adagios and the largo of Beethoven's late A minor String Quartet—it also broke the barrier of music into what could only be called spirituality. I could always depend on it to take me away from myself and my problems into a realm of timelessness.

So there I was, the music stopped and I was lying flat on my back, wondering whether I should get up and put some other music on the turntable or just stay there and read, when something very curious happened.

Suddenly I was no longer looking up at my studio ceiling. I was somehow on the ceiling, looking down at myself. I blinked my eyes, but I was definitely still up, looking down, seeing myself lying on the daybed looking up at myself. Between my selves, I could barely make out an undulant, glittering line or rather thin tubing as though from navel to navel. Even though I'd used LSD twice and mescaline more than twice, I'd never had such a totally disorienting sensation. And I was cold sober; hadn't had a drink or joint in several days. Even odder, I could sense that my stocking feet against the ceiling were being drawn to the window, open from the top, my entire body being tugged, sliding along the ceiling. If I didn't stop myself, I would slip out of the window entirely.

I remember thinking, *God! Wouldn't that be great! Light as I am, I could probably fly!*

And the next second thinking, *Fly? Hell! I'll fall four stories down to the street!*

I shut my eyes tight, and when I opened them, I was back on the daybed looking up. I leapt to my feet and felt my body to make sure all of it was there. Then I busied myself with little chores and tasks around the apartment. But I couldn't get rid of the sensation until I went outside for a long, tiring walk around the Village, and even so it lingered.

By the next day I'd forgotten about the experience. But in some way, I sensed that its occurrence meant that I felt trapped and needed to escape. Taking that in its literal sense, as soon as I saw the super of 51 Jane again, I told him I had to move and that I was prepared to lose a month's rent in advance. He thought the landlord would agree to that. I phoned Bob Herron and told him I'd move into his building. I didn't know I would remain at 43 Jane Street for the next ten years, long after my life had utterly changed.

* * *

"Now, Phil," Bob began, "you've promised that you won't talk about the war in Vietnam and you won't say a word about drugs and you won't go on about the U.S. government or anything else you think you know so much about but don't really."

That last because I'd told Bob earlier that I'd bumped into a former high-school classmate, Mario Savio, and promised to join him and the rest of the gang in the SDS in demonstrations that coming August at the Democratic National Convention in Chicago. What I hadn't mentioned was that I'd known Mario in high school when he'd been a Young Republican and had worn a suit and tie and carried an attaché case and called himself Bob because his given name was "too ethnic."

"Don't worry," I told Bob, "I'll pretend I'm a deaf-mute."

"Now, see, Phil! That's exactly the attitude I'm talking about."

"C'mon, Bob," Ken warned, "lay off." He was getting as irritated as I was with Bob's lecturing me.

"If he's got to come along at all, he's got to act like a civilized human being."

"Orlan *has* gone to a lot of trouble to arrange this gathering," Ken admitted.

The gathering was the prophesied—from my point of view, foredoomed—meeting with the great poet W. H. Auden, who was a friend of Orlan's. We were to meet with him for no more than two hours at Orlan's apartment, at which time Orlan would whisk the bard off to dinner, *à deux,* and we'd be left to our own devices, doubtless stunned into contemplative silence by the experience. I considered Auden—like every other figure of authority or importance in the world at that time—a fraud and of no importance. I had no interest in putting on a jacket and tie and sitting amidst adorers hanging on his every word.

"I promise," I said, just to make peace.

Bob was reknotting his tie in the mirror. "I just know this will end in disaster," he commented.

Finally he was ready, and the three of us got into a taxi and sped up to Orlan's Chelsea apartment.

My first surprise was that other people were present: Kenneth Libo, whom I'd met walking along a Village street the week before with my friend Joseph Mathewson; and James Wilhelm, a pale, thin, high-voiced but altogether nice and very intelligent man who'd taught the Dante and His Times seminar I'd aced in my last term at Queens College. I never discovered how they knew Orlan.

What was obvious was that they were all quietly excited about meeting Auden. Jim Wilhelm, my former professor, could barely keep his eyes on me as he talked about his current project, a translation of Catullus, which he said would be "a bit shocking, as I plan to translate every word and connotation."

I was pumping him on exactly what those connotations could be—were they homosexual? I thought perhaps they were—when I noticed everyone standing up. I turned and vaguely, and only partly, given the bad angle I was at, saw someone come into the apartment, give his coat to Orlan, then repair to the kitchen. Auden had arrived.

I was still pumping Jim about Catullus when Orlan and Auden came into the room, our host carrying what looked like a lemonade pitcher, which he placed on the table at the far end of the long living room. Auden sat down there, waved a general benediction in our direction and proceeded to pour and drink three good-sized glasses of the stuff.

"Carry on," Orlan said to us in a stage whisper. "As soon as Wystan has had his three martinis, he'll join us."

During this interim, people tried to pick up their previous conversation, but it couldn't help but be strained.

I was shut-mouth silent. The great poet W. H. Auden, who sat not ten feet away sipping martinis, turned out to be the same dizzy British auntie who had almost killed George and me with a flowerpot on St. Mark's Place.

After some time Auden wiped his mouth on a handkerchief, then turned toward the room.

"That's better! Orlan, you'll introduce your friends?"

One by one we stood up and were brought over to meet him. I held back as long as possible, uncertain what to do or say. When we were introduced, he gave no inkling at all that he recalled our encounter. Fine with me.

About a hour had gone by, during which Auden had moved to an armchair in the center of the room and had imbibed another martini or two and was speaking—a bit pompously, I thought—about something or other while everyone listened in rapt attention, when he suddenly stopped, propped himself up and stared at me closer.

I thought, *He remembers me.*

But as he went on speaking as before, I guessed he didn't want our previous meeting mentioned.

About ten or fifteen minutes passed; Auden excused himself from the room.

Amidst all the chatter, Orlan came over to me, puzzlement all over his face, and said. "Would you mind coming with me a minute?"

Auden was in the kitchen, seated at a table. He motioned me to come closer. When I was inches away from his huge, square, folded and wrinkle-enfolded face, he said, "Why you *naughty* young man! I *know* you!"

"You certainly do!" I said, bold as brass. "And I know you too!"

I could hear Orlan groan behind me.

"You and I spent a *love*ly after*noon* together. With . . . that *love*ly faunlike young man."

"My friend, George."

"How *is* young George?"

"He's going to London to make a film with Franco Zeffirelli."

"And you weren't going to *breathe* a *syll*able. *Were* you?" Auden asked.

"Not a diphthong!"

"You're *very* naughty. Why not?"

"I thought you'd forgotten."

"How could I *pos*sibly for*get*?"

"I'm sure you've got plenty on your mind."

"Why, that *same* evening I told Vera and Igor *all* about you! They wanted to *know* why I hadn't *brought* you two a*long* for *din*ner. You *should* come *next* time," Auden insisted.

"Stravinsky?" I asked.

"They're *lovely* people. She more than he, lately. Poor health has drawn him *back* into the capacious fold of *Mother* Russia in the form of the Orthodox Church. *Quite* dis*turb*ing, in *my* opinion," Auden declared. "Or*lan*! This is the young man. Or *one* of them, I told you *all* about." Auden stroked my hair. "How *beast*ly. clever of you to *find* him for me a*gain*."

He dismissed Orlan and insisted I sit by him. "What *was* that *clev*er riposte of young George? Ah, yes. Someone had *told* him he was *most ed*ible. And he replied, 'Fifty *bucks* before you *put* the *bite* on me!' "

We talked and laughed for another ten minutes until Orlan made an appearance and Auden realized he had to return to his other guests.

"Now that I've *found* you a*gain*, you *shan't* escape *quite* so easily," he told me fondly.

We all left Orlan's apartment together. Orlan and Auden got into a cab headed uptown. Bob, Jim, the two Kens and I wandered through Chelsea until we found a restaurant Ken Libo knew.

Throughout dinner, I was a Sphinx about what had happened in the kitchen. Torture wouldn't have made me breathe a word about it to Bob or Ken, not that night or later.

Auden did get my phone number and did call me and we met several times in the next year, usually at his St. Mark's Place digs, before he made what turned out to be a fatal decision to leave New York and move back to England. He was always sweet and open and a little dizzy with me: not the great poet and scholar he'd been with strangers at Orlan's place but the British Auntie he'd been the first time we'd met. We never spoke about poetry or literature except in the most glancing manner; in fact, we talked of nothing but silly, superficial matters and we thoroughly entertained each other. I suppose because of Orlan's interest in the leather scene, Auden was fascinated by it. He sent me to Keller's and the Eagle's Nest and listened to my reports and we fantasized dressing him in full harness and chaps and entering him into the Mr. Leather contest.

In a more serious mood, he once told me, "I was wrong, you know. I wrote that poetry doesn't mean anything in the real world. But I found out that wasn't true."

He went on to tell me of a trip he'd taken in an American Air Force plane near the end of World War Two. He'd been asked by the U.S. government to be involved in something or other he never adequately explained to me. As he told it, he was the only civilian passenger in a plane designed for parachutists. It had been a bumpy and stormy nighttime ocean crossing, and as they approached the coast of Ireland, two German planes appeared and began harassing the U.S. plane. The American pilots didn't want to endanger Auden, and opened up a radio channel to the German planes. But they didn't speak German, and the Germans didn't speak English.

"Mother was com*plete*ly terrified of dying in the *o*cean," Auden told me. "And I could *hear* them all speaking, as there was no wall between the cockpit and what there was of a cabin. We were *doomed*. Mother *flung* herself toward them, *grabbed* the radio phone and *shouted*, 'Ich bin Auden. Der Dichter!' telling them in German, you see, that I was Auden. The poet. *Odd* that in that panic, Mother count*ed* on that to save her skin. But it worked. The Germans have *such* respect for poets! We talked another minute, and they let us go. Mother *threw* herself back onto the tarpaulin and promised she'd do *some*thing to pay back those sweet boy pilots."

Which he did, he said, when he translated Goethe's *Italian Journey* several years later.

In the few years he was away, we exchanged only one letter. His bemoaned the irony of having lived in high-crime Manhattan for decades in perfect safety, whereas within one week back at Oxford his apartment had been burgled.

Some months after Auden died, a great literary establishment commemoration was held at Riverside Church. I guess because I was in his address book, I received an invitation, but by then I was working on the night shift at a fancy bookstore. As I waited after midnight for the E train, I found that I missed Wystan terribly. Using the inside blank page of the paperback I was reading, I sketched out:

> No solemn music
> in uptown cathedrals
> suffices . . .

After a lot of writing and re-writing of the rest of the poem, those words would stand as written, opening the third part of my elegy for Auden.

I always wondered what he would say if he'd lived long enough to see me end up becoming a writer. I'm not sure he'd be too pleased. He never thought it was a reputable vocation.

At the end of March 1968, I moved a studio's worth of furniture into a (small) four-room apartment down Jane Street. The apartment had been (ho-humly) cleaned and vacuumed and (poorly) painted an off-white, thus revealing all sorts of architectural features such as ten-times-overpainted original moldings. My bed went into the tiny bedroom. My daybed and *faux-bois* table into the little study. My stereo system and bookshelves and my bentwood rocker left plenty of space in the largest room. The floors turned out to be in nastier condition than I'd expected, and I found an inexpensive carpet to cover at least the living room. A painted-over antique gateleg table and three somewhat matching chairs helped fill the space in a style appropriate to the era of the place, i.e., turn of the century.

Other furnishings came my way in a more roundabout way. Since my return from Europe, I'd partied on the fringes of the Warhol Factory crowd, mostly as a result of propinquity: they seemed to be at Max's Kansas City or the Electric Circus and a few even came into Julius's, although they stood out among its preppier denizens. And Paul Morrissey was as central a figure in the Factory as one got in those days. Since Paul had worked in a neighboring unit in the same large room with me at the Department of Welfare before I'd gone to Europe, spending most of his time there either on the phone or looking through reels of film, we'd struck up a distant acquaintance, which was equally coolly picked up at this time.

I suddenly began meeting my brothers at various trendy parties, places and functions where the Factory crowd gathered. Both Bob, older than me by three years, and Jerry, younger by four years, arrived with their own friends or groups, although we all eventually mixed and overlapped, and especially within the Brownian motion of the larger shindigs, we ended up sharing and exchanging friends and acquaintances.

It was Jerry, still living at home, who told me my mother was getting rid of her older "den" furniture and who managed to find a truck and gather together several of his more reliable methedrine-head buddies to move the huge old sofa and armchair into my apartment. In turn, I opened up my apartment to Jerry for whenever he happened to be in Manhattan and needed a place to crash, and to a few of his friends that I'd come to like—Boy Ondine, Lou Reed, Nico— for them to drop in, hit up in the john, then come chat with me over a cup of tea.

They—and especially Ondine—would bring by all sorts of things in their large leather shoulder bags: a wall hanging, a set of pirated Callas records (Ondine adored Callas and all conversation would stop when she sang Lady Macbeth's sleepwalking *scena*), or merely some object they'd passed in a store window and bought on impulse. In this way, within a few months, my apartment gathered furniture and achieved a casual if au courant decor. As I retained the apartment for years while around me people moved every few months from apartment to loft to apartment, from uptown to downtown to midtown, from Manhattan to San Francisco to Los Angeles and back to New York, they left things with me for keeping. Once I had three complete dining-room sets—all in conflicting styles—and once five pairs of ice skates. At times I didn't even know they'd left something behind. In the summer of 1975, John Cale knocked on my door and asked if I still had my sofa. He came in, rummaged inside a rip in the upholstery I didn't even know existed near the left armrest and pulled out the lyrics and music for three then-new *Velvet Underground* songs he'd stuffed inside during a bout of paranoia years before.

Meanwhile I was settling down into being editor at *Graphique* with more or less good grace. Boelmann, luckily, was still in Europe dealing with the other parts of his small publishing empire, so I didn't feel too much pressure. My article on *Harper's Baazar* appeared in the February issue to many compliments from the magazine world, including a thank-you note and second invitation to lunch with La Vreeland. My equally in-depth article on videotape came out in the March issue and it proved to be even more widely read and discussed in advertising and film offices. So, more by chance (and my superior's insistence) than plan, I'd developed the sort of instant credit among regular readers of *Graphique,* which softened the blow of Will's sudden leaving and my ascension. The regular contributors to the magazine eagerly met with me, and as eagerly discussed future plans. Several had particular obsessions or pet peeves which Will had perhaps wisely held in check during his stewardship, but which in my ignorance and desire to please I gave them free rein to write about, and, so mollified, they supported me: Their columns continued to arrive on my desk.

Carl's work as news editor improved so rapidly, I soon found myself looking for topics to have him write about at more length. As long as they were technical, he was on sure ground. Roberta continued to do her work without having to make any sort of alteration at all. I got the sense that she'd more or less tolerated Will and would more or less tolerate me, without giving it much thought, as long as I didn't poach on her territory. I had no intention of doing so: Roberta produced reams of copy totally apt for the magazine without appearing to expend much thought or effort. Because we'd always been standoffish with each other before my promotion, we didn't have to in any way adjust our working relationship now that I was her boss. If anything, she was now a bit friendlier and more open with me. But withal she was utterly placid.

The day my silver cover for the Art Director's Show issue arrived turned out to be both a high point and a low one for me.

The cover was gorgeous. Remarkable. Unquestionably it would be talked about and influence the industry. The arrival of the sample—printed and folded as it would appear but not bound in yet—caused a sensation in the office that morning. Jerry and I toasted our cleverness and innovativeness at lunch with two martinis apiece.

From that high, I returned to the office to find Tonia, our production manager, poring over some invoices while deep in consultation with someone on the telephone. She signaled to me that we had to speak as soon as she was done with her call.

Five minutes later she came into my office, sat down, ashen-faced, and said, "Disaster!"

"They can't bind the cover in time for the show?" I asked, my worst fear.

"They'll have it well in time for the show."

I relaxed.

"This is how much your quilted silver foil cover is going to cost."

She thrust the invoice at me, and as I looked it over, she went on. "It's *twice* the price of our regular cover. Boelmann's going to hit the roof when he finds out."

"Twice the price? But I thought—"

"*Twice* the price," she repeated grimly. "Evidently it requires a special binding machine and can only be sent through fifty copies at a time instead of the usual hundred at a time. Meaning more manpower and more man-hours, meaning a higher price for binding."

"We can raise the newsstand price," I said. The price had not been printed on the cover, and I thought we could get away with a twenty-five-cent, even a fifty-cent, price increase for this one special issue. "They'll pay."

"True, but sixty-five percent of our sales are through subscription. We can't change the price there."

"Figure out how much higher we'll have to go on the newsstand price to compensate."

"I already have. Fifty cents per issue. And we have to sell out."

"We don't usually?"

"The special issue always does best of the twelve. It usually sells about seventy-five percent of what we put out on the newsstands. Given this issue does as well, we'll drop this much in income."

It wasn't much. But it was still too much.

"And if we sell out?"

"It'll just skim by," she said. "But it won't sell out."

"Yes it will," I declared. "In fact, I want you to contact both the paper manufacturer and binder and work out figures for reprinting more copies. A twenty-percent overrun."

Tonia looked at me as though I were out of my mind.

"Do it!" I commanded.

"Boelmann will be here for the awards ceremonies. He'll see the invoice. He'll—"

"Don't give him the invoice unless he asks for it. Meanwhile get prices on those reprints. And work up profit figures on a ten-percent and twenty-percent newsstand increase in sales. Oh, and tell Budd Singleton to make some phone calls to our biggest distributors and dealers. Have him send them the sample covers and ensure prime display spots for the issue and bigger orders than usual. Ron is where? California? Have him get some samples too. That should generate sales."

Tonia stared at me.

"What are you waiting for?" I asked.

"I'm waiting for sanity to descend."

"Get out of here," I said.

The minute Tonia left, not sanity but blackness descended. While she'd been there I'd held back all of my doubts. I knew that as perpetrator of the error I had to keep the most positive outlook on it, so that would become the attitude around the office. Now that I was alone again, my decision haunted me. I suspected that reality would intrude and that my silver-foil issue would be the last issue I'd publish for *Graphique*—or any other magazine.

I was banging my head quietly on the desk when the phone rang. Hesitantly I picked it up.

"You *clever* thing!" It was Budd Singleton. "I'll push this issue as though it were '*Life* Goes to the Movies.' "

"Make sure Ron works his butt off too," I said.

"Don't worry. I'll tell Ron you'll give him a big bonus. Say, a fifth of Four Roses and all the head he can stand?"

"You say a word and I'll murder you and burn your tutu!"

Bob's play, *Arrangement for Children,* was finally being premiered at the Eugene O'Neill in Connecticut, and I was invited. In fact, I was given two tickets and so I invited George, who'd just returned from London.

Bob had been up in Connecticut several days readying the production. I'd been in the city, working, watering his plants and feeding his cat Ceila—a recent acquisition named after the single female character in his play. In all fairness to him, Bob had had his hands full of late, what with Joan's crisis

and his job and his play. Even so, I felt that our reconciliation had been virtually nonexistent, that he'd not taken
nearly enough time to be with me and that he'd done
absolutely nothing to change my belief that whenever he
traveled, he whored around. He'd still not satisfactorily
explained away that young man I'd seen coming out of his
apartment. I was looking for a fight.

Ken was aware of my pique, and while he went out of his
way to keep me occupied while Bob was away—dinner at
the One Potato, drinks at Julius's, even a visit to Orlan
Foxx—Ken told me that he'd known Bob for more than a
decade (since college) and he'd never known Herron to be in
any way monogamous, never mind faithful. In fact, even
counting a woman some years ago, my relationship with
Bob—only five months in duration so far—was the longest
Ken had seen in Bob's life. All their mutual friends—Sally,
Tom—although they agreed that I was a terrific person,
were also astonished it had lasted this long. Ken advised me
to let Bob have more "room," not to let Bob think he was
under pressure.

Somewhere during this talk I wondered if Ken had been
sent as an emissary. I never did discover if Ken had seen the
unraveling of our affair and had decided to step in himself, or
whether he was acting on a more objective basis—sort of
amicus curiae. Both, I suspect.

In vain did I attempt to explain that I'd had little interest
in a relationship with Bob—or with anyone else. Without
giving names or details, I referred to a "difficult" love affair
in Europe that had left me scarred and untrusting. I showed
Ken how everything that had happened so far between Bob
and myself had been Bob's doing. He was the one who'd
come on to me like gangbusters in that movie theater. He
was the one who'd insisted on me sleeping over every night.
He'd set the times and places and terms of our every
meeting—and their frequency. I'd been a passive bystander,
pleased by his attentions, sure, and happy to meet his friends.
I was willing to admit that for me it had been an easy and

convenient affair while it lasted, but if Bob wanted out, that was okay with me.

I said more. I told Ken that if I was interested in any man, it was that dreamboat Luke Harms I'd met at Jonathan and Oliver's party. After all, since it seemed I was going to be gay, I might as well have a lover who was drop-dead handsome and sweet-tempered like Luke. I went on at some length about Luke, more than was absolutely necessary, partly to keep Ken's own possible fantasies about me dampened, and also so he'd have something to report back to Bob. But as I talked about Luke I began to convince myself that I really ought to do something about seeing him again. I'd already pretty much concluded that my hundred-dollar New Year's limousine trick had happened not because I was angry with Bob that evening and seeking revenge, but because I'd been excited by meeting Luke. The man in the limo had been a stand-in for him. I decided to phone Luke at home in Brooklyn Heights and ask him out for dinner that very weekend.

I guess Ken did report back to Bob, which would explain an elaborate phone call explanation from the theater of why Bob had to be away so long and how much he missed me. What he didn't say was more important. The play was premiering on a Saturday night and would have a matinee and evening performance on Sunday, then run for the next three or four weekends. Bob planned to remain up in Connecticut all that weekend. But he didn't invite me to sleep over, and more importantly, he didn't make any excuses about it. It was clear he was keeping his sexual preferences from the Foundation.

Bob's phone call came at work late on a Friday afternoon. Even before I'd hung up from speaking to Bob, I'd made a decision. I dialed Luke, and although I was as nervous as any young man asking a young woman out on a date, I relaxed the minute he recognized my voice. He'd told me he was a free-lance copy editor and worked at home, and when I said I hoped I wasn't interrupting, Luke graciously said

he'd just been thinking of taking a break. Dinner turned out
to be impossible over the weekend. He was busy Friday
night, I Saturday night. We made the date for lunch, Sunday afternoon, and Luke asked if I minded coming out to
Brooklyn Heights. I didn't say it, but I would have gone
anywhere to meet him for lunch. Even Queens.

Meanwhile I still had to get through Bob's premiere and
seeing Bob again. That was why I called George, and although I didn't tell him exactly why I wanted company, I let
him know I'd really appreciate it.

George arrived at my apartment around five o'clock that
evening, dressed as though he were auditioning for the part
of Alan A-Dell in some remake of *Robin Hood*. Baby-skin
soft tan leather pants, a pale violet silk *blouson* casually
closed at his sternum by a wide black velvet cravat, a suede
Deerslayer jacket cut like a sports coat but with generous
fringe, cream-colored cowboy boots with chocolate trim and
silver tips. He'd allowed his already long, straight butterscotch-
colored hair to grow. George looked both extremely hip and
extraordinarily fashionable. He'd also never looked so handsome, and I told him so.

After a few tokes of grass we went through my meager
wardrobe until George had managed to dress me so as to be
a not too unflattering companion. Given how little was
there and how boring it was, he did wonders.

"I thought we'd catch the six-ten train up from Grand
Central," I said. "A jitney from the theater meets most
trains."

"Where are we going?" he asked again. I'd told him a
half dozen times before and now reiterated it.

"That's near Stratford, isn't it? The Shakespeare theater
up there?"

"The next town, I believe. Why?"

George was dialing my phone and he ignored me.

"Dahhllllingggg!" he intoned in the oddest accent I'd
heard out of him yet: a parody of a slightly tipsy Kentish
woman of a certain age. "Il Principe and La Contessa re-

quire a Berline and eight large Arabs to whisk us off to
some plague-stricken drama house in the depths of Nueva
England. What can you offer for our amusement?"

His face lit up with amusement at the answer; I realized
that I was being treated to George's Countess persona.

"I couldn't possibly offer Il Principe that! No, no, impossible! The offense would be too grave. Not to mention the
difficulty of placing it inside his . . ."

Five minutes of such conversation put George in a very
good mood, not to mention into an attitude as stylish as his
apparel. He hung up the phone, lit the pipe and said, "We
go, then!"

"Should we grab a cab?"

"Leave it all in my ultra-capable hands."

We walked to the corner, crossed Eighth Avenue, and
there facing us and waving at the traffic was a bizarre
sight—a heavyset baldish man in full British Banker regalia,
complete with rolled umbrella and homburg, attaché case at
his side and a type of leather suitcase he later referred to as
a Palmerston.

"Dahhlllllingggg!" he greeted George, seeing us approach.
"Trip me a Checker, will you?" in what I took at first to be
a stage-British accent.

George bowed deeply and went to do his bidding.

I stood there looking at the apparition.

"You must be the 'little charmer'!" he said, and I realized
that his accent was real.

A cab screeched to a halt at the sidewalk. The driver was
an ordinary-looking fellow who stepped out and opened the
trunk for our companion's baggage. George opened the
back door. Our portly friend waved George in. I followed
and he joined us.

"Phil, this is my friend George Rose," George introduced
us. "We were in *Royal Hunt* together."

"Charmed, I'm sewer!" Rose said, kissing a spot in the
air between us. "I note, Signor Atahualpa, that you are
looking, shall we say, *completely* edible this evening."

"Too many thanks." George made a kissing gesture with his fingers I'd seen only in productions of Shakespeare.

"Where to?" the cabbie asked.

"Just drive on a while, my good man," Rose said. He was hunting in his attaché for something and finally pulled out a bottle of champagne and three fluted glasses.

"To *la vie* and all her whorish sisters!" he toasted.

"*La vie!*" George and I seconded, and drank.

"Perhaps our Charon would like to imbibe some bubbly?" Rose leaned forward and offered some through the cab's internal window.

"Where we going?" the driver, not unreasonably, asked again.

"You're certain you won't have any?" Rose insisted.

"Not while I'm driving, mister. Where to?"

"Stratford, Connecticut," Rose said. "And step on it!"

"You're kidding, right?"

"Not at all," Rose said. "Would you like to see my folding money?" he asked, as though it were the most obscene object in the Continental U.S.

"I don't have to go out of the city, you know," the cabbie said.

"My good man, if you wish, we'll not only pay you well, we'll also buy you dinner in Stratford and take this cab back home."

"You guys actors?"

"Alas!" Rose sighed.

"Okay. A hundred dollars. All night," the driver said, then when we began to giggle, "I mean, there and back. Dinner'll be extra."

"You are a virtual paragon of sense—not to mention sensibility," Rose declared. "And think of it, someday you'll be able to tell your grandchildren about this journey."

The cabbie spun left, heading for the West Side Highway, and we settled back comfortably in the roomy backseat.

"You may take a seat, Mr. Worthy," Rose said across me to George in a voice redolent of antimacassars and winter gardens. "I feel bound to tell you that you are *not* down on my list of eligible young men, although I have the *same* list the dear Duchess of Bolton has. We work together in fact. However I am *quite* ready to enter your name, should your answers be what a really affectionate mother requires." Rose paused, pretense pencil poised in stubby fingers. "Do you smoke?"

George answered, "Well yes, I must admit, I smoke."

"I am glad to hear it." Rose sighed with relief. "A man should always have an occupation of *some* kind. There are *far* too many idle men in London as it is. How old are you?"

And on they went from memory, to my surprise and delight, until they'd completed the scene, and I was laughing so hard, George had to hold me back.

Then they switched places, George becoming an amazingly imperious Lady Bracknell and Rose becoming Jack Worthing for the third-act encounter and verbal duel between the two.

By this time we were passing Yonkers, and we'd finished the champagne and the two Georges ("As in Thackeray," George Rose explained. "If you wish, you may be George Third, my mentally deficient grandson, the one"—he paused significantly—"who lost the Colonies.") decided to pull off the highway and locate a liquor store for more champagne, which we did.

Their whistles rewhetted, they sailed unabashed into Beatrice and Benedict's sparring scenes from *Much Ado*, switching parts at whim, and those proved so much fun, they sidled into a dialogue from *Waiting for Godot*, which they completed just as the second bottle of champagne was finished and the cabbie pulled up to the Eugene O'Neill Theater. There George ("the Second") and I disembarked with much bowing and curtsying to George Rose ("the First").

After that hour-long barrage of brilliant acting of brilliant lines and in such intimate quarters, Bob Herron's play couldn't help but be a letdown. Even so, everyone else liked it, and it was clearly a hit.

As the evening wore on, it also became quite annoyingly clear that Bob Herron was not only *not* going to acknowledge me to his new theater friends as someone special in his life, he was going to treat me as though I were a distant, and not very well-known, acquaintance. The first hint of this came during the intermission when I went up to speak to Bob while he was chatting with a distinguished-looking man and woman I didn't know but who might well be anyone. Bob saw me coming and signaled me with his hand to pass on by.

I stood there in disbelief. Once again he waved me aside and went on talking to the couple. I stalked away, furious.

I couldn't help but tell George, who attempted to explain it by saying that perhaps the couple were Broadway producers—although he didn't recognize either of them. I should stay calm and await an explanation.

All the Jane Street Girls, as well as Bob's other friends whom I'd only met once or twice—Sally, Tom, Orlan Foxx—had come up for the premiere and all were at the cast party held afterward at a local restaurant. A half hour after we'd all gathered, Bob arrived with the director, cast and crew of the show and I thought, *Now he'll come up to me and apologize for his earlier rudeness.*

He didn't. He remained surrounded by people from the show, receiving his old friends as though he'd won the Nobel Prize for Literature. I was embarrassed and disgusted with his behavior and kept my distance. The one time Bob even acknowledged me occurred when he passed the buffet table where I was fixing myself a salad plate. Bob stopped briefly to ask me how Ceila was eating and if she'd developed hair balls. "Phil's taking care of my cat," Bob explained to the female lead in the show as he swept her away from the buffet. "He's such a good neighbor!"

If Bob ignored—and infuriated—me, George immediately saw what was going on between me and Herron and scarcely left my side. George—and his outfit—made a considerable stir during intermission and at the cast party. Theater people who were present recognized him from the TV soap and from *Royal Hunt* and a few had heard rumors about Zeffirelli's project and George's role in it and went up to ask him if he were looking at Bob's play as a new "vehicle." I also heard someone ask Bob the same question: which naturally irritated Bob and which naturally pleased me. Besides, I realized that merely through George's body language, which he made sure at all times included me, that people we were first meeting assumed that George and I were together. I felt wanted for the first time that night.

Evidently, despite his bout of extreme egotism, Bob also read George's body language, and it, along with his own bad behavior toward me, must have finally come to haunt him, because while the party seemed to go on for a long time, the minute the room appeared to be thinning out, Bob got up the nerve to come over to talk to me.

Seeing Bob on his way toward me, I told George, "Let's get out of here." We began heading in the opposite direction.

I heard Bob call my name, a hint of something—perhaps panic—in his voice, and I half turned to see him rushing forward to keep us from leaving.

I moved even faster—directly into the bulk and encompassing arms and winy breath of George Rose, who clasped me and loudly sputtered, "Apprised, sir, of my daughter's sudden flight by her trusty maid, whose confidence I purchased by means of a small coin, I followed her at once by a *luggage* train!"

"And *found* her!" I asserted in the same theatrical vein.

Rose hugged me, drew George the Second into his capacious embrace and announced to the company as well to Bob Herron, who'd stopped on a dime some feet away, "Our coach and trusty driver awaits. Adieu, good people. Adieu!"

I could see Bob's bewildered face among several other more amused ones as George Rose wafted us out of the restaurant and into the Checker's backseat, where fresh champagne was uncorked and where they made me laugh all the way back to Manhattan.

*   *   *

The April awards issue of *Graphique* arrived three days before the Art Director's Awards ceremonies, and once again spirits rose in the office. Using cover dummies of the magazine, Budd Singleton and Ron Mallory had managed to get far larger newsstand orders than I'd expected, although to keep it as much a surprise as possible, the issue wouldn't be shipped until the morning after the show itself.

By noon of the day of the awards, Boelmann still hadn't arrived from Zurich and I kept hoping the publisher would arrive too late for anything but the ceremonies. I was counting on such a terrific response to my cover from everyone at the show that Boelmann would feel the higher price was worthwhile. In truth, there was no realistic or logical reason to believe this would happen. If I knew anything about Boelmann in the short time I'd worked for him, it was that like all successful businessmen, he thought art and innovation were all fine enough, so long as they aided, and didn't contradict, his profit. But what could I do? I was desperate.

When I returned back to the office from the very late lunch I'd taken, I could see from a single glance at Tonia and a second glance at the ajar door of the publisher's office that Boelmann's plane had not gone down over the Atlantic, as I'd prayed it would all morning. Tonia was tight-lipped as she told me that he was in a meeting with Budd Singleton. He'd taken *all* of the latest invoices with him.

I spent the next hour or so thinking that Budd would manage to charm or somehow distract Boelmann—anything to keep him from seeing that invoice. And for a while it seemed to be so. True, every time the phone rang on my desk, I jumped half a yard and wouldn't answer until I'd once again unsuccessfully steeled myself to be called into Boelmann's office. Finally it was five o'clock.

Unconscious of what was going on, Roberta and Carl left for the day, promising to see me again at eight at the Palm Court at the Plaza Hotel, where the ceremonies were being held.

I waited another fifteen minutes, then began to head for the door, planning to sneak out. Unfortunately the publisher's office door was now wide open, and to get out I would have to pass directly in sight of Boelmann himself in clear view at his desk, looking over papers and scowling. I still might escape if I were very, very quiet.

"There you are!" Boelmann called out. I'd been spotted.

I decided to brass it out. "You made it! How was the trip!"

"Not bad once the fog lifted at Orly," he said. He gestured me closer, saying, "Come in. I don't want to have to shout."

In a childhood street game called May I? you ask the person who's "it" if you may advance toward them to tag them, with very specific requests: "May I take two scissor steps?" Or "May I take three elephant steps?" Or "May I take ten baby steps?" Without asking may I, I was taking the tiniest baby steps I'd ever taken in my life, all the while trying to check over his desk for the telltale invoice.

"Sit down!" Boelmann said. "I've been talking with Budd. He tells me the April issue has received the largest newsstand orders of any issue we've ever done. And he showed me why that was." Boelmann held up a copy of the offending periodical. "Quite nice. I asked for something quite special and that's what you gave me."

I couldn't for the life of me figure out whether he was pleased or irate. My smile was frozen on my face.

"Yes, quite special," Boelmann went on. "I'm certain it will make a big stir among all the art directors. And that you will make a name for yourself because of it."

"It was Jerry who art-directed it and who—"

"No!" he interrupted. "Jerry is a craftsman. You are the imagination. It was all your doing, wasn't it? Wasn't it?" he insisted.

Caught, I admitted it was all my doing.

"Then it will be a good thing if we sell more copies," he said.

He'd broached the topic: I wouldn't back down. "We *have* to sell more copies. Otherwise we'll lose money on it," I replied. "That's why Budd pushed newsstand orders."

"And if it doesn't sell more?"

I didn't answer.

"You're taking a risk, aren't you?"

"I didn't think so at the time I ordered it. There were hidden costs."

"Anytime one does something innovative there are hidden costs."

Fury I could have taken. Not this compassionate and ultra-sane moderation. I saw no way out. "I'll resign if you want," I said.

"Don't you think that's a bit premature?" Boelmann asked.

"Not if I screwed up."

"You told Tonia this issue would sell twenty percent more than usual. That means it should earn a larger profit than usual. That's scarcely grounds for resignation. Don't you want to stay around to see your prediction come true?"

There it was, the knife twisting.

"I said that to lift her spirits. To keep a positive attitude. That's all. It was hokum. Bluff."

"Perhaps," he said. "But isn't part of being a leader to bluff? To keep a positive attitude?"

"I guess."

"You'd better go home and change into your evening clothes. The car will pick you up at seven-thirty, then come get me here and we'll go to the Plaza."

I went home, showered, changed into my rented tuxedo, met the rented limo, rode up to the office where Boelmann, also dressed for the occasion, stepped in, and we sped up to the hotel. Roberta, Carl, Budd and Jerry were already at our table in the Palm Court, and it was a glittery affair, a superb dinner followed by the awards ceremonies.

Throughout it all I suffered. Boelmann had done worse than merely berate me. He'd challenged me to make good what I'd begun. That meant I would have to follow newsstand sales of the issue on a daily basis, suffer day by day, week by week, until I knew whether the magazine was selling well or not.

It didn't help that toward the end of the ceremonies my issue of *Graphique* was given a special Art Director's award for Overall Editorial and Graphic Excellence, nor when Boelmann went to the dais to accept the award and graciously asked Jerry and me to stand for applause. It didn't help that, as the publisher had predicted, during dinner and intermission and after the ceremonies, dozens of art directors came over to talk about the magazine and especially its cover.

I'd discovered two things that evening. First, that a catastrophe needn't be sudden and total, it could take weeks to achieve its fullest effect, and it could slowly drain one's energy and spirit with worry and anxiety, alternating hope with despair. And I learned that in the real world, the world of adults and work, that those sudden inspirations and flashy effects that I'd depended upon for years in lieu of sustained thought and perservering labor, meant nothing unless they were backed up by something tangible and lasting.

It was a sobering realization, and even though the issue went on to become the best seller *Graphique* ever had— more than doubling its usual circulation—and the most profitable by far as the months went by, I found that in time I couldn't even look at that quilted silver cover without feeling a great deal of irritation tinged with that smidgen of nausea that always accompanies a failure narrowly averted.

My first date with Luke occurred the next day, a splendid spring afternoon, and it was altogether charming. I met him at the top-floor apartment in Brooklyn Heights he shared with another editor: a light-filled, high-ceilinged flat above the Promenade with views straight across the East River to the Manhattan Battery. We walked around the Heights, which I didn't know (although I'd grown up in Queens, the other boroughs except for Manhattan might have been on Mars for all I knew of them), and ended up at the Norwegian Sailor's Home, which put on a superb ethnic buffet in its spacious first-floor dining hall. It was old and full of beautifully crafted wood with authentic nautical detail. However, it wasn't open to the public, and Luke was anything but an old tar from Oslo, so I never did discover how we got in. It was evidently a favorite spot of his, and its hushed atmosphere seemed somehow appropriate. We followed lunch with another walk through a newly developing Arabic neighborhood on Atlantic Avenue, then sauntered along the Promenade. By nightfall I was on the subway headed back to the Village.

I hadn't had such a pleasant day in weeks. Luke was so easygoing, so unruffled, so quietly certain of himself, that I found myself not missing Bob's mercurial high spirits. If Luke was considerably slower in his thought and even hesitant in his speech than I was used to from the Jane Street Girls, he proved to be eloquent when he did speak, and his words always seemed to be well considered. Those flashes of sensitivity I'd sensed in him the first time we'd met seemed genuine—tiny, refreshing pools wherein I might dive at will and at my own speed. Clearly there were hidden depths to the man. Yes, I was pleased with myself for having phoned Luke. Despite his strong sense of privacy, his almost palpable air of restraint, I didn't feel I'd forced myself on him. We made a second date for midweek.

That took place in my neighborhood. We met at a local restaurant for dinner, had a martini before, wine with it, a brandy afterward. As we walked back to my apartment, Luke's arm encircled my shoulders and it seemed to go there easily. In fact, everything about our being together seemed natural, unforced: as we lolled on my daybed looking through an oversize picture book just arrived from England, our faces came together unhurriedly over a marvelous seventeenth-century lithograph detailing the design and construction of St. Paul's Cathedral: we almost *had* to kiss. As naturally, as easily, we slid the book to the floor to give ourselves more room.

He made love to me more slowly than I've ever experienced, with a kind of solicitude I thought both terribly sensual and oddly methodical. We seemed to take an enormously long time to reach the point where our shirts could be drawn out of our belts, another age until those shirts were unbuttoned, exposing that new field of erotics, our cotton T-shirts. A decade eroded each loafer off our feet, another decade or so our socks. A half century was required to pull up my undershirt; every few inches required his intimate attentions. He seemed incapable of taking in more of me than a bicep or kneecap or collarbone at a time; any group of longer muscles had to have at least an era of kisses to confirm their substance, to connect them to the next area of flesh to be caressed. A mini-aeon after he'd begun, my chinos and Jockeys were finally sliding down my ankles. Luke propped himself up on one arm, gazing at my body as though he'd previously anatomized me, already completely predicted me and was now checking the reality against his diagram. I sensed I would never discover precisely what he was thinking. Although I felt he was pleased, I wondered whether even he would be able to explain what he was thinking. And if he could, if I'd ever understand. Effortlessly he removed his own clothing, and then he slowly covered me as though he were a carpet draping itself upon parquet. His body felt like a warm stratocumulus cloud.

In the span of immeasurable time that ensued, I was slowly, inexorably, totally possessed. He fitted himself completely to me, filling in every possible crevice between us until I felt as though I might have donned a form-fitting cloak of human skin softer than any leather. When, at last, he began to move, our bodies took on the consistency of molasses heated long before and not quite cooled. In the midst of this maceration by adoring, he would sometimes stop, look at me, brush his lips against mine, and suddenly

everything in the universe hinged upon the precise depth
and duration of a double-tongued kiss.

Only afterward, when finally, reluctantly, unendurably,
we allowed our bodies to move apart so that only two thirds
of our skin abutted, only then did I realize that he'd already
entered me, brought us both to orgasm, and retracted himself. As we lay there, flesh to flesh, eyelashes meshed and
fluttering synchronously, neither of us seemed able to speak.
Wordlessly he slowly separated from me—strands of hot
taffy pulling apart to chill—dressed, left.

My entire body felt so utterly fondled, I was scarcely able
to think. I could imagine no sensation possible other than
rest. Yet in those floating moments before I was wafted into
sleep, I remember remarking to myself that lovemaking
with Luke had been more like a visitation than sex: not the
Greco-Roman grappling of two muscled bodies that I'd become familiar with but the sculptured ecstasy of two Baroque
saints.

Of course, by the next morning I was convinced that I was
in love with him. My flesh still tingled. Every five minutes at
my desk I would recall some detail of our lovemaking and
almost swoon: how he'd stroked my upper thigh as though
memorizing it; or how he'd suddenly lifted one of my arms
back and buried his face in my armpit; or how one time he'd
bared his teeth and softly bitten my left nipple, then glanced
up, eye to eye, for my reaction. Naturally I wanted to see
him again as soon as possible, yet I didn't call him; not
because I was waiting for him to call me first but because I
suspected that he might need as much time as I to recover
from the experience.

Meanwhile I was waiting for Bob to apologize to me. I'd
warned our receptionist at work to tell him I was out should
he telephone. But either Bob was unaware of what he'd
done to me, or he considered it of little importance since by
Tuesday of the week following the premiere of his play, he'd
not called me at work nor at home; he hadn't even done the
most natural thing now that I was living in the same build-

ing: knock on my door. I was still inexpressibly angry with him, but those flashes of white-hot fury I experienced were brief and constantly undercut by the thought that I'd already moved beyond my relationship with Bob into a far more titillating, uncharted one with Luke.

By midweek Luke phoned me at work and we planned another weekend date. A warm front had swung in from the west and the weather had turned from early spring to midsummer. So I wasn't surprised when on Friday he called and suggested we have a picnic at Kings Park that coming Sunday. His roommate, whom I'd still not met, and someone he was dating would complete a foursome. We'd take a hamper, prepare sandwiches and drinks beforehand. It sounded exactly like the kind of afternoon that Luke would feel most comfortable with and be at his best in, so I agreed and took on the responsibility of making cold salads. We planned to meet at his apartment around eleven.

I'd still not seen Bob by Friday evening when I returned home from work, but Ken was perched reading on the concrete stoop, enjoying the warm spell, and though he was even more diplomatic and delicate than usual, he let fall several pieces of information for me to ponder over. First, Bob had taken it as a personal insult that I'd arrived at the Eugene O'Neill with George, who'd inadvertently stolen thunder from what was supposed to have been Bob's occasion. Bob had been even more insulted that I'd left with the two Georges, and in such a public fashion. Second, Ken— and several of Bob's friends—had witnessed the incident of Bob waving me aside while he spoke to that couple, and they'd been as mortified as I. When Ken and Sally had brought it up to Bob, he'd not only not accepted their point but defended his actions with the blanket statement that it had been necessary under the circumstances, and if I was too immature to understand, then that was *my* problem. Ken thought I shouldn't expect an apology and while he couldn't bring himself to support Bob's point of view, their long friendship meant he must support Bob in a more general way; Ken was genuinely disturbed that he might be drawn into a conflict he felt unable to settle.

I let Ken off the hook by telling him I expected nothing further from him, that I realized his position and that he and I would continue our own budding friendship with appropriate slowness and tact. About Bob I merely said that the premiere had made clear what had been long brewing: Bob and I were through, apology or no. I saw no reason why— even living in the same building—we ever had to speak to each other again.

The morning of the picnic provided one of those postcard skies photographers desire and Tennessee Williams called "Della Robbia blue." By the time I stepped out of the subway stop in Brooklyn Heights, someone had mixed zinc onto the palette. The sky continued to whiten as I walked to Luke's building; when I entered, it was so white, he was backlighted as though by the first second of a thermonuclear detonation. We kissed, we looked through the sandwiches he'd packed, the salads I'd brought, the bottles of gin and vermouth to make our pitcher of martinis.

His roommate telephoned. He was still in Manhattan at his friend's place, and something inexplicable was holding them up. He promised to call back shortly. Luke mixed a half pitcher of drinks while I stared out the windows, watching the zinc-white sky over the Battery streak with pewter. He joined me there with glasses, and we sipped and talked and watched the pewter turn to battleship gray, the streaks revealed as an enormous flotilla of storm clouds launched from somewhere over Newark.

We sat down in the window seat but we found less and less to say and settled for gazing outside as the glass and stone sides of huge and distant skyscrapers swirled with cloud shadow before darkening. The atmosphere grew gusty and tiny cyclones of newspaper and dust gathered to spin on the Promenade below, shoving baby carriages into railings, forcing couples and children to scatter for shelter. The air seemed to be sucked out the windows, out of our throats and in its place only electrical charges remained, so the merest brush of a finger or touch of cloth upon cloth sizzled and stung. The wallop of thunder was almost a relief, skirling sheets of hot rain a release. We moved back to his sofa and watched the rain.

Sometime during the storm his roommate called again with new qualifications and obstacles. I could hear Luke's deep, gentle voice, only slightly exasperated as he patiently explained how he'd grown up with thunderstorms in West Texas; this one would be over in minutes.

After the phone call he mixed more martinis, brought the pitcher to the sofa and refilled his glass. He lay my head in his lap and he began to stroke my hair and to speak of what it had been like growing up in the dry, hardscrabble hills of the Texas Panhandle: how every tenth person was struck by lightning by the time they were twenty and would show you the scar; how the infrequent rain teemed so hard, when it did come, it tore up new-sown fields and slammed down four-story metal silos; how one hailstorm had killed a dozen head of steer at a local farm; how at midnight heat lightning was so constant, it would illuminate a room so you could read all of Ecclesiastes. He spoke softly, quietly, stopping often to sip from his glass or refill it, and he spoke as though telling not me, right there in his lap, but someone in another room. He told me of a desperation of baked-mud houses with half-caulked windows and plank doors, with dirt floors and the ineradicable odor of wet wood fires and pan-fried bread. He evoked sultry August nights in packed-flesh revival meetings, the open-flap tent lit from without by a circle of auto headlamps, and of respectable citizens who became instant sinners, screaming and ranting and rolling on the ground, babbling in strange voices he called the gift of tongues. He told me of overwhelming floods from gullies dry as a chromium fender an hour before and of dust devils taller than the Chrysler Building which appeared so precipitously from out of a clear sky and alighted so skittishly here and there, they would demolish a row of main-street storefronts in seconds. So thoroughly that only a week later would a missing shopclerk be discovered six miles away, still encased in frozen slush, still bent forward in the gesture of scooping a pound of hominy; the metal scoop, the sack of grits, the entire shop's contents littered across the landscape—and only a hint of surprise playing about his days-dead lips.

I listened and sometimes looked up and back at his face, and sometimes urged him to tell me more, and I listened for the doorbell to ring, signaling the roommate's return and I heard the glass emptied and refilled and his voice unchanged, untiring, reciting, as though he'd saved it up since he was a child, rehearsed it for Judgment Day. At one point I slumbered.

When I awoke, my head wasn't on Luke's lap but on a pillow. I didn't see him at first, then I did see him, half kneeling at the far window, one hand raised as though a blinder against the glare. He was still speaking, still reciting, but without human listener, and his eyes seemed to shine with a glaze beyond any amount of liquor.

I called his name, and instead of reply or recognition, I heard the drone of his voice narrating, explicating, supplicating. I went closer and took his shoulder. But no response was forthcoming, only the endless drone. I thought about speaking in voices and revival meetings, and I let go of him and backed up and backed up, recalling what he'd said about men who gained the strength of ten and had to be restrained with dray-horse harnesses, of skinny old women exhibiting the strength of Samson and pulling down cedar trees when the fit was on them. From where I'd backed up into the foyer, I could see down the long living room to the three tall windows where the storm had vanished and a jaundiced glare now filtered in. For a moment I thought he was doing as he must, speaking with, thanking the sun itself. But I knew the truth. He was mad.

The strangeness of it all swept over me, girdling me with ice coldness, the blade tip of fear. I spoke his name once again, just to be certain, but he was gone—from the room, from me. I spun around and the apartment door opened into me.

My panic must have been apparent on my face, and in how startled I must have been at that instant. A blond man stood there, and, behind him, someone else. I scarcely saw them. The man with the keys blocked my way, and I think I said something. Then he asked, "How long has he been like this?" I don't know what I answered, because he was already past me, saying something to the other man, who drew me out into the hallway as the door slammed shut on us. Everything about the corridor and staircase looked fake: cut out of cardboard and in all the wrong colors. I staggered and half fell, half sat on the staircase where I began to shudder uncontrollably.

After a while the door opened and the roommate thrust my sport coat at his friend and barked out more words I didn't quite get. Then I was being ushered down the stairs and out of the building and walked to the subway station. The air refreshed me, drew me out of that terrible inner place I'd been consigned to by the incident, and I decided I had to go back and help Luke.

"I don't think so," my new companion said. "I'll phone and check in, but it's more than likely that I'll take the next train into the city."

"But what . . . ?" I didn't know how to formulate my question and still avoid the answer I didn't want to hear.

"Bill told me that Luke sometimes gets like this. Luke used to be a Baptist minister, you know," he explained. "He was defrocked back in Texas."

He heard the train coming and pushed me down the stairs, shouting, "Hurry or you'll miss it!"

Douglas was house-sitting for a music critic who had a large ground-floor duplex with backyard garden off Central Park West. At the end of May, Miss Sherry Jackson was at last given an unceremonious heave-ho from the small two rooms he'd been squatting in on Thompson Street when the owner of the building decided to renovate. While Sherry waited for a dirt-cheap apartment on Bedford Street to become vacant, he moved in with Douglas. Naturally they had to celebrate this stellar conjunction with a party.

The Jane Street Girls were invited and not all but most of us arrived, George and I, Ken with a new—very preppy and quite pretty—beau, Jonathan, Oliver, and some people we didn't know, among them an attractive and cheerful man I'd seen at some of the Washington Square parties named Chuck, who lived with a handsome lover in what Miss Sherry told me was a *marriage blanche*, meaning that they no longer slept together and thus were fair game. Sherry knew Chuck as an employer—having worked as a domestic without pay for room and board so long, Sherry had decided to become a bona fide professional housemaid for upscale Village homosexual couples and their pets, of which there turned out to be a surprising number. I'd flirted with both Chuck and his lover at Julius's and the above-mentioned soirees, and the minute I stepped into the Douglas–Sherry duplex party, Chuck made it clear that he was alone and that this was a perfect time for us to get to know each other more intimately.

I'd gotten over Luke's vision of the deity a lot easier than he had. He wouldn't answer the phone, or his roommate wouldn't let him answer. A few days later I heard from the fourth member of the ill-fated picnic that Bill and Luke had gone upstate, address unknown, where Bill had family. Not even Jonathan—who seemed to know everything about everybody—was able to tell me the location.

Since the incidents with Bob and then Luke, I'd become a bit put off by romance. Then I told myself they were merely aberrations, I would play the field, be what Miss Sherry called a "gay blade on the loose—and I do mean loose!"

As a result, regarding Chuck, my flesh was certainly willing, but alas, that evening my attentions were divided. For among the guests was my friend and neighbor Joseph Mathewson, whom I'd brought to the Douglas and Miss

Sherry temporary household with the specific intent of turning him on to marijuana—an event discussed at some length beforehand. And eagerly anticipated by several present, if Douglas's demonic giggle when we arrived was any indication. Knowing Joseph best, and also knowing that people sometimes reacted oddly to the drug (even if it was old-hat to me) naturally, I promised to remain with him as much as possible.

We decided to stay on the bottom floor of the apartment where the crowd would be thinnest and where we might relax in the homier environment of the huge, long eat-in kitchen with its Colonial furnishings, hooked rugs, comfy sofas, and of course its Dutch doors, open to the backyard and the night.

George arrived looking as distinctive as ever and gave Joseph and me great sweeping eighteenth-century bows and his countess voice as he presented us with a record to enhance our pleasure—an LP recorded at the Columbia University Music Department with pieces of electronic music by Arel, Blunt and Ussachevsky to serve as background music. Joseph and I had smoked several pipefuls of quite good Mizhoacan grass and he was already beginning to sail into the unknown. George and I smoked a bit more and chatted with Douglas, who frequently dropped downstairs for tea, coffee and merely to snoop on Joseph's progress.

George and I had talked often about going to Europe on a motorcycle tour, and on this occasion we planned it more definitely. He would be in London in the next few weeks to begin shooting *Romeo and Juliet* with Zeffirelli and should be done by the end of August. Somehow or other I'd made good enough at work to be settled in as editor at *Graphique*, and as a result, I'd been granted a two-week vacation with pay which I might take that summer. I decided to take it in August, following a meeting in Boelmann's main office in Switzerland. I'd buy a bike in Zurich and drive to Paris, where I'd meet George driving down from London.

Toward this end, and George admitted, also to practice

motorcycle driving (and I suspect also to impress me of his seriousness), he'd that very morning bought a brand-new Kawasaki 500, which he had parked outside on the street. George offered me a ride, and I was about to take him up on it when Ussachevsky's music began to twitter, and Joseph sat up very straight and began quite evidently to hallucinate a flock of migrating birds. I thought I'd better stay and keep my eyes on any further extenuations.

George went upstairs to join the others. Douglas and Ken came downstairs with some nonsense that claimed even Joseph's scattered attention so successfully that he left off "those lovely, lovely birds," and I felt somewhat more at ease. So much so that a short time later, when Chuck dropped downstairs and invited me out into the garden to look at the moon, I was able to leave Joseph laughing and chatting with the others.

The night was warm and balmy, and the moon was gibbous and more than ordinarily bright. Chuck knew the music critic's garden, and as we sauntered, he told me what each bush and flower were, many of them quite visible in the moonlight. None of it necessary except perhaps to keep us talking, together, alone, and away from the others. I was as drawn to Chuck as he to me, touched by his courtliness, delighted that he was scarcely able to hold back his lust for me. We were at the farthest end of the garden leaning over a tall bush of white roses gleaming almost as brightly as at midday when our heads came together suddenly and lightly bumped as we bent to smell a blossom. Its fragrance was correlative to the night, and he kissed me.

I pulled back, and there, far away, framed by the doorway, was a backlighted silhouette which I immediately knew from its pose was George. I was about to say something, to call him into the garden, when Chuck blocked my view and kissed me again. A few long minutes later, when I looked toward the doorway, George was gone.

After another course around the garden and a few more passionate kisses, Chuck and I returned indoors, where I remained by Joseph's side—no longer as high as before yet thoroughly thrilled with the experience—sipping cold coffee, talking and listening to pop music, until we cabbed downtown together and I'd gotten him safely back to his apartment. Chuck had meanwhile gone upstairs in the duplex and left shortly before we did with the friends he'd arrived with.

When I asked about George, Miss Sherry said he had cycled off, making a great deal of noise. Knowing how itchy he'd been to go for a ride on his new motorcycle, I thought nothing of it.

The following day at *Graphique* was a "closing" day for the June issue, the last chance to make changes before it would be printed, so I was frantically busy both morning and afternoon. Midday was taken up with a "business" lunch with a young art director at Young and Rubicam I'd met whose brilliantly photographed TV commercials I'd admired. I was trying to get him to write an article or at least do an interview for the magazine.

We met at his office and he was still in production when I arrived, so I asked for the key to the executive washroom from his assistant to freshen up. As I stepped in, I was surprised to see someone at one of the large marble sinks, half visible behind a partition, quickly roll down a shirtsleeve. He stuffed something into his jacket breast pocket, threw his suit jacket over his shoulder and rushed past me out the door. Oddly furtive behavior, I thought, but it was only when I was about to wash my hands at the same sink he'd used that I noticed two tiny drops of blood marring the surface's malachite perfection. He'd been shooting up! Methedrine, given the speed with which he'd moved.

At lunch, Roger confirmed my assumption, saying that virtually everyone under forty at the executive level in advertising took some sort of speed; almost had to, to stay sharp, to keep up. "Not just Madison Avenue, but Wall Street is speeding too," Roger added. His source was a friend who worked at a highly reputable downtown firm. "And who knows what other areas of American business life." I thought about the tiny amounts of meth which Boy Ondine and the others would leave on my mantelpiece after they'd used my bathroom to hit up, and how I'd taken to bringing it to work and snorting it for a lift on those afternoons when work seemed piled up on my desk. "For all we know," Roger concluded, "they're probably all on speed at Congress and the Pentagon."

The idea that speed freaks in three-piece suits were running the government seemed to explain the current madness regarding Vietnam. It not only made sense but it somehow pleased me: Reality wasn't what Ken and Bob thought it was from reading newspapers and magazines, it was far more chaotic, influenced by unpredictable factors like drug use and infidelity.

There was a call on my notepad from Miss Sherry when I returned to work, but I wasn't able to call back until sometime after five. When I did reach him, Sherry was breathless from running down several flights in the town house he'd been vacuuming.

"Mandy Rice had an accident," he sputtered.

"George? When?"

"Last night. On the motorcycle. I guess right after he left the party."

Sherry gave the name of the hospital and the room number.

"Is he all right? What happened?"

"I'm not sure. Mandy was so doped up from the operation when I phoned."

"Operation?"

"On his knee. He smashed his knee. The operation to put it back together again took two hours, Mandy said. He came out of anesthetic once during it and they had to put him under again."

"Only the knee? Nothing else?"

"Nothing else. Oops, one of my employers is home. Gotta go."

I hung up the phone, quite shaken. Poor George! I dialed the number Sherry had given me and after many rings a nurse answered. She said that George was out of the room being fitted for a knee brace. Evening visiting hours began at seven.

I stayed at the office until the cleaning lady arrived and kicked me out, then I stopped and bought flowers and chocolates for George, and because I still had time until it was seven o'clock, I stopped in a bookstore and picked up a copy of a Balzac novel I'd never read—never even heard of before—titled *Splendors and Miseries of Courtesans*. George and I had talked of Balzac before, and I knew he loved both the author and the period.

George was in the hospital bed when I arrived and he was still a little stoned—not only from the anesthetic: Douglas had a key to George's apartment and had arrived during mid-afternoon visiting hours, bringing things from George's place—his Japanese kimono, among other items, which he now wore—a bottle of Scotch, and his stash of grass, both of which George admitted he'd utilized in quantity since the painkillers the hospital gave out were few and ineffective.

His right leg was not only in a cast up to the top of the thigh but also in some sort of metal framework: the brace, which he explained was actually a sort of pincushion designed to keep the shards of reconstructed patella in place so they might eventually grow back together into some semblance of a kneecap.

I'd never seen George so stationary before—he'd always been on the move, gesturing, dancing around, curtsying, slowly turning, acting with his entire body—and I couldn't help but wonder how seriously the accident was and how long it would take for him to recover. I didn't ask, of course, but instead I listened to him tell about the accident, about the various characters among the ambulance drivers and emergency staff and doctors and nurses he'd encountered. In less than twenty-four hours George had already populated and evaluated and even nicknamed the people in this new world he'd been thrown into. He was doing his best to entertain and amuse me. God, he was brave!

The man who shared a room with him began to receive visitors, and George had me find a wheelchair and help him into it, which took some doing with his brace and cast. He directed me to roll him up in the elevator to the huge, windowed and now dimly lit top floor sun room. We settled there and smoked more grass.

"Franco's been wonderful," George said as he sipped Scotch and handed me the half-empty bottle. "He sent Anne as soon as he heard, and she was there when I came out of surgery. He's offered to put me on his production books so his medical insurance will pay the bills. Naturally he can't stop production just for me, so I'll miss it, but there will be other films, other parts."

He talked on, telling me how long the doctors expected his knee would take to heal, and what he could hope for in terms of full recovery and what he should be prepared to expect in terms of partial use, and as he talked, he and I drank more booze and smoked more grass and got more and more depressed until he suddenly said, "Let's race!"

"Race?"

"We passed an unused wheelchair back by the elevator. Go get it and we'll race."

We raced around the huge chilly sun room, circling each other, laughing as the Scotch bottle slid out of George's hands onto the floor, then skittering around in the wheelchairs as we manuevered to see who could reach it first. We kicked at the bottle like a hockey puck, George utilizing his cast and brace as a stick, carrying on until suddenly the lights were thrown on very brightly and a most stern and completely scandalized head nurse chased us out.

I brought George down to his room and stayed with him while he picked at his snack—he'd already charmed one of the floor nurses into bringing him a late meal—and commented on the most likely, thoroughly inedible, origin of each dish. Soon afterward he began to read the Balzac paperback.

I didn't leave the room until the book had slid out of his hands and I'd contented myself that George was asleep.

I was going home, honest I was, but George's visit had depressed me pretty thoroughly, especially his courage in the face of losing the role he was born to play, which an entire multi-million-dollar film had been devised to exhibit. So I ended up in Julius's. Well, stayed there a while. I was known as a close friend of George's, and everyone who'd ever glanced at him on the Village streets came up to me and asked about him until I was sick of repeating my rather limited story. Arnie Deerson, ever frank, took me aside and said, "Darling! Philly!" in that tone of voice of his that promises at the least a revelation. "You look like something the cat dragged in—then threw out again!" I knew it was time for me to go home.

Crossing Seventh Avenue at the lethal trisection of Eleventh Street and Greenwich Avenue, I saw a somewhat familiar figure unsuccessfully waving down a cab. He was tall and wearing a trench coat and swaying a bit on his feet and—it was Ron Mallory!

"Ron! What are you doing here?" I asked, as yet another taxi driver he'd spoken to pulled away from the curb with squealing tires.

"Huh?" He focused on me momentarily, then seemed to ignore the evidence of his eyes. "I'm trying to get a cab."

"These are all going downtown. Don't you want uptown?"

"They can turn around!" he slurred angrily.

"Sure! And the sun can rise in the west. Come on. I'll walk you to Hudson Street. That goes uptown."

Despite his general air of hostility, he followed my lead, and I felt like the little engine that could as I steered Ron's slow bulk through traffic and around sidewalk obstacles.

At the corner of Perry and Greenwich he stopped and demanded, "What are *you* doing here!"

"I live near here. Jane Street."

"Got any liquor?" His green eyes were cunning, interested.

"Scotch."

"Atta boy!" He linked his arm in mine, and from there his speed doubled as he half dragged me to my building.

Good thing I'd moved to a first-floor apartment; just getting there seemed to use up all of Ron's energy. He collapsed on my sofa, and I helped him get off his gear, almost having to peel his raincoat off him. For a moment I thought he was about to pass out, but at the last moment of full consciousness he came alive and said, "What about that drink?"

"Coming up."

"Bring the bottle!"

I brought the bottle and he was insistent, literally pulling me over to join him on the couch. There I poured and he drank. He also loosened his tie and opened his shirt halfway, revealing the tautly muscled chest I'd supposed would be there, and almost invisible whirls of sparse blond chest hair. When he'd emptied his first glass and poured another, I thought, *Great! Having Ron in my apartment and on my couch is just what I've wanted. Now how do I get rid of him?* To my surprise, he suddenly seemed to sober up.

"You wonder where I've been lately?"

"Chicago?"

"Right here! I was fired. That little twinkletoes got me fired."

Budd? I hadn't known that. "When?"

"Two days ago. Or was it three?" He poured himself another drink. "He's running the show now. Just as they planned. In fact, everything's just as they planned."

"What are you talking about?"

"Well, they planned to get rid of Will and they hired you. And they planned to get rid of me. And they did."

It sounded like alcoholic paranoia; I didn't believe him.

He narrowed his eyes at me. "C'mon, you mean to tell me you weren't in on it?"

"I walked into *Graphique* off the street. I was living in Europe until the day before I got the job."

"Aha!"

"In London. And before that Rome. I'd never heard of Boelmann or the magazine. And I never stopped in Zurich. Honest!"

"All right"—another long swallow of the stuff—"I believe you."

I wondered if he was telling the truth about me being hired all along just to boot out Will. It was a terrible thought. I *liked* Will. Respected him. Boelmann had said Will was unhappy there. Had he lied to me? That would explain how suddenly Will left.

"I guess you're okay," Ron said. Sure, I was; he was drinking my liquor. "Only thing is," and he suddenly leaned over me—liquor breath and those flecked green eyes and those shapely lips—"you're a little too pretty for a guy. Know what I mean?"

Oh, please, I thought, *I hope this is not what I think it is.*

"Know what I mean?" Ron repeated. "No? Maybe you should do something to yourself. Grow a beard." Suddenly he was rolling up his shirtsleeve, but it wouldn't go far enough up his arm because it was too tight, so he pulled the shirt off with some effort and showed me a not very faded tattoo on his bicep honoring the Marine Corps. "USMC. Know what that means?" Ron demanded. "USMC? You suck my cock."

Lord, I thought, it *is* what I think it is. How did I get myself into this mess?

"No offense, okay?" Ron said in a different tone of voice. "You been in the service?" He didn't wait for my answer, but instead filled up his glass, then he noticed mine wasn't drunk from and he glared at me suspiciously, until I picked it up and sipped.

"Well, it's true!" he declared, and as I wondered what was true, he added emphatically, "Twinkletoes and small-titted women taking over the whole damn city."

"Like Judy?" I asked, meaning our overendowed receptionist and hoping to change the subject.

"Ah!" He dismissed her. "She thinks like a small-titted woman! Acts like one!"

"I'm sorry you were fired."

"Naaah. 'T's okay. I'll get unemployment. Find a new job when I want to. You live here alone? Whatsamatter? Whyn't you drinkin'? 'Fraid I'll make a move for your drawers?" He leered and almost fell onto me. I pushed him back, thinking, *I don't* need *any of this, not tonight of all nights!*

"C'mon. Don' be like tha'!" Ron insisted drunkenly. "You're alone. I'm alone. Need a little rub-a-dub-dub. You ever do that? Rub-a-dub? Where I come from we call it dry humping. Whadda you call it?"

I tried to get away from him but he grabbed me surprisingly fast given his condition and held me tightly, and I thought, *Please, Lord, I've had a hard day. I just want to go to sleep.*

And evidently said it aloud because he responded. "Okay! We'll *both* go to sleep!"

I'd ended up still gripped by him, but seated in his lap. Panic grew as I tried to get free and couldn't. Then just as quickly, it subsided. For a moment I felt totally at ease, totally comfortable. I turned around and suddenly I was eight or nine years old again and he wasn't a drunken, impetuous unemployed near stranger but the Taystee Bread man—he looked enough like him!—and I found myself saying, "You were always nice to me. You always treated me the best of anyone. Right from the start."

To my surprise Ron was no longer gripping me, he wasn't leering or aggressive, wasn't ambiguous and dangerous. He was nice, he was gentle and strong, he was the Taystee Bread man. He patted my head and said, "Sh! Tha's okay. I won' do nothin', okay?" I could tell he hadn't heard my precise words, only heard my tone of voice. "We'll jus' sleep. You 'n' me. Hell! Tha's all I'm really good for righ' now, anyway. Okay?"

That's what we did. He stretched out on the sofa against its back, and I easily fitted into his length, and he put his arms around me and held me closely but not too tightly against himself, and we used his trench coat as a blanket and he soon began to snore, and I thought about poor George and I thought about how both of us—Ron out on his ass and me now editor—had been manipulated by a person or persons unknown for reasons unknown. I fell asleep and slept dreamlessly.

The day after Robert Kennedy was shot at the Ambassador Hotel, I came home from work to find a note slipped under my door. "It's very important that Kenny and I speak to you. After the news," it read. From Bob Herron.

Almost two months had passed since Bob's play had premiered in New Haven and I'd not seen or spoken to him since; although we now lived in the same building, our hours were now quite different, and since I could see anyone coming in the front door, I could avoid him.

It had been an awful day for me. RFK was the antiwar candidate: the only candidate, in fact, who stood even vaguely for anything that could connect me and many of my friends to the country again. His winning the California primary race made him finally seem like a viable candidate; and now, now he lay mortally wounded in an L.A. hospital, and with him the future. Deep in my heart I knew he wouldn't pull through. It seemed the Weathermen's predictions would come true, and before the next election there would be bloodshed in the streets of every large city in the nation. The last thing I wanted was to see or speak to Bob Herron, but reason won out: I thought it might have something to do with the building, so at seven-thirty I knocked on his door.

Ken was in the wing-back chair, looking as though he'd rather be anywhere else. Bob, on the other hand, seemed quite pleased with himself. After letting me in, he sat himself down in the "magic chair" and said, "This is very serious."

"You're telling me," I said.

"We're *not* discussing the news," Bob said. He cleared his throat and began again. "It's come to our attention—Kenny's and mine—that not everything you've told us about yourself is exactly true."

He then went on to tick off certain statements I'd made, and the facts. When he was done, he sat back, quite contented with himself.

"You hire a detective or what?" I asked, half amused.

"*How* we found out is not important."

I looked at Ken. "Whatever this cost you, you were gypped!"

"Phil!" Bob interrupted. "I don't think you realize the gravity of the situation."

"Evidently I don't. Why don't you explain it as only you can, Bob?"

"Well, it means you lied to us."

I felt like Alice in Wonderland wandering down a rabbit hole. Was this real? "So what?"

I thought his eyes were going to bulge out of his head. "So what! Here you are living a floor away and you . . . you . . ." he sputtered.

"Neither of us," Ken said much more sedately, "think dishonesty is a quality friends of ours should have."

"I told both of you that my past was none of your business. I still don't see how it is."

"Of course it is!" Bob shouted.

"The *hell* it is!" I shouted back.

"Phil! Bob!" Ken tried. "Perhaps Phil is right that it isn't any of our business. But even so, the fact remains that you lied to us. Which would lead us to conclude that you'll do so in the future."

"I've never lied to you, Ken"—ignoring Bob—"about anything of the *least* importance."

"Your college, your father's business!" Bob insisted.

"Means absolutely nothing to me, and shouldn't mean anything to you."

"Of course it means something to you!" Bob insisted. "Otherwise you wouldn't have lied about it."

"I lied about it for two reasons. First because it was none of your business. And second because it gratified your bourgeois ego."

"*My* ego?" Bob demanded.

"Not mine. I'm satisfied to have graduated with honors from Queens College. I'm satisfied I was considered for a Woodrow Wilson Grant and got into Columbia's grad school and was accepted into the Iowa Writing School. I also thought it all complete bullshit. As is where I went to school. As is my father's business. I've been paying my own bills since I left home at the age of sixteen. The person I am now has nothing to do with my father!"

"You still lied," Bob doggedly insisted.

"Fine, I lied. End of absurd discussion." I got up to leave.

"Wait just one moment, young man." Bob jumped up and blocked my way.

"I'm done," I said.

"No, you're not!"

"Don't you think you at least owe us an apology?" Ken said.

"Don't you see, Ken? This isn't about *me*. This is only a way for Herron to save face and feel superior. Don't you see? He dished himself so throughly in Connecticut, he's got to rebalance it somehow. Don't you hear his ego screaming for vengeance?"

"What are you talking about?" Bob demanded.

"If what I said to you were lies, and as I said before totally unimportant ones, the way you live your entire life is nothing but a lie."

Bob all but threw up his hands. "I don't believe this!"

I went on. "You've become such a hypocrite, you can't judge what's important anymore."

"Because I wouldn't fawn all over you at the Eugene O'Neill?" Bob scoffed.

"Didn't you know every person there over the age of twelve knew you were gay?"

"Phil!" Ken warned.

I wouldn't be stopped. "Because if you don't, you're even more deluded than I thought. You're leading an entire life based on the lie that you're not homosexual. Where you work, at the theater, everywhere but right here. It's . . . obscene!"

"I *knew* I shouldn't have invited you."

"You shouldn't have picked me up at that movie, Bob. *That* was your first mistake."

"Phil, don't you think you're going too far?" Ken tried to reason. "You know as well as I that you can't be openly homosexual and hope to . . . you know, get anywhere."

"I am. I did. I haven't hidden my homosexuality from anyone, and at the ripe old age of twenty-four I'm editor of a magazine with a salary higher than either of you, *and* an expense account, *and* three-martini lunches every day with Madison Avenue movers and shakers."

"That's an isolated case," Ken said.

"Like the cases of all the other gay men I lunch with?"

"You're insane," Bob said. "You're going to destroy yourself."

"Hold on, Bob!" Ken went on. "Honest, Phil, I wish I could do the same where I work."

"You can, Ken. No one cares whether their architect is gay or not."

He shook his head. "It's just not practical. Not realistic."

"What would happen," Bob argued, "if every faggot in America did what you're doing?"

"For one thing, America would see how many faggots there actually are," I said. "Sorry, Ken. This is going to have to be yet another one of those areas where we're diametrically opposed. And, Bob, I'm not going to apologize, make that I'm *never* going to apologize. Because I don't care what you think of me. And if you want to use your influence to kick me out of the building, well, go ahead."

"Just don't drag *us* into your madness," Bob insisted.

"Don't worry, Bob. Your 'secret' is safe with me."

I left the apartment and could hear Herron explode behind the door, and Ken's voice also rising as he tried to reason with him. I went down the stairs and outside for some fresh air.

A few weeks after this confrontation I woke up feeling as though someone had been dancing the rumba on my back all night long. It was all I could do to get up, go to the john and urinate. The face that greeted me in the mirror was something out of *Tales of the Crypt*. Good thing it was a Saturday. I went back to bed.

I woke up again at three P.M., only because the phone was ringing. I don't recall who it was or what I said, but I knew I was ill, thought it might be the flu. Around seven P.M., I awakened again, fixed myself scrambled eggs and toast, ate a third of it and went back to bed.

Sunday brought no relief: I woke up after having slept fifteen hours and felt worse than before. I spoke to George, who was getting out of the hospital, and told him that unless I made a miraculous recovery I wouldn't be able to help him move his belongings to his apartment. It had taken that long—and several more operations on his knee—for him to be well enough to return home.

It was George who first said that my symptoms sounded like mononucleosis. He gave me the name of his doctor, thankfully only two blocks away. I slept through most of the rest of Sunday, called in sick on Monday and saw the doctor at noon. He said it might take a few days for the blood tests to confirm his findings, but it looked like mono. He gave me a shot of B-12 and said there was nothing to do but rest. I returned to my apartment, called Budd Singleton, had him contact Boelmann in Zurich to phone me at home and dozed while I waited for him to return my call.

We'd just put the July issue to bed, and aside from news items and other late-breaking items Roberta and Carl could handle, the August issue was done, and most of the September one. Boelmann told me to rest and return when I could.

By Wednesday it was clear that I wouldn't be recuperating soon. I slept twelve, fourteen hours at a stretch and awakened without feeling in any way refreshed. The doctor called to confirm his diagnosis. George had alerted our other friends to my plight, and Douglas, Miss Sherry and finally even Ken knocked on my door with groceries and especially fresh produce. I would get out of bed, greet them, and doze off between the time they began to broil my steak and it was ready to be eaten. I was a mess. After two weeks of this and no change, the doctor began to talk about hospitalization. I didn't see the point.

Someone, possibly Ken, contacted my younger brother, who was at the time working for my father, and my family began harassing me to return home, at least until I felt able to take care of myself. When my younger brother—whose motives I never suspected were anything but affectionate—insisted on it, I gave in and he drove me to my parents' home.

I ended up spending all of July there. I recovered, slowly, partly due to the natural course of the disease, partly due to the great cooking and nursing care my mother lavished on me. I lay in the backyard closely inspecting insect life through the slats of garden lounges, reading mystery novels and the lightest literature my mother could find in the local library. I also developed a taste for Iris Murdoch novels and read most of Proust. Mostly, however, I ate and I slept.

There was plenty of time to think about the past year, about Djanko and Bob Herron and Luke Harms. In retrospect, it seemed that I'd managed to hook up with three of the oddest men on the planet. With the most dismal results.

Worse, I no longer cared what happened to me. I had enough savings to pay rent on my apartment, which my younger brother watched and sometimes stayed in that summer, but when Boelmann called yet again and asked yet again how I was feeling and when I thought I would return to *Graphique* and yet again I had to tell him I had no idea, he finally said he thought he would have to replace me. I said that seemed like a good idea. Of my friends, only Barbara came to visit. No surprise, since my parents now lived in the suburbs, and it required a car or endless train then bus rides to get there from Manhattan. And while I sometimes spoke to people on the phone, that happened less and less. By the third week of July I was only well enough to walk a block to buy a newspaper. I felt ninety-eight years old.

Sometime in early August I suddenly felt much better. A week later I returned to my apartment: It would take the next year or so for me to put my life back together. I applied for unemployment benefits and was given a run-around from that office to the work disability office. The fact that I'd once been a city employee helped me a bit in dealing with the bureacracies but not much, and periodically I'd go into a complete physical slump, miss appointments, not give a damn. Someone had replaced me at *Graphique*, but I didn't look for work again. Instead, when someone told me that a terrific scene was happening in California, I flew to San Francisco. The weather of that climatically temperamental city was amazingly regular, sunny and warm: summer lasted well into October. I took lots of LSD and lived in a commune off the Haight and when I returned to Manhattan for Christmas, my hair was long and curly, I had a beard, I wore granny glasses, I was practicing Zen meditation, using the *I Ching*, and the last thing I was interested in was a job.

During the months I'd been gone, a great deal had changed around me. Not my apartment on Jane Street, which I'd let my younger brother and his friends use, and not Bob or Ken. Although in the months ahead Ken would relax into the new scene that developed in the Village, he would do so his own way, in his own manner, at his own speed, without ever losing sight of who he was and what he valued. Ken retained his individuality in the midst of all the changes that ensued, and that made him valued and admired by even the wildest drug heads he would encounter.

It would take Bob several more years before he'd loosen up, smoke grass or come to accept being gay. I was never certain whether he accepted and changed out of real belief, from a basic Gemini adaptability, or simply because it was the best way to meet young men. Bob and I settled into an on-again off-again neighborly acquaintance, but unlike with Ken, I never felt I could trust Bob, and I had no regrets that our lives went in very different directions thereafter.

George had recovered enough to do a late summer stock production of a Harold Pinter play in Connecticut, playing opposite Brian Bedford, but he was still having trouble with his knee, still seeing doctors, and was in and out of court trying to recover a large insurance claim to cover his medical expenses.

People we knew told me that George had changed, and when I finally located him, George was indeed different although I couldn't put my finger on how exactly. He was using a lot of different drugs—ups, downs, coke—and was hanging out with a new group of people: his own brother and sister, who came down to the city often, and someone named Bobby Brown, who later on became my roommate. George had become embittered by his experiences, naturally, which he did his best to disguise, especially when Zeffirelli's film of *Romeo and Juliet* opened to ecstatic reviews that spring and became enormously successful, and Michael York—in George's role—became an instant star.

I felt that George and I could no longer communicate as we used to. But he denied it was personal and told me that we had to rethink the meaning of things like friendship in light of the times we were living in, which declared that "nothing was real." He still planned to go to Europe, only now he would be alone, traveling by rail. After acting in the one play he made no efforts to get other roles, claiming that his leg—stiff because of the knee pins—was a major disadvantage, which it probably was.

George had always prized his freedom, his ability to live without attachments, to come and go at whim, and that now became George's mode of existence. At times I had no idea where he was living, if he was in Manhattan, in Europe or up in Plymouth, Massachusetts, his hometown, where his siblings were the center of a small local "hip scene." In my telephone book his name took over an entire page, then two pages as he moved around the city, the country. As I and Arnie Deerson and Joseph and a few other of the Jane Street Girls moved into a new scene with new people in the following months, George would sometimes appear and be charming and witty and enigmatic, providing us with flashes of his old self, then he would as suddenly disappear.

"Honey moosha pie!" Jemima bussed both my cheeks. "Why, I haven't seen you since the last time Harry plugged Bess Truman's plumbing. So very glad you could come." An effusive greeting, I thought, since I was certain that Jameson Metcalf didn't remember me in the least.

As you might have guessed, Jameson was having another lease-break party. He'd moved to Sheridan Square following the Chelsea eviction and had taken a lovely apartment on the eighth floor, facing much of the southernmost of the two adjacent open triangles which together comprise the misnamed area. I hadn't seen him since the last party, and if I weren't in such a generally draggy mood I wouldn't have come to this one, but it was one of those humid, overly warm late-June evenings, and a mutual friend—not Joseph, who was down south with family—was going and said why didn't I come.

The Jane Street Girls—or "Janettes," as Jemima called us—were not present in any force this evening, but I knew several of the other guests from the Village bars and other parties. One of them, a smiling, slender, attractive young man named Buzz, decided to take me in hand about ten minutes after I arrived and, to this end, walked me into the kitchen where he played Miss Congeniality with me and Mr.

Bartender with the guests. I suppose we also talked. I'm certain we smoked some hash—the last of my hash, alas! —and then he discovered among the still paper-bagged bottles brought by guests an exotic-looking flask of tequila. It was in a flat, concavely curved bottle with Spanish writing I could only half decode. Inside the bottle, floating at the bottom, appeared to be what looked like a long white worm.

"Oh, my!" Buzz said. "This is the best tequila there is. We used to drink this stuff. Or at least my Daddy and older brother did, back in Texas."

Remembering Luke, I declared, "If you say you belonged to the Baptist church, I'm leaving."

"Lord, no! We were Methodists. Uppity Methodists."

"Fine by me. What's the worm doing?"

"Well, it looks day-ed to me." Buzz had uncorked the bottle and was rummaging about in the refrigerator for something. "Wait. I re-call. The worm gives it flavor."

"Uggk! I'll pass."

"No, it's gooo-od!" He held out two lemons and had located a small box of kosher salt. "It's the best tha-ang!"

He sliced the lemons, spilled out the salt on the table and poured us each a stiff glassful.

"Now, the way to do it is to wet the snuff spot on the back of your hand—that's it!—put the salt there. You take a long sip of tequila, then lick the salt, then lick the lemon slice. Ready?"

"You go first."

He did and I watched. It seemed easy enough and I followed. The tequila was smooth and quite flavorful, but it hit my stomach like a bolt of lightning.

"Bar's closed," Buzz said to someone stumbling in. He forced a bottle into the outstretched hand, then shut the door. "We'll just hide in here," he said and snapped off the lights.

For the next fifteen minutes or so we sat side by side in folding chairs, and sipped and licked and licked again. I don't remember much talk after we'd begun seriously drinking. Nor, despite the efforts we were making, did I feel much of an effect. After all, I was already laced on the hashish.

Buzz began to giggle. "We're coming up on that worm now. We'll split it."

"What are you talking about?"

"Gotta eat it."

"I've put some nasty things in my mouth, but not that."

"Suit yourself."

I watched him eat his half of the worm.

"What's it taste like?"

"Sol-id fuckin' te-qui-la."

"Nothing else?"

"Nope."

"Okay I'll try it."

Squeamishly I did, and he was right. Either the liquor had already completely deadened my mouth or it was ninety-nine percent tequila.

The liquor gone, we decided to go into the other room.

Bad decision. Buzz fell off his chair, and trying to get him up, I fell off mine. We were now on the floor, under the kitchen table, the legs of which appeared to me as great twisted roots in some primeval jungle.

"Jesus, am I hallucinating or what?"

Definitely, unquestionably hallucinating. The effect of the tequila was like peyote or something. Twisty and strange and . . . but how? That worm!

Time passed, we extricated ourselves by slowly crawling out of our private kitchen forest and into the living room, which was a scene of a completely different sort, if equally strange, far more changeable and a great deal less definable. I would sit back and my mind would suddenly check out for a while, then it would be back again and I'd be doing something, plumped on objects I recognized as big pillows on what was purportedly a sofa, or leaning against an imitation wall, half propped up by someone who'd had smashing, almost perfect, plastic surgery, duplicating someone I knew.

Eventually I found Buzz again, and he and I thought several previous bad decisions called for one more: We'd leave the party and go home together.

It didn't help that the elevator operator resembled a king cobra, nor that the lobby was decorated like the antechamber of the Spanish Inquisition filled with tottering ancient women who'd evidently been tortured for decades. Nevertheless we managed to get out onto the street.

That section of the Village is fairly busy on any warm night. This night it was . . . well, Buzz and I just couldn't believe *how* busy! People seemed to be running around a great deal, dozens of sirens seemed to be wailing, cars racing through the area. We crossed Waverly Place and huddled in the little doorway that lopped off the tip of the triangle of what was then the Greenwich Bookstore. The view of the northern part of Sheridan Square that greeted us, we instantly agreed, could be nothing but a result of the tequila: A batch of police cars was filling the streets, and scores of cops appeared to be massed in front of one of the storefronts. Despite their mass, however, they appeared to be under attack. People surrounded them, throwing flaming bottles, flaming wooden boxes, flaming purses, flaming anything. Buzz and I thought that we saw leather queens up in trees hurling abuse and various objects down at the police. A taxi seemed to have been rolled over, and all of its windows were smashed. One police car appeared to have been pushed into a fire hydrant that had split up from the sidewalk and was geysering water. Despite this deluge, the police car suddenly shot up in flames. And the shouting and the sirens and . . .

"Boy! This tequila is something else!" Buzz slurred out the words. "I'm seeing the damnedest th-angs!"

"Me too. In our condition, we might do something dangerous," I slurred back in reply. "We'd better get home."

Still holding each other up, we left the doorway and headed straight across the triangle, threading our way through people running and milling about both in and out of uniform, people shouting, people calling into megaphones. Buzz stumbled over a thick black boa of a fire hose on the ground, and as I propped him up, someone ran up to us and asked, "Is he wounded? Does he need medical attention?" But we ignored him and kept on pushing through what looked like a half dozen fire trucks and mostly gawking firemen. After what seemed like ages and adventures equal to Sinbad's, we got to my apartment, where Buzz fell on his knees and loudly blessed the Lord. Shortly thereafter we passed out.

The next morning, my phone was ringing off the hook. I looked at the clock and thought, *Omigod! It's so damn late! I missed an appointment!*

Without asking who it was, I moaned into the receiver, "Food poisoning last night. Must have eaten something off."

"I'll just *bet* you ate something off! Right off *somebody!*"

"Douglas?"

"Well, it ain't Mary Queen of Scots!" He switched into his Butterfly McQueen voice. "Get up, girl! It's a lovely day and there's riotin' in the streets. Dah queens is at war! There's mascara streaked across Miss Sheridan Square thicker than my lover's dong. And policemen? Girl! Half the force! More'n even you can shake your stick at. It's like a dream come true for those uniform fairies. They're all marchin' away and demonstratin' and checkin' out details on the uniforms. It's like Miss Heaven come to dah earth."

"Who is it?" Buzz asked from bed. Then, "Where am I?" Then, "Who are you?"

"Wrong questions," I replied. "You should ask what's going on."

"You don't believe me?" Douglas was asking. "Turn on Miss News. Ten-Ten A.M."

I found the bed-table radio and turned it on. Sure enough, the announcer was talking about a riot in Greenwich Village, evidently sparked by the closing of a homosexual bar.

"Well?" Douglas asked.

"I guess you're right."

"When has this queen been wrong? Meet us in Miss Sheridan Square in ten minutes. We're all demonstrating. Dress up fine. There'll be lots of neat meat there."

"We'd need at least a half hour," I protested. "And who's we?"

"We are every single male-woman of any importance in Miss New York City! And who's at your place?"

"Buzz."

"Buzz, whom you ate off last night?"

"We'll be there in half an hour."

"Don't be late! It's going to be fab-u-lous!"

I hung up the phone and got a glass of ice water and returned to bed, where Buzz and I sipped and listened to the news until the announcer moved to another topic. We turned the radio off and looked at each other in disbelief.

"We were there!" Buzz declared.

"It wasn't the tequila at all!" I said.

We laughed all the while we had coffee and showered and dressed and went out to join the crowd, which by noon had grown to twice the size of the gathered police force and was still growing. We were given hastily composed placards, and we marched and chanted and cheered guys like ourselves who were speaking through megaphones, railing against city corruption and police Fascism, demanding the release of the people arrested the previous night and calling for gay rights. And, just as Douglas had predicted, it was pretty exciting. Okay, fab-u-lous!

It would be some time before I realized that Stonewall was a watershed, not only in gay politics but also in my life. For one thing, it was probably the last time that the younger Jane Street Girls were all together, and it clearly delineated us and served to separate us from many of the older generation of homosexuals, who were terrified of such "radicalism."

While they continued to hang out at Julius's and their duplex parties, we ended up at the Firehouse, a Soho space taken over for meetings, debates, and on weekend nights, for gay-only dances in what had once been a Lower Manhattan Fire Department Hook and Ladder Company. But even there, among hundreds of others like ourselves, we came to feel that we belonged to something larger, a real community, rather than a group small enough to gather in a living room and watch television. As the months went on, I began to see even less of the other Janettes, and then only by accident.

It was in a relatively quiet corner of the Firehouse during a Saturday night dance sometime in early 1970 where I bumped into Miss Sherry. David had kept up with the others a bit more than I and he told me that George had gone "mad" the previous winter and left New York for good. Sherry or Douglas would sometimes get notes or phone calls from George. He'd tell them he was in the New Hampshire woods teaching art at a school for disturbed children, or he was in Plymouth, between jobs, or he'd been in the Village for only a day.

My own life had changed. From being a young man on the make—consciously or not—I'd taken on an entirely new attitude toward work, toward ambition. During the following years I would look for jobs lasting at most six or eight months; remain on the job only long enough to earn the money to live on another six to eight months. I was trying to become a writer and felt I needed stretches of free time to do so. The jobs I got were chosen so I wouldn't get too involved at work and could quit easily; clerking in bookstores, that sort of thing. Sometimes I'd return home from work to find scrawled and mostly illegible messages from George stuck in the edge of my foyer mailbox showing he'd been there. One time he left with a neighbor a book of Hopkins's poetry he'd borrowed from me years before. Whenever I thought about George, I would always spend that evening unable to shake off my sadness. It didn't help that those who saw him more frequently than I reported a certain "mad glint" in his eyes. I do recall the one time George did find me home. I immediately dropped what I was doing, we went out to eat, then walked around the Village most of a summer night, talking about all sorts of things just as we had in the old times. I thought, Hey, George is okay, after all! But in the middle of a sentence, he suddenly leapt into the street, hailed a cab and without a word of explanation or even a good-bye, he took off.

It would be another five years before I saw George again, and it would be a complete shock. I was at an orgy at someone's apartment Douglas had invited me to and which I'd gone to late and only after I'd had my own date for the evening canceled. I needn't have worried. Even with Douglas present—using his "butch voice" and on his best behavior—it turned out to be a very hot orgy indeed, filled with sexy men. While I was taking a break I heard someone say, "Hi, Phil!" and turned to see an obese, mostly naked man with a full head of hair and beard. It was dim in the room—dim in the whole apartment—and I wondered who he could be: almost no one called me Phil anymore. Only after he came closer and in an amused voice asked, "Are you *that* stoned?" did I see his eyes: tawny hazel-brown, unforgettable: George! After I got over my shock, we sat down and talked for a while, but I couldn't hide how surprised I was to see him, and it was a strained conversation. After a while George said, "No one here is interested in me. And I can't blame them." This from a man whose looks only a few years before had been legendary. I didn't know how to deny the fact with any honesty. George smiled ruefully, and soon afterward he left the orgy.

Several years later George moved back to Manhattan. He'd taken an apartment on East Fourteenth Street just past Avenue B, and he was working for a poster printing company on Union Square in a sort of supervisory capacity, which he never really clarified. George had become an artist, he was painting now and making his own lithographs—I suppose using the company's facilities on his own time—and I saw enough of his work to believe he showed a great deal of style, energy and originality. Although I was very busy during this period, in and out of town, busy with friends and

boyfriends, busy with my press, busy writing books, I made
a point of seeing George whenever he would call up or drop
by my place.

During these times he made it clear without ever really
discussing details that he'd had a mental breakdown of some
sort over the years, and let me know that he was still a bit
fragile and vulnerable. Again, without actually saying so,
George more or less told me that he didn't expect or even
want to recover our friendship with the closeness it had once
possessed; he preferred a gentlemanly reserve and restraint.
On the other hand, he very seldom had the "mad glint" in
his eyes I'd seen that day he fled from me into that taxi, and
I thought he would progress well and, if he stuck at it,
eventually make a name for himself as an artist.

George had lost some of the weight that he'd gained and
though he still had long hair and a beard and somewhat
resembled a nineteenth-century Impressionist painter, he
looked well enough to audition for and get an acting job.
He was Lord Darlington in a very small company's Off-Off
Broadway production of *Lady Windemere's Fan*, and he was
wonderful in the role, his presence as commanding as ever,
his baritone voice richer and more modulated than before,
even the way he moved about the stage was more authorita-
tive, more physically graceful than before his accident.

It was a showcase, only twelve performances, and not
reviewed or well attended, but his little success onstage
renewed George's confidence. He discussed with me turning
Diderot's brilliant, odd little novella, *Rameau's Nephew*,
which I'd given him to read a decade before, into a dramatic
monologue for the theater—a one-man show. We worked at
it together and he presented it before me in his apartment.
It seemed to me that it was only a matter of time before
George broke out into the limelight again.

That was in the early eighties. George had been living in
the city about a year. Then, suddenly, everything became
too much for him. The dirt, the noise, the crime, the people
at his job, the noisy neighbors in the building he lived in,

the unending grind of poverty, the endless auditions for parts he was wrong for, the attempts to secure a cheap little theater for his production, the suicide of his friend Bobby Brown, and finally the devastating illness of friends he'd known for years: among them Douglas. One day he phoned me, not to arrange another dinner date as he usually did, but to say he was leaving. A week later George was gone. No one—among the few people he knew in Manhattan who are still alive—has heard from him since.

"What I'll never understand is why George did it," I said.
"Did what?" David Jackson asked.
"You know, got that motorcycle, took that chance! There was so much of a future waiting for him. Why would he risk all that just to ride a motorcycle? Or could the self-destruction have been built in all the time? Was it just waiting to erupt?"
We were sitting in a French Provincial antiques store on upper Bleecker Street in the spring of 1981. David had been working there for the past two years. Despite the summer heat outside, the shop was cool, even with the air-conditioning off. It had to be turned off, because he was afraid of anything that might bring on another attack of pneumonia. David was thin, close to gaunt, and no longer the handsome man of only a year and a half before when he'd starred in a French porno movie titled *Le Plus Gai Manhattan*. David was now wearing a blousy light cotton gray shirt with long sleeves to hide the KS lesions on his arms. Amidst all that Norman frou-frou, brass and crockery he moved slowly, a shrunken facsimile of the person I once knew.
I'd taken to visiting David at least once a week at the shop in the midst of my errands. He was usually sitting on huge pillows to cut down the pain of bones against wood— often doing nothing more physically taxing than bookkeeping or inventory. He remained seated as long as possible if a customer came in to browse. He often asked me to move items or to help customers with heavier objects. He was so matter-of-fact about his illness that the few times he did

complain, I was surprised. What David mostly complained about was that so few people he knew ever phoned or came by. I knew my visits weren't much, either, but David had never asked much of the world, so I was on his short "Gay Angel" list.

My expostulation about George had been greeted by David's silence.

"No one's heard from him," I went on. "You haven't, have you?"

"Not I. Would you look at these gay ashtrays. I'm supposed to mark them up to eighteen bucks!"

"They're nice. But eighteen dollars!"

"These rich old biddies who shop in Pierre Deux pass by the window and buy them by the gross."

"Did he ever tell you why?" I asked. "George, I mean."

"He didn't tell me. Didn't have to. I already knew why."

I looked at David. He wasn't acting like someone who was about to unravel a mystery now over a decade old.

"Well? Tell me!"

"Remember that gay party Douglas and I gave uptown at . . . I don't remember his name. Joseph got ripped, as who didn't get ripped."

"Sure, the night of George's accident."

"Well, his gay highness suddenly swept out of the place like someone had burned his ass and he hopped onto that bike and took off like fifteen women were after his one-of-a-kind gay slip."

"George?" I asked.

"Concentrate! Yes, George."

"You mean he was angry when he left the party and it was in his anger that he drove off and had the accident?"

"You got it!"

I was still befuddled. "What was he angry about?"

"Well, as he left, I said, 'Going so soon, Mandy?' and he replied, 'Why not? No one *here* wants me!' "

"Meaning what exactly?"

"Well, I didn't know exactly, until I happened to look

into the garden and saw you and someone we both know who shall remain nameless if not blameless wrapped in a *très gai Screen Romances* embrace."

I remembered. Remembered Chuck holding out that white rose and kissing me and me pulling back and seeing the silhouette of George in the kitchen doorway. I would always remember that.

"I still don't get it," I said.

"Well, look in the gay mirror!" David said, shoving a brass-frame hand mirror he'd just unpacked from a large crate toward me.

"You mean because I wouldn't ride with George?" I asked. "But he knew I couldn't go. I told George I'd promised Joseph I'd stay and—" I stopped as a thought came to me. I brushed it away and said, "Sherry, explain what you mean."

"Forget it," David said. He grabbed the mirror and slapped a gummed price tag on the frame.

The thought wouldn't go away. I remembered a score of incidents, tiny and insignificant in themselves when they'd occurred, which now, together with what Miss Sherry had said, seemed to form themselves into a pattern, a strange one because never before had it been perceived from precisely that angle: how George had stared at me so ambiguously from his hospital bed whenever I visited, how he'd insisted that I know how much pain he was in from the knee pins and brace, how much the cast itched, how shrunken his leg had gotten in the cast, how limited his walking was. I remembered other looks, after he'd gotten out of the hospital, sudden glances I'd catch from him where I'd read one thing and where I now saw another; I remembered how during his most recent stay in the city he'd told me about a flirtation he'd been carrying on for months with a straight lad at work and how George had gone on about it every time we'd seen each other and I, from sympathy, had once said, "Lord, that must be painful," and George had knitted his brow at me, then smiled and said, "It's what I do best!

And, after all, it's not as though I haven't had practice!"
Could he have meant . . . ? Had he thought all those years
that I . . . ?

"You're wrong!" I said to David. "George and I were
friends. Good friends! Nothing else! We never . . . He
never . . ."

David was exasperated. "Fine! Since you've already made
up your gay mind about it." He reached over the edge of
the table for the box of hand mirrors.

"You're making this up, Sherry. It's not true. George
never said a word. He never intimated . . . ! I mean, we
were together a lot and never once . . . !"

David tried to lift the box and couldn't, so I helped and
watched as he slowly pulled it along the desk to where he
could reach the hand mirrors better.

I couldn't shut up. "You are completely wrong to think
that just because Chuck was kissing me and George left in a
huff that it was because of me! Completely wrong to believe
that because I would not return an affection I never even
knew existed, George went off on that motorcycle and had
that accident and . . . and . . . and . . . ruined his life!
Because of me!"

David didn't look up from the table, where he was now
assiduously marking gummed labels with a felt-tip pen.

"Miss Sherry Jackson, nee David," I tried one final time,
"say you're making this all up!"

The chimes on the door jangled and two of the rich old
biddies he'd mentioned before came in to browse.

David ignored them—and me—until it was obvious they
were more than browsing and needed his attention. After a
while David stood up, and as he moved away from the table
toward them, he made it plain that our discussion was over.
As I was leaving the shop, David suddenly said, "Even so. I
know what I know."

A week later when I went to see him again, the shop was
closed. I knew why. By the time I'd located the hospital
David had gone into, his parents had taken his body back to

Philadelphia to be cremated. If there were services or a memorial, I never heard of them. I wondered if George knew about David's death. If so, it would only confirm his reasons for leaving New York.

A month later the antiques shop was closed and the space emptied. Many months went by before I noticed someone renovating it. A few weeks later it opened as a beauty salon. Not one of those chic Village-Chelsea unisex places with punk beauticians you'd expect given the neighborhood. No, a real fifties beauty salon like you'd find in Maspeth or West Passaic, its name on a huge hot pink sign, with gauzy curtains over the windows and inside pink and red Naugahyde chairs and hair-drying machines, and women in square-heeled white shoes and white uniforms with their names embroidered in pink across the front, names like Laverne and Madge, women in their late forties and fifties with tight-curled hairdos I haven't seen in decades, who smoke filterless Luckys and call everyone "honey" and who can be seen hanging out weekly specials discreetly on the door: MANICURE/ PEDICURE $10 or DEPILATION—NAIR USED. ASK FOR PRICES.

To my surprise, it's become a great success; lasted for years now. And every time I pass that shop I think of sitting there that last time with David, and I recall our conversation, which I will never discover the truth of, and I remember George and Douglas and all of the Jane Street Girls and how innocent we were and how much fun we had. But mostly I smile a little, and think that if there is such a thing as ghosts or spirits and David's ever returned to the place of his last employment and saw that beauty salon, how very, *very* pleased the immortal spirit of Miss Sherry Jackson would be.